SIMUL 2025

The Seventeenth International Conference on Advances in System Simulation

September 28th - October 2nd, 2025

Lisbon, Portugal

SIMUL 2025 Editors

Sibylle Fröschle, Technische Universität Hamburg, Germany

Printed from e-media with permission by:

Curran Associates, Inc.
57 Morehouse Lane
Red Hook, NY 12571

Some format issues inherent in the e-media version may also appear in this print version.

Printed with permission by Curran Associates, Inc. (2025)

International Academy, Research, and Industry Association (IARIA)
412 Derby Way
Wilmington, DE 19810

Phone: (408) 893-6407
Fax: (408) 527-6351

petre@iaria.org

Additional copies of this publication are available from:

Curran Associates, Inc.
57 Morehouse Lane
Red Hook, NY 12571 USA
Phone: 845-758-0400
Fax: 845-758-2633
Email: curran@proceedings.com
Web: www.proceedings.com

Table of Contents

SIMUL 2025

Forward

The Seventeenth International Conference on Advances in System Simulation (SIMUL 2025), held on September 28 – October 1, 2025 in Lisbon, Portugal, continued a series of events focusing on advances in simulation techniques and systems providing new simulation capabilities.

While different simulation events are already scheduled for years, SIMUL 2025 identified specific needs for ontology of models, mechanisms, and methodologies in order to make easy an appropriate tool selection. With the advent of Web Services and WEB 3.0 social simulation and human-in simulations bring new challenging situations along with more classical process simulations and distributed and parallel simulations. An update on the simulation tool considering these new simulation flavors was aimed at, too.

The conference provided a forum where researchers were able to present recent research results and new research problems and directions related to them. The conference sought contributions to stress-out large challenges in scale system simulation and advanced mechanisms and methodologies to deal with them. The accepted papers covered topics on social simulation, transport simulation, simulation tools and platforms, simulation methodologies and models, and distributed simulation.

We welcomed technical papers presenting research and practical results, position papers addressing the pros and cons of specific proposals, such as those being discussed in the standard forums or in industry consortiums, survey papers addressing the key problems and solutions on any of the above topics, short papers on work in progress, and panel proposals.

We take here the opportunity to warmly thank all the members of the SIMUL 2025 technical program committee as well as the numerous reviewers. The creation of such a broad and high quality conference program would not have been possible without their involvement. We also kindly thank all the authors that dedicated much of their time and efforts to contribute to the SIMUL 2025. We truly believe that thanks to all these efforts, the final conference program consists of top quality contributions.

This event could also not have been a reality without the support of many individuals, organizations and sponsors. We also gratefully thank the members of the SIMUL 2025 organizing committee for their help in handling the logistics and for their work that is making this professional meeting a success. We gratefully appreciate to the technical program committee co-chairs that contributed to identify the appropriate groups to submit contributions.

We hope the SIMUL 2025 was a successful international forum for the exchange of ideas and results between academia and industry and to promote further progress in simulation research. We also hope that Lisbon provided a pleasant environment during the conference and everyone saved some time for exploring this beautiful city

SIMUL 2025 Steering Committee

Carlo Simon, Hochschule Worms - University of Applied Sciences, Germany
Frank Herrmann, University of Applied Sciences Regensburg, Germany
Sibylle Fröschle, TUHH - Hamburg University of Technology, Germany

SIMUL 2025 Publicity Chair

Lorena Parra Boronat, Universidad Politécnica de Madrid, Spain
Sandra Viciano Tudela, Universitat Politecnica de Valencia, Spain
Jose Miguel Jimenez, Universitat Politecnica de Valencia, Spain

SIMUL 2025

Committee

SIMUL 2025 Steering Committee

Carlo Simon, Hochschule Worms - University of Applied Sciences, Germany
Frank Herrmann, University of Applied Sciences Regensburg, Germany
Sibylle Fröschle, TUHH - Hamburg University of Technology, Germany

SIMUL 2025 Publicity Chair

Lorena Parra Boronat, Universidad Politécnica de Madrid, Spain
Sandra Viciano Tudela, Universitat Politecnica de Valencia, Spain
Jose Miguel Jimenez, Universitat Politecnica de Valencia, Spain

SIMUL 2025 Technical Program Committee

Petra Ahrweiler, Johannes Gutenberg University Mainz, Germany
Saleh Abdel-Afou Alaliyat, Norwegian University of Science and Technology, Norway
Chrissanthi Angeli, University of West Attica, Greece
Ozgur M. Araz, College of Business | University of Nebraska–Lincoln, USA
Alfonso Ariza Quintana, University of Malaga, Spain
Natesh B. Arunachalam, The University of Texas at Austin, USA
Michel Audette, Old Dominion University, USA
Souvik Barat, Tata Consultancy Services Research, India
Ana Paula Barbosa Póvoa, Universidade de Lisboa, Portugal
Marek Bauer, Politechnika Krakowska, Poland
Sahil Belsare, Walmart / Northeastern University, USA
Massimo Bertolini, University of Modena and Reggio Emilia - UNIMORE, Italy
John Betts, Monash University, Australia
Maria Julia Blas, Instituto de Desarrollo y Diseño (INGAR) | UTN-CONICET, Argentina
Paolo Bocciarelli, University of Rome Tor Vergata, Italy
Stefan Bosse, University of Bremen, Germany
Jalil Boudjadar, Aarhus University, Denmark
Christos Bouras, University of Patras, Greece
Lelio Campanile, Università degli Studi della Campania "L. Vanvitelli", Italy
Yuxin Chen, University of California, Davis, USA
Franco Cicirelli, ICAR-CNR, Italy
Fábio Coelho, CEG-IST Instituto Superior Técnico | University of Lisbon, Portugal
Federico Concone, University of Palermo, Italy
Duilio Curcio, University of Calabria, Italy
Andrea D'Ambrogio, University of Roma TorVergata, Italy
Gabriele D'Angelo, University of Bologna, Italy
Luis Antonio de Santa-Eulalia, Business School | Université de Sherbrooke, Canada

Ettore Lanzarone, University of Bergamo, Italy
Herman Le Roux, Council for Scientific and Industrial Research (CSIR), South Africa
Fedor Lehocki, Slovak University of Technology in Bratislava, Slovakia
Stephan Leitner, University of Klagenfurt, Austria
Laurent Lemarchand, University of Brest (UBO), France
António M. Lopes, University of Porto, Portugal
Fabian Lorig, Malmö University | IoTaP, Sweden
Emilio Luque, University Autonoma of Barcelona (UAB), Spain
Johannes Lüthi, University of Applied Sciences - Fachhochschule Kufstein Tirol, Austria
Imran Mahmood, Brunel University London, UK
Fahad Maqbool, University of Sargodha, Pakistan
Eda Marchetti, ISTI-CNR, Pisa, Italy
Romolo Marotta, University of Rome "Sapienza", Italy
Omar Masmali, The University of Texas, El Paso, USA
Michele Mastroianni, Università degli Studi della Campania "Luigi Vanvitelli", Italy
Andrea Matta, Politecnico di Milano, Italy
Radek Matušů, Tomas Bata University in Zlin, Czech Republic
Roger McHaney, Kansas State University, USA
Nuno Melão, Polytechnic Institute of Viseu, Portugal
Roderick Melnik, MS2Discovery Interdisciplinary Research Institute | Wilfrid *Laurier* University, Canada
Adel Mhamdi, RWTH Aachen University, Germany
Owen Molloy, National University of Ireland, Galway, Ireland
Mahathir Monjur, University of North Carolina at Chapel Hill, USA
Sébastien Monnet, LISTIC / Savoie Mont Blanc University, France
Federico Montori, University of Bologna, Italy
Emilio Moretti, Politecnico di Milano, Italy
Jérôme Morio, ONERA (the French Aerospace Lab), France
Paulo Moura Oliveira, Universidade de Trás-os-Montes e Alto Douro (UTAD) / INESC-TEC Porto, Portugal
Andrzej Mycek, Cracow University of Technology, Poland
Nazmun Nahar, University of Jyvaskyla, Finland
Luis Gustavo Nardin, National College of Ireland, Ireland
James J. Nutaro, Oak Ridge National Laboratory, USA
Alessandro Pellegrini, Sapienza University of Rome, Italy
Tomas Potuzak, University of West Bohemia, Czech Republic
Manon Prédhumeau, IRIT | University Toulouse Capitole, France
Dipak Pudasaini, Tribhuvan University, Nepal / Ryerson University, Canada
Francesco Quaglia, University of Rome Tor Vergata, Italy
Abdul Rahman, Deloitte, USA
Marco Remondino, Università degli Studi di Genova, Italy
Dupas Rémy, University of Bordeaux, France
Oscar Rodríguez Polo, University of Alcala, Spain
Kristin Yvonne Rozier, Iowa State University, USA
Cristina Ruiz Martin, Carleton University, Canada
Julio Sahuquillo, Universitat Politecnica de Valencia, Spain
Nandakishore Santhi, Los Alamos National Laboratory, USA
Victorino Sanz, ETSI Informática | UNED, Spain
Paulo Jorge Sequeira Goncalves, Instituto Politecnico de Castelo Branco, Portugal
Li Shi, Snap Inc., USA

Patrick Siarry, Université Paris-Est Créteil (UPEC), France
Carlo Simon, Hochschule Worms - University of Applied Sciences, Germany
Leszek Siwik, AGH-UST University of Science and Technology, Krakow, Poland
Yuri N. Skiba, Universidad Nacional Autónoma de México, Mexico
Azeddien M. Sllame, University of Tripoli, Libya
Giandomenico Spezzano, CNR-ICAR, Italy
Sven Spieckermann, SimPlan AG, Germany
Renata Spolon Lobato, UNESP - São Paulo State University, Brazil
Mu-Chun Su, National Central University, Taiwan
Grażyna Suchacka, University of Opole, Poland
János Száz, Corvinus University, Hungary
Kumar Tamma, University of Minnesota, USA
Elena Tappia, Politecnico di Milano, Italy
Ingo J. Timm, Trier University, Germany
Felix Tischer, Virtual Vehicle Research GmbH, Austria
Abtin Tondar, Stanford University School of Medicine, USA
Klaus G. Troitzsch, University of Koblenz-Landau, retired, Germany
Hasan Turan, University of New South Wales, Australia
Alfonso Urquía, UNED, Spain
Edson L. Ursini, University of Campinas - Technology School, Brazil
Vahab Vahdatzad, Harvard Medical School, Boston, USA
Bert Van Acker, University of Antwerp, Belgium
Durk-Jouke van der Zee, University of Groningen, Netherlands
Antonio Virdis, University of Pisa, Italy
Frank Werner, OvGU Magdeburg, Germany
Kuan Yew Wong, Universiti Teknologi Malaysia (UTM), Malaysia
Yang Yang, Cornell University, USA
Irina Yatskiv (Jackiva), Transport and Telecommunication Institute, Latvia
Xinrui Zhang, Carleton University, Canada

Copyright Information

Enhancing Building Retrofit Decision-Making: A Synergistic Approach Combining Calibrated Simulations and Machine Learning

Navid Shirzadia, Meli Stylianou
CanmetENERGY-Ottawa
Natural Resources Canada,
Ottawa, Canada
e-mail: navid.shirzadi@nrcan-rncan.gc.ca

Abstract— **Achieving energy efficiency and reducing greenhouse gas (GHG) emissions are critical goals for building retrofitting. This study tackles challenges such as limited data and scenario generalizability by adapting the U.S. ComStock database for Canadian buildings using a Euclidean distance-based matching algorithm, achieving a 92% success rate for matches below a 2.43 threshold. Machine learning models, Random Forest (RF) and Extreme Gradient Boosting (XGBoost), were selected due to their effectiveness in handling high-dimensional, non-linear datasets and were applied to predict Energy Use Intensity (EUI) and GHG emissions. XGBoost, with optimized hyperparameters, outperformed RF, achieving R^2 values of 0.91 for EUI and 0.86 for GHG emissions, with lower RMSE and MAE values, showcasing its capability in handling complex, high-dimensional data. A comparative analysis highlighted significant environmental benefits of transitioning Heating, Ventilation, and Air Conditioning (HVAC) systems to cleaner fuels, such as air-source heat pumps. The proposed distribution-based method, leveraging 100 buildings across diverse climates and types, offers a robust framework for policymakers to guide energy-efficient retrofitting decisions.**

Keywords- smart building retrofitting; energy efficiency; greenhouse gas emissions; machine learning.

I. INTRODUCTION

The construction and operation of buildings contribute significantly to global energy consumption and greenhouse gas (GHG) emissions [1][2]. In Canada, existing buildings alone account for over 40% of emissions in major urban centers [3][4]. Consequently, enhancing energy efficiency and minimizing the environmental impact of existing buildings have become critical priorities within the building sector.

Despite government initiatives such as the Canada Greener Homes program providing financial support [5], retrofitting buildings faces numerous challenges and uncertainties for building owners [6][7]. Key obstacles include a lack of information and awareness, which complicates decision-making processes. Retrofitting decisions typically depend on the expertise of energy advisors and audits—often time-consuming and expensive processes designed to identify potential retrofit measures [8][9].

Another approach involves physics-based energy models that simulate building energy use and define retrofit scenarios based on these simulations. For instance, a historical building in Italy was modeled using EnergyPlus in [10], while Rahman et al. [11], simulated an office building in Australia, exploring major retrofit scenarios that achieved approximately 42% energy savings. Similar physics-based approaches have been applied in various cases [12]-[15]. However, these models often face significant uncertainties and energy performance gaps, which are rarely considered in final evaluations. Furthermore, their complexity, reliance on specialized expertise, and time-consuming processes render them less accessible for many building owners.

The rise of artificial intelligence has spurred interest in Machine Learning (ML) and data-driven approaches for building retrofits. A key challenge in applying data-driven models to retrofit scenarios is the availability of reliable retrofit data. Common issues include uncertainty and subjectivity in data quality [16] and sometimes the privacy issues about gathered measured data. As a result, researchers often rely on artificial data or surrogate models to analyze retrofit scenarios [17]. While surrogate models mitigate some expertise and computational demands associated with physics-based simulations, they do not resolve uncertainties or performance gaps inherent in these models.

Recently, a highly granular tool named ComStock [8], [18][19], developed by the National Renewable Energy Laboratory (NREL), has provided a database of over 300,000 buildings, containing detailed building characteristics and information. The simulation results in this database are highly calibrated, incorporating stochastic models to more accurately reflect occupant behavior. This level of detail addresses the data availability issue for developing data-driven models. However, ComStock is limited in its geographic scope, being tailored to locations within the United States. Extending its utility to other regions, such as Canada, requires innovative approaches to ensure compatibility and relevance.

This study addresses the challenges through an integration of data-matching techniques and machine learning models. The key contributions of this research are:

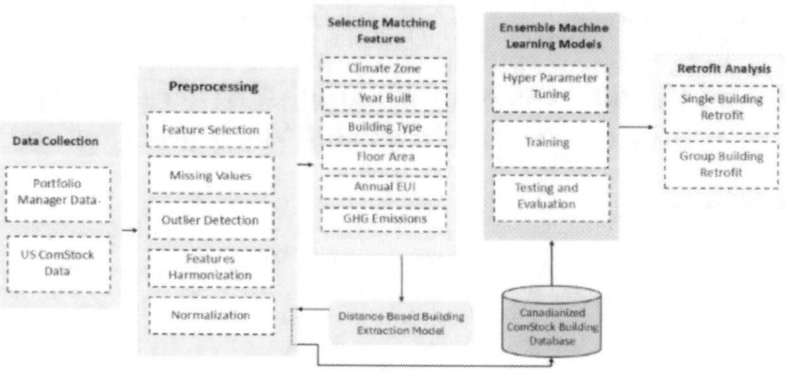

Figure 1. Workflow for developing retrofit scenarios from raw data to analysis

- Data Matching for Enhanced Model Accuracy: The study leverages a highly calibrated simulation database (ComStock) using a Euclidean distance-based algorithm to identify and extract data from buildings that closely match Canadian counterparts. This approach addresses the data scarcity challenge and ensures reliable inputs for data-driven analysis.
- Scalable Retrofit Evaluation Framework: A distribution-based method was proposed to generalize retrofit impacts across a diverse sample of buildings, considering variations in type, location, and climate zone. This method offers a robust framework for policymakers and stakeholders to make informed decisions.
- Environmental and Energy Impact Insights: The research highlights the benefits of some retrofit scenarios such as transitioning HVAC systems to cleaner fuel sources, demonstrating their potential to significantly reduce GHG emissions.

This study not only advances the application of machine learning for building retrofits but also provides a scalable framework for evaluating retrofit scenarios in diverse contexts, contributing to sustainable energy and environmental management in the building sector.

The remainder of this paper is organized as follows: Section II details the proposed methodology, outlining steps from data extraction and preprocessing to the development of data-driven models, Section III presents and discusses the results of the case study. And finally, Section IV concludes the paper and highlights directions for future research.

II. Methodology

The overall process of developing retrofit scenarios from raw data is illustrated in Figure 1. The workflow begins with data collection, utilizing real user-input data from the Energy Star Portfolio Manager (ESPM) database—a database derived from Canadian user inputs—combined with the U.S. ComStock database. The preprocessing stage involves several steps, including feature selection, handling missing values and outliers, and feature engineering. For the ESPM database, a climate zone feature was generated using the heating degree days (HDD) metric for each building. In the ComStock database, a filtration process was applied to exclude buildings located in climate zones not present in Canada.

Six features were selected for the building extraction process, implemented through a distance-based matching model. Categorical features underwent harmonization to ensure consistency between the datasets. The extracted buildings then went through the preprocessing pipeline again, starting with feature selection, followed by normalization. The preprocessed data was then used to train ensemble learning models, followed by a detailed retrofit analysis.

A. Matching Process

To adapt the ComStock database, originally created for buildings in the USA, for use in Canada, the portfolio manager database, which is based on Canadian user inputs, is employed. Six key features are selected for the matching process: climate zone, building construction year, building type, gross floor area, annual energy use intensity, and annual greenhouse gas (GHG) emissions. Categorical features in the dataset are transformed into numerical representations to ensure compatibility with the distance-based matching process. Specifically, one-hot encoding is applied to categorical variables, converting them into binary feature vectors. This transformation allows categorical attributes to be incorporated alongside numerical features without introducing ordinal biases. Once categorical variables are encoded, all features undergo normalization to eliminate discrepancies in scale and ensure that no single attribute dominates the distance calculation. The normalization process standardizes numerical features to a common range, facilitating a fair comparison between different building attributes during the matching process. Euclidean distance (Formula 1) is used to calculate the similarity between buildings in the two databases.

$$D(A,B) = \sqrt{\sum_{i=1}^{6}(a_i - b_i)^2} \quad (1)$$

Where a_i and b_i represent the feature values of buildings A and B, respectively, for the i-th feature.
In the matching process, each target building, buildings in the ESPM database, was iterated through, and the closest matched building in the ComStock database was identified based on pre-computed distance values. For each target building, the already matched ComStock buildings were filtered out, and the closest building was selected by finding the minimum distance. The index of the closest building was recorded as the match, and the building was marked as used to prevent it from being selected again. This process was repeated until all target buildings were matched, ensuring that each building in the ESPM database was paired with the closest available building in the ComStock.
To statistically show the accuracy of the matches, a threshold is first calculated based on the below formula using the mean and standard deviation of the minimum distances between buildings to establish a threshold. The threshold is a distance value that helps define what is considered a good match.

$$Threshold = \mu + k.\partial \qquad (2)$$

Where μ is the average of the minimum distances, ∂ is the standard deviation of the minimum distances and k is multiplier which adjusts the sensitivity of the threshold.
Then to calculate the good matches by counting how many of the minimum distances between buildings are less than the threshold previously calculated.

$$Good\ Matches = \sum_{i=1}^{n} minimum\ distance < Threshold \qquad (3)$$

$$percentage\ of\ good\ matches = \frac{Good\ Matches}{n} \times 100$$

Which n is the number of minimum distances in the minimum distance array.

B. Machine learning models

Two powerful ensemble learning techniques, Random Forest (RF) and XGBoost, were used to predict EUI and GHG emissions. RF was chosen for its ability to handle high-dimensional feature interactions and provide interpretability, while XGBoost was selected for its superior predictive performance through gradient boosting and optimized learning. RF is an ensemble method that creates multiple decision trees using random subsets of the data, then combines their predictions to enhance model robustness and accuracy [20]. This approach is particularly effective at reducing overfitting and managing high-dimensional data. In contrast, XGBoost is a boosting-based technique that trains weak learners iteratively, focusing on minimizing errors from prior iterations. Its gradient boosting framework, along with features like regularization and efficient handling of missing data, enables it to capture complex patterns within the data effectively [21].

To optimize the performance of these models, RandomizedSearchCV method, which is a package of Scikit Learn library [22], was used for hyperparameter tuning. This method efficiently explores the hyperparameter space by randomly selecting combinations and evaluating their performance based on cross-validation. Key parameters, such as the number of estimators, maximum depth of trees, and learning rate, were tuned for both models. The results of this tuning process, including the best parameters and corresponding performance metrics, will be detailed in the results section. This tuning ensured that the models were well-suited to the dataset and provided reliable predictions for retrofit scenarios.

C. Evaluation metrics

This study employs three primary evaluation metrics: R-squared (R^2), Mean Absolute Error (MAE), and Root Mean Squared Error (RMSE). These metrics assess the performance of the trained model on the training data, which is then tested using the testing data. The corresponding formulas are provided below:

$$R^2 = 1 - \frac{\sum_{i=1}^{n}(y_i - \hat{y}_i)^2}{\sum_{i=1}^{n}(y_i - \bar{y})^2} \qquad (4)$$

$$MAE = \frac{1}{n}\sum_{i=1}^{n}|y_i - \hat{y}_i| \qquad (5)$$

$$RMSE = \sqrt{\frac{1}{n}\sum_{i=1}^{n}(y_i - \hat{y}_i)^2} \qquad (6)$$

Where n is the number of data points, y_i is the actual value, $\hat{y}_i$ is the predicted value and $\bar{y}$ is the mean of the actual values.

III. Results

This section presents the key findings derived from the dataset, highlighting the steps taken to ensure its relevance and applicability to Canadian building stock characteristics.

A. Matching and data evaluation

The ComStock database was initially filtered based on climate zone, reducing the dataset from 336,149 to 193,741 buildings to better align with Canadian conditions. The

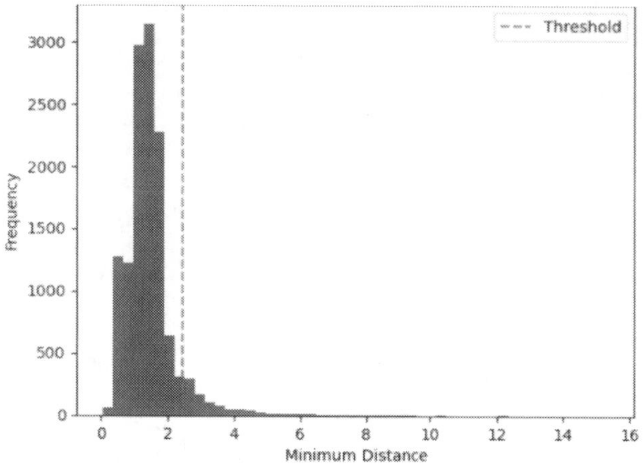

Figure 2. Distribution of minimum distances

matching process aimed to find the most similar buildings for 12,865 target buildings from the Portfolio Manager (PM) database. To achieve this, we utilized a Euclidean distance-based approach across six key features, ensuring a robust and consistent comparison. Each target building from the PM database was iteratively matched to its closest counterpart in the filtered ComStock dataset, prioritizing similarity while preventing duplicate matches. The quality of these matches was assessed using a threshold-based validation method, which determined that approximately 92% of matches were within an acceptable distance threshold of 2.43 (with the multiplier set to 1). Figure 2 presents the distribution of minimum distances, highlighting a peak in frequency just before reaching the threshold, indicating the effectiveness of the matching strategy in pairing buildings with similar characteristics.

Evaluating the extracted matched buildings, the boxplots for EUI and GHG emissions (Figure 3) reveal significant variability among building types, underscoring the influence of operational characteristics on energy consumption and greenhouse gas output. Quick Service Restaurants and Full-Service Restaurants consistently exhibit the highest median values for both EUI (above 100 kWh/ft²) and GHG emissions (20,000–40,000 kg CO_2). This is likely due to the energy-intensive nature of their operations, including frequent use of cooking equipment and extended operating hours. In contrast, building types such as small offices, medium offices, warehouses, and hospitals show narrower distributions, reflecting more uniform energy use, though the limited hospital sample size may artificially reduce observed variability.

Interestingly, while large offices have slightly higher median EUI compared to medium offices, the latter demonstrates higher median GHG emissions. This disparity may reflect differences in energy source mixes or operational efficiencies. The extended whisker lengths for Quick Service and Full-Service Restaurants in the EUI plot, along with the longer whiskers for medium offices and Full-Service Restaurants in the GHG plot, highlight significant variability

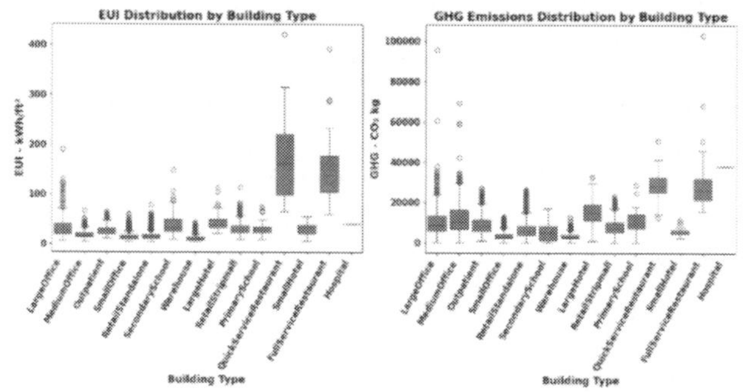

Figure 3. EUI and GHG emissions distribution across building types

within these categories, possibly due to diverse building designs or operational practices. While outliers are present in both plots, particularly for Large Offices and restaurants, they were retained as they represent simulated variations intended to capture diverse building performances. These trends emphasize the importance of tailored energy and emissions management strategies for different building types.

Based on Figure 4, Zone 7 has a medium EUI compared to other climate zones but records the lowest GHG emissions. In contrast, Zone 6 exhibits the highest average GHG emissions despite not having the highest EUI. This suggests that factors beyond energy consumption, such as the type of fuel used, play a significant role in GHG emissions. As shown in Figure 5, buildings in Zone 7 primarily use cleaner energy sources like electricity, natural gas, and district heating, which contribute to its lower GHG emissions. Conversely, a significant portion of Zone 6's GHG emissions is attributed to the use of carbon-intensive fuels like fuel oil, which lead to higher CO_2 emissions despite moderate energy usage.

The challenge with zones like Zone 7 or Zone 8 is that they do not encompass buildings with a wide variety of fuel sources, which can reduce the accuracy of the training process. To address this limitation, a key future step is to update the Portfolio Manager data used to extract the datasets and include a broader range of buildings from the source database. This would ensure more comprehensive representation and improve the reliability of the analysis.

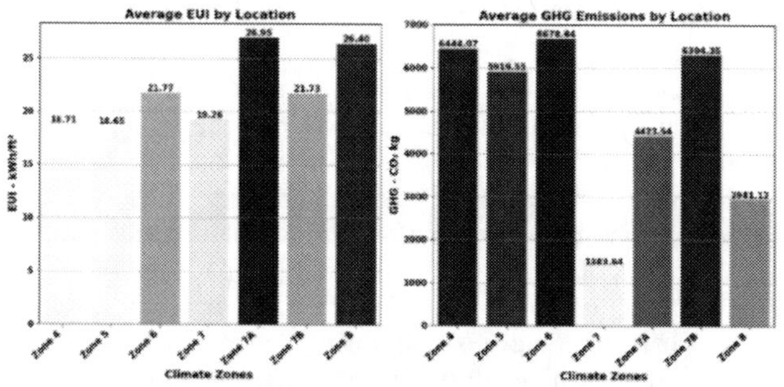

Figure 4. EUI and GHG emissions by climate zone

TABLE I: HYPERPARAMETER RANGES AND OPTIMIZED VALUES FOR XGBOOST AND RANDOM FOREST MODELS USING RANDOMIZEDSEARCHCV

XGB Params	Range	Optimum	RF Params	Range	Optimum
Number of estimators	[100, 200, 400]	400	Number of estimators	Randint (50, 300)	169
Estimator max depth	[3, 6, 10]	6	max depth	[None, 10, 20, 30, 40]	40
Estimator learning rate	[0.01, 0.05, 0.1, 0.2]	0.1	Min sample split	Randint (2, 10)	2
Estimator subsample	[0.7, 0.8, 0.9]	0.8	Min sample leaf	Randint (1, 10)	3
Estimator colsample bytree	[0.7, 0.8, 0.9]	0.8	max_features	['sqrt', 'log2', None]	sqrt
			Bootstrap	[True, False]	False

B.Model training

Table 1 summarizes the hyperparameter ranges and the optimized values for the two machine learning models used in this study: XGBoost (XGB) and Random Forest (RF). The purpose of this parameter tuning is to improve the predictive performance of each model by identifying the optimal combination of hyperparameters. The tuning process was conducted using RandomizedSearchCV method, which performs a randomized search over the specified parameter ranges to find the best-performing configuration.

The hyperparameters chosen for the Random Forest (RF) and XGBoost models reveal important aspects of their optimization and performance. For example, max_features in the RF model defines how many features are considered at each split, with "sqrt" being the optimal value here. This parameter contributes to the diversity of the decision trees, a crucial element in improving generalization while maintaining computational efficiency. Similarly, the number of estimators (optimal value: 169 for RF and 400 for XGBoost) governs the ensemble size, directly affecting both model accuracy and training time. The selection of a higher number of estimators in XGBoost suggests its ability to handle larger ensembles effectively, while the smaller optimal value for RF indicates a balance between computational efficiency and predictive power.

Another point of interest is the learning rate in XGBoost, which controls the step size during optimization. The optimal value of 0.1 strikes a balance between convergence speed and overfitting prevention. On the other hand, parameters like min samples split and min samples leaf in RF are essential for controlling tree growth and preventing overfitting by requiring a minimum number of data points at splits or leaves. The interplay between these parameters highlights how RandomizedSearchCV has fine-tuned the models to suit the dataset's characteristics. These optimal values reflect the need to manage trade-offs between model complexity, overfitting, and computational demands, providing an essential balance for practical implementation. The selected optimum values were then utilized during the training process to ensure the models were fine-tuned for optimal performance.

The model was trained using 90% of the data and then tested on the remaining 10%, which includes over 1,200 different buildings. The training evaluation results (Table 2) highlight that XGBoost outperforms Random Forest in predicting both EUI and GHG emissions, as shown by higher R^2 values and lower RMSE and MAE metrics. XGBoost achieves an R^2 of 0.91 for EUI prediction compared to 0.83 for Random Forest, and similarly, an R^2 of 0.86 for GHG emissions prediction compared to 0.75 for Random Forest. This superior performance underscores XGBoost's capability to handle complex patterns in the data effectively. For example, in EUI prediction, the reduction in RMSE from 5.05 (Random Forest) to 3.54 (XGBoost) reflects its ability to better capture underlying relationships, while the drop in MAE from 2.94 to 1.99 shows improved precision in its predictions.

The high-dimensional input vector, consisting of approximately 48 predictors, plays a critical role in XGBoost's superior performance. XGBoost is particularly adept at managing complex feature interactions and identifying important predictors, thanks to its gradient boosting framework and regularization techniques. This is especially beneficial when working with many predictors, as it reduces the risk of overfitting and effectively prunes less relevant splits. Random Forest, while robust, may struggle with high-dimensional data, as it treats all features more equally and lacks the inherent optimization for feature selection and interaction modeling. The results are visualized in Figure 6, using plots that show the relationship between predicted and measured values, with the red dashed line representing perfect predictions. These graphs highlight the performance of both models. The scatter plots demonstrate how closely the predicted values align with the measured values, with the red dashed line indicating the ideal prediction scenario. It is evident that XGBoost offers a more accurate fit for both EUI and GHG emissions data, as reflected by its higher R^2 values and smaller deviations from the perfect prediction line. This makes XGBoost the superior model in terms of predictive power and accuracy.

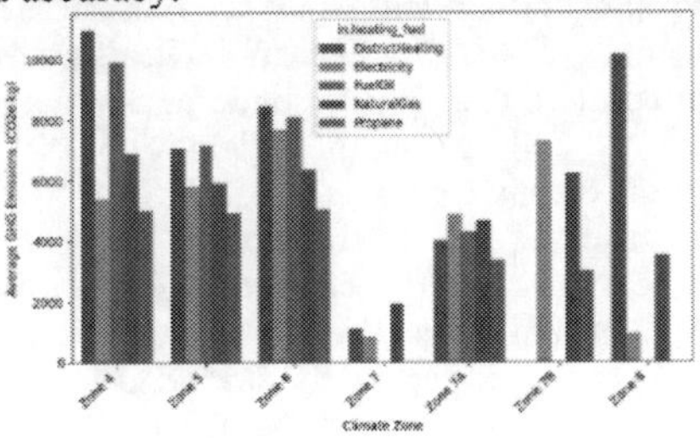

Figure 5. Average GHG emissions by heating fuel type and climate zone

TABLE II: TRAINING EVALUATION

	EUI Prediction			GHG Emissions Prediction		
Model	R^2	RMSE (kWh/ft2)	MAE (kWh/ft2)	R^2	RMSE (kg-CO2)	MAE (kg-CO2)
Random Forrest	0.83	5.05	2.94	0.75	2440.59	1481.82
XGBoost	0.91	3.54	1.99	0.86	1840.10	1012.21

C. Retrofit evaluation and savings

Figure 7 provides a clear comparison of how switching HVAC heating types affects both EUI and GHG emissions. For example, transitioning from a Furnace with Propane as its fuel source to an air source heat pump (ASHP) using Electricity results in a notable reduction in both metrics. The EUI decreases from approximately 29.5 kWh/ft^2 to around 27.5 kWh/ft^2, indicating improved energy efficiency. Similarly, the GHG emissions drop significantly from around 3,612 kg-CO_2 to just above 2,348 kg-CO_2, highlighting the environmental benefit of switching to a cleaner fuel source. This comparison underscores the potential of fuel changes in HVAC systems to achieve both energy and emission savings. While the evaluation presented in Figure 7 for a single building is valuable for specific retrofit scenarios, it is generally insufficient for policymakers and organizations involved in building retrofits. Decisions are rarely made based on the performance of a single building; instead, stakeholders prefer to evaluate retrofit savings across a broader portfolio of buildings [23]. To address this need, a sample of 100 diverse buildings across different climate zones was selected from the original database, and two distinct datasets—pre-retrofit and post-retrofit—were created for analysis.

The pre-retrofit dataset represents the baseline scenario, where all buildings maintain their existing features except for the retrofit-specific variables (in this case, HVAC Heating Type and Heating Fuel Type), which were standardized to Furnace and Propane. Conversely, the post-retrofit dataset includes the same buildings with identical features as the pre-retrofit dataset, but with HVAC Heating Type and Heating Fuel Type changed to ASHP and Electricity to simulate the retrofit. Additional post-retrofit scenarios were created by varying the HVAC and fuel types, consistent with the single building retrofit analysis.

The resulting distributions of EUI and GHG emissions for various retrofit scenarios are shown in Figure 8. In this context, 'positive savings' refers to reductions in EUI and GHG emissions compared to the base case. Retrofitting from Furnace/Propane to options such as Furnace/Natural Gas, ASHP/Electricity, and Electric Resistance/Electricity demonstrated more than 70% of buildings achieving positive energy savings, highlighting the reliability of these scenarios for energy efficiency improvements. On the other hand, the transition from Furnace/Propane to Furnace/Fuel Oil exhibited the lowest positive change in GHG emissions, with nearly 98% of buildings showing negative savings. This outcome aligns with expectations, as Fuel Oil typically results in higher GHG emissions. Retrofitting to ASHP and Electric Resistance systems also showed high positive changes in GHG reductions, reinforcing their effectiveness in lowering carbon emissions across a diverse building sample.

For District/District Heating, while the exact methodology for calculating heating energy and GHG emissions in the ComStock database is not explicitly detailed, the results presented in Figure 8 highlight the significant variability in district heating impacts among buildings. This variability is largely due to differences in fuel sources used within district heating networks, which can range from renewable energy sources to fossil fuels. For instance, in the case of the building depicted in Figure 7, the energy source could predominantly be renewables, resulting in very low GHG emissions alongside reasonable EUI. In contrast, other buildings, likely relying on fossil fuels for district heating, exhibit markedly different results, with higher EUI outcomes. Although, on the other hand, the positive GHG emissions observed for a group of buildings suggest that other attributes may influence district heating GHG emissions and even EUI. These attributes could not be accounted for due to a lack of available information. It is also worth noting that while 99% of the buildings using District/DistrictHeating show positive GHG emissions, the average GHG emissions of this group are 4526 kg-CO2, which is lower than buildings using Furnace/Propane (base case) with an average of 6365 kg-CO2, yet notably higher than the example building shown in Figure 7. This suggests that, despite the variability in district heating sources, the overall emissions performance of these systems may align more closely with that of fossil fuel-based systems like Furnace/Propane.

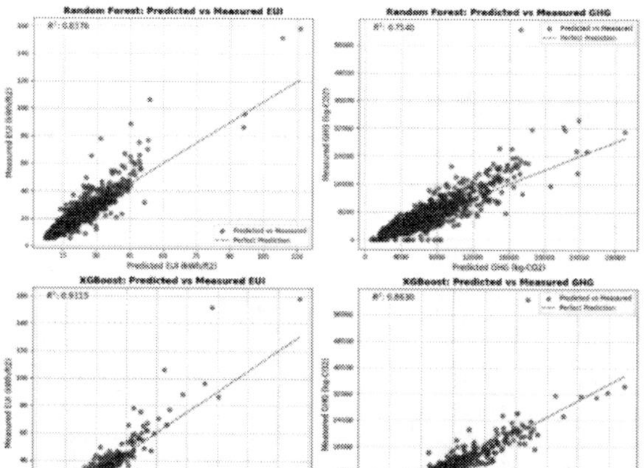

Figure 6. Comparison of predicted vs. measured EUI and GHG emissions for Random Forest and XGBoost models

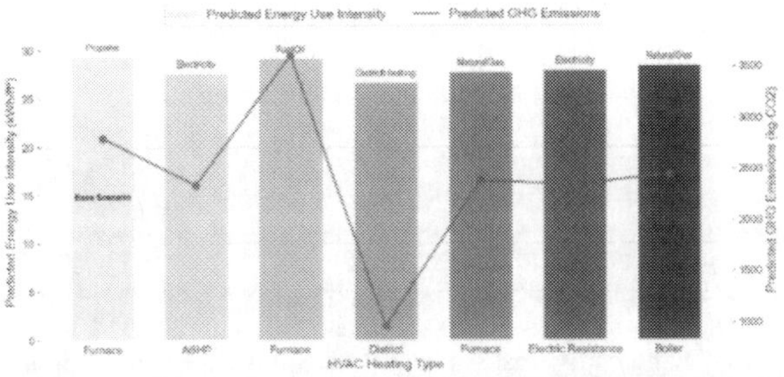

Figure 7. Comparative analysis of predicted energy use intensity (kWh/ft²) and GHG emissions (kg-CO_2) across various HVAC heating types

These findings highlight the need for further investigation into the specific factors influencing emissions variations across different building groups.

There may be some inaccuracies in the results due to the limited data used for training the regression model and its inability to accurately predict certain combinations of features. Other retrofit scenarios, such as changing window types, wall materials, or window-to-wall ratios, can also be evaluated using the same proposed methodology. While combining multiple retrofit scenarios could provide a more comprehensive evaluation, it introduces complexity, making it challenging to isolate the impact of each individual scenario.

IV. CONCLUSION AND FUTURE WORK

This study addresses the critical challenge of improving energy efficiency and reducing greenhouse gas (GHG) emissions in existing buildings, which contribute significantly to global emissions. While traditional methods such as physics-based energy simulation models offer valuable insights into retrofit scenarios, their limitations, including expertise requirements, time-consuming processes, and inherent uncertainties—can impede their practical application. Similarly, data-driven approaches using ML models face challenges due to the lack of reliable measured data and privacy concerns.

To bridge these gaps, this research integrates data-matching techniques with highly calibrated simulation databases to overcome data limitations for ML-based retrofitting analyses. By employing a Euclidean distance-based matching algorithm, this approach successfully identifies comparable buildings and extracts valuable data, achieving a high success rate. Ensemble learning models, specifically Random Forest (RF) and XGBoost, were trained on the matched data to predict EUI and GHG emissions. The optimized XGBoost model outperformed RF, demonstrating superior accuracy and robustness with R^2 values of 0.91 for EUI and 0.86 for GHG emissions.

The study further demonstrated the environmental and energy efficiency benefits of transitioning HVAC systems to cleaner fuel sources, such as air-source heat pumps. To enhance the generalizability of the findings, a distribution-based method was introduced, which analyzed retrofit impacts across a sample of 100 buildings of various types and in different climate zones. This method provides actionable insights and a scalable framework for policymakers and stakeholders to make informed, data-driven decisions on building retrofits.

By combining advanced data-matching techniques with machine learning and proposing a scalable evaluation framework, this research contributes to the growing body of knowledge on sustainable building retrofits. The scalability lies in its ability to generalize retrofit impacts across a diverse range of building types, climates, and geographic regions. Future work could focus on:

1. Adding cost as a target variable to evaluate the economic aspects of retrofits, providing a more comprehensive assessment that integrates energy, environmental, and financial impacts.
2. Updating the portfolio manager data dynamically with new inputs from users to enhance the adaptability and applicability of the proposed framework, ensuring it remains relevant and effective in real-world scenarios.

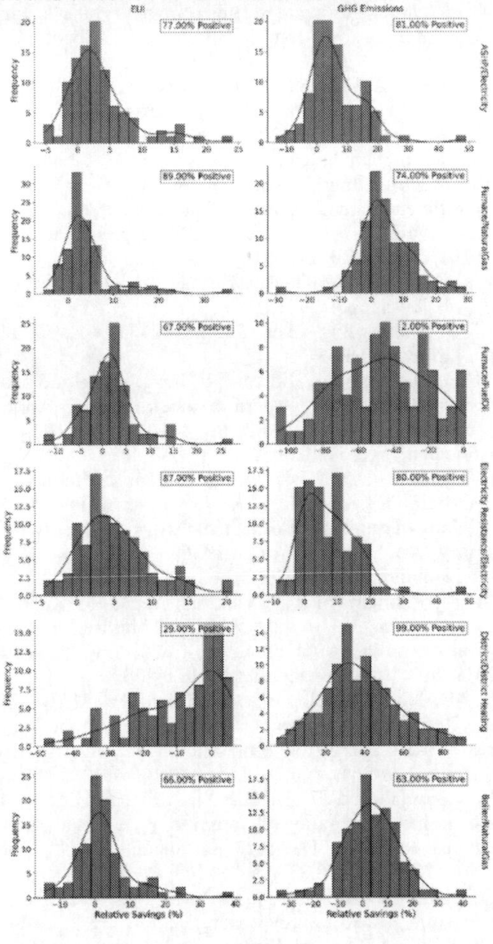

Figure 8. Distributions of EUI and GHG emissions savings for various retrofit scenarios of heating HVAC and fuel type across a 100-building sample

ACKNOWLEDGMENT

Thanks to Natural Resources Canada's Office of Energy Efficiency for funding this research.

REFERENCES

[1] E. Asadi, M. G. Da Silva, C. H. Antunes, and L. Dias, "Multi-objective optimization for building retrofit strategies: A model and an application," Energy Build., vol. 44, pp. 81–87, Jan. 2012, doi: 10.1016/j.enbuild.2011.10.016.

[2] Z. Ma, P. Cooper, D. Daly, and L. Ledo, "Existing building retrofits: Methodology and state-of-the-art," Energy Build., vol. 55, pp. 889–902, Dec. 2012, doi: 10.1016/j.enbuild.2012.08.018.

[3] D. Malomo, Y. Xie, and G. Doudak, "Unified life-cycle cost-benefit analysis framework and critical review for sustainable retrofit of Canada's existing buildings using mass timber," Can. J. Civ. Eng., vol. 51, no. 7, pp. 687–703, Jul. 2024, doi: 10.1139/cjce-2023-0222.

[4] N. R. C. Government of Canada, "National Energy Use Database." Accessed: July. 28, 2025. [Online]. Available: https://oee.nrcan.gc.ca/corporate/statistics/neud/dpa/data_e/databases.cfm

[5] N. R. Canada, "Eligible retrofits and grant amounts." Accessed: July. 28, 2025. [Online]. Available: https://natural-resources.canada.ca/energy-efficiency/homes/canada-greener-homes-grant/start-your-energy-efficient-retrofits/plan-document-and-complete-your-home-retrofits/eligible-grants-for-my-home-retrofit/23504

[6] A. Akhatova and L. Kranzl, "Agent-based modelling of building retrofit adoption in neighbourhoods," Energy Build., vol. 328, p. 115172, Feb. 2025, doi: 10.1016/j.enbuild.2024.115172.

[7] S. Ebrahimigharehbaghi, Q. K. Qian, F. M. Meijer, and H. J. Visscher, "Unravelling Dutch homeowners' behaviour towards energy efficiency renovations: What drives and hinders their decision-making?," Energy Policy, vol. 129, pp. 546–561, Jun. 2019, doi: 10.1016/j.enpol.2019.02.046.

[8] F. Re Cecconi, A. Khodabakhshian, and L. Rampini, "Data-driven decision support system for building stocks energy retrofit policy," J. Build. Eng., vol. 54, p. 104633, Aug. 2022, doi: 10.1016/j.jobe.2022.104633.

[9] T. Hong, L. Yang, D. Hill, and W. Feng, "Data and analytics to inform energy retrofit of high performance buildings," Appl. Energy, vol. 126, pp. 90–106, Aug. 2014, doi: 10.1016/j.apenergy.2014.03.052.

[10] F. Ascione, F. De Rossi, and G. P. Vanoli, "Energy retrofit of historical buildings: theoretical and experimental investigations for the modelling of reliable performance scenarios," Energy Build., vol. 43, no. 8, pp. 1925–1936, Aug. 2011, doi: 10.1016/j.enbuild.2011.03.040.

[11] M. M. Rahman, M. G. Rasul, and M. M. K. Khan, "Energy conservation measures in an institutional building in sub-tropical climate in Australia," Appl. Energy, vol. 87, no. 10, pp. 2994–3004, Oct. 2010, doi: 10.1016/j.apenergy.2010.04.005.

[12] B. Abu-Hijleh, A. Manneh, A. AlNaqbi, W. AlAwadhi, and A. Kazim, "Refurbishment of public housing villas in the United Arab Emirates (UAE): energy and economic impact," Energy Effic., vol. 10, no. 2, pp. 249–264, Apr. 2017, doi: 10.1007/s12053-016-9451-x.

[13] H. Abdullah and H. Alibaba, "Retrofits for Energy Efficient Office Buildings: Integration of Optimized Photovoltaics in the Form of Responsive Shading Devices," Sustainability, vol. 9, no. 11, p. 2096, Nov. 2017, doi: 10.3390/su9112096.

[14] C. Citadini De Oliveira, I. Catão Martins Vaz, and E. Ghisi, "Retrofit strategies to improve energy efficiency in buildings: An integrative review," Energy Build., vol. 321, p. 114624, Oct. 2024, doi: 10.1016/j.enbuild.2024.114624.

[15] T. D. Mora, A. Righi, F. Peron, and P. Romagnoni, "Cost-Optimal measures for renovation of existing school buildings towards nZEB," Energy Procedia, vol. 140, pp. 288–302, Dec. 2017, doi: 10.1016/j.egypro.2017.11.143.

[16] E. Thrampoulidis, G. Mavromatidis, A. Lucchi, and K. Orehounig, "A machine learning-based surrogate model to approximate optimal building retrofit solutions," Appl. Energy, vol. 281, p. 116024, Jan. 2021, doi: 10.1016/j.apenergy.2020.116024.

[17] S. A. Sharif and A. Hammad, "Developing surrogate ANN for selecting near-optimal building energy renovation methods considering energy consumption, LCC and LCA," J. Build. Eng., vol. 25, p. 100790, Sep. 2019, doi: 10.1016/j.jobe.2019.100790.

[18] A. Parker et al., "ComStock Reference Documentation: Version 1," Renew. Energy, 2023.

[19] J. Landsman et al., "Leveraging NREL's ResStock & ComStock Dataset to Evaluate Building Stock Electrification," 2024.

[20] Z. Wang, Y. Wang, R. Zeng, R. S. Srinivasan, and S. Ahrentzen, "Random Forest based hourly building energy prediction," Energy Build., vol. 171, pp. 11–25, Jul. 2018, doi: 10.1016/j.enbuild.2018.04.008.

[21] D. Ma, X. Li, B. Lin, Y. Zhu, and S. Yue, "A dynamic intelligent building retrofit decision-making model in response to climate change," Energy Build., vol. 284, p. 112832, Apr. 2023, doi: 10.1016/j.enbuild.2023.112832.

[22] L. Buitinck et al., "API design for machine learning software: experiences from the scikit-learn project," Sep. 01, 2013, arXiv: arXiv:1309.0238. doi: 10.48550/arXiv.1309.0238.

[23] T. Walter and M. D. Sohn, "A regression-based approach to estimating retrofit savings using the Building Performance Database," Appl. Energy, vol. 179, pp. 996–1005, Oct. 2016, doi: 10.1016/j.apenergy.2016.07.087.

Highly-Modular and Immersive Human-in-the-Loop Driving Simulators Using the CARLA Simulation Environment

Patrick Rebling, Lars Beeh, Philipp Nenninger, Reiner Kriesten
Institute of Energy Efficient Mobility
Karlsruhe University of Applied Sciences
Karlsruhe, Germany
e-mail: {patrick.rebling | lars.beeh | philipp.nenninger | reiner.kriesten}@h-ka.de

Abstract—**Driving simulators are a common industry tool for verifying driver assistance systems with human involvement. However, there is considerable variation in the hardware and software specifications of these simulators. Consequently, the development of such simulators is often a lengthy process due to the need to create custom software or the high cost of commercial solutions. The goal of this project is to integrate the simulation software Car Learning to Act (CARLA) into highly modular and immersive driving simulators. This will result in the creation of an open source, reconfigurable hardware abstraction that will facilitate the easy and rapid construction of driving simulators that prioritize modularity and extensibility.**

Keywords-simulation; testing; human-computer interaction; automotive.

I. INTRODUCTION

In past years, the development of autonomous driving has been accompanied by a series of optimistic assumptions [1][2]. However, despite significant progress, the road to fully autonomous vehicles capable of seamlessly handling all possible driving situations remains an ongoing challenge [3]. One of the most prominent challenges is the proliferation of mixed traffic scenarios, in which the road is shared by different entities, including automated and autonomous vehicles, cars with human drivers, as well as vulnerable road users, such as cyclists and pedestrians. Understanding, predicting, and replicating human driving behavior in these complex and dynamic environments has emerged as a central but challenging facet of autonomous driving research. The need to address this challenge is not only rooted in safety concerns, but extends to the broader goals of gaining public acceptance [4] and trust [5] in Artificial Intelligence (AI), particularly in the area of self-driving cars [6].

This is the domain in which the Human-In-The-Loop (HITL) methodology is applicable, which is particularly suited to understanding human behavior in complex driving situations without endangering the test subjects. However, there are several challenges associated with HITL driving simulator software. Achieving a high level of realism is critical, as visual, auditory, and tactile feedback must be convincing to ensure realistic driver responses, which requires high-quality graphics and precise input/output synchronization. Ensuring minimal latency between the driver's actions and the simulator's responses is essential, as any delay can disrupt the driving experience and affect the accuracy of the data. The integration of different subsystems can be complex due to different communication protocols and data formats, especially for hardware-related input and output devices, such as realistically behaving force feedback (FFB) motors, different visualization systems, and different driver positions and therefore visualization angles. Designing an intuitive and user-friendly interface is essential for efficient control and quick adjustments. Overcoming these challenges improves the test and verification processes for driver assistance systems in driving simulators, leading to safer and more reliable automotive technologies. The software must be open and adaptable to different driving simulators and scalable for future enhancements without extensive redevelopment.

However, to the best of our knowledge, there is no freely available open source framework that considers all requirements and provides a highly modular hardware abstraction of components for immersive simulators, including realistic steering wheel behavior and easily configurable input and output devices based on the Car Learning to Act (CARLA) simulation environment [7]. The objective of this research is to address the above issues by developing a solution that enables driving simulators to be quickly built and deployed, and that allows them to be connected all over the world.

Section II presents related work to this paper, including highlighting new elements and the need for such a modular, open-source framework for easily integratable driving simulators. In Section III, the approach and implementation of the modular framework is presented. Section IV concludes this paper and highlights areas for further research and development.

II. RELATED WORK

Modularizing software for abstraction is a common practice in software development. The use of Hardware Abstraction Layers (HALs) [8] allows the development of easily reconfigurable software. A popular HAL technology is virtual machines, which simulate operating systems on different host systems [9]. Robot Operating System (ROS) [10] is also widely used for hardware abstraction, as it allows software to be developed in a modular fashion so that hardware-related components can be easily replaced. For example, in the automotive industry, the AUTomotive Open System ARchitecture (AUTOSAR) [11] standard is a common way of abstracting hardware. Furthermore, [12] have developed a HAL for embedded systems with time-triggered hardware access. Simulation environments, such as CARLA on the open source side, or SILAB [13] on the commercial side, often provide a naturally modular architecture with a focus on software interfaces for testing autonomous driving functionality and testing driver assistance systems. In 2008, [14] presented an approach based on MATLAB/SIMULINK for customizable vehicle dynamics in HITL simulators. In the context of driving simulators, [15] presented a modular software-based architecture for integrating developed software for model-based testing of automated driving functions, but focused on specific simulator configurations and lacking open source features. [16] developed modularization in terms of interchangeability of hardware mock-up modules. For example, Realtime Technologies [17] commercially offers its RDS-Modular simulator mock-ups, which can be assembled from predefined modules to meet customer requirements.

To the best of our knowledge, there is currently no freely available open source framework that comprehensively addresses all potential requirements while providing a highly modular hardware abstraction for components used in immersive simulators. This includes features, such as realistic steering wheel behavior and easily configurable input and output devices, all integrated into the CARLA simulation environment. This also allows simulators based on the same simulation environment and framework presented in this paper to be connected all over the world. Thus, the next chapter presents an approach to address these challenges by developing a solution that enables rapid construction and deployment of driving simulators.

III. Approach

The overall concept of our approach for integrating the CARLA simulation environment into a driving simulator is shown in Figure 1.

To achieve a high degree of modularity and extensibility, the processing of driver input, control of environmental variables, display of images, FFB for the steering wheel, and vehicle control are divided into several separate ROS nodes as shown in Figure 2. ROS is a state-of-the-art framework for automated and autonomous driving research, as it enables highly modular software design (see, for example, [18]–[20]). Therefore, a simulator that enables testing of automated driving functions with HITL should also be based on ROS. The nodes communicate via ROS messages with the CARLA-ROS-Bridge and with each other or, if needed, as clients directly with the CARLA server via the API. The vehicle control interface to external driver assistance systems is formed by six ROS topics, allowing testing of, for example, Cruise Control (CC), Lane Keeping Assist System (LKAS), and Lane Change Assist (LCA), and can be easily extended to include further functionality. The following subsections provide a more detailed explanation of each node.

A. Input handling

The *Input Handling* node is responsible for handling all user input from the steering wheel, buttons, pedals, and keyboard. The Python library Pygame [21] is used because it is platform-independent and generally compatible with all game controllers and other input devices. A configuration file contains the assignment of inputs to various program functions, such as activating a turn signal, changing gear, or changing weather conditions. This gives users the flexibility to change assignments and use hardware with different numbers of buttons and axes. A ROS message is issued when an input event occurs. In addition, a CANopen interface is available to publish Controller Area Network (CAN) messages within the ROS environment and to control the ego vehicle via CAN.

B. Time and weather control

The *Weather Controller* node is responsible for controlling the weather and time of day within the simulation. A configuration file contains an expandable list of preset time and weather conditions. At the user's request, the system switches to the next or previous preset by passing the corresponding parameter values to the CARLA-ROS-Bridge, where they are applied to the simulation.

C. Display control

Camera sensors are added to the simulated vehicle at the start. The number of cameras M is equal to the number of monitors or video projectors used in the driving simulator. This value is specified in a configuration file which also contains information about other parameters, such as the resolution, the width of the monitor b, the width of the side monitor frame k, and the distance between the screens and the driver's head d as described in Figure 3. The *Display Controller* node uses these values to calculate the angle f (see (1) and Figure 3) and the horizontal rotation angles o_i (see (2) and Figure 3) of the camera sensors, ensuring that the simulated scene is displayed in a realistic manner.

$$f = 2 \cdot \arctan\left(\frac{\left(\frac{b}{2} - k\right)}{d}\right) \tag{1}$$

where b is the width of a single monitor, d is the distance from driver's head to the monitor surface, and k is defined by the frame width of the monitor. While f remains constant for all camera sensors with identical monitors, the rotation angles o_i of these cameras vary by a factor i, where i is calculated based on whether the number of displays M is an even or odd integer. Thus, i represents a list of numbers for the partial rotation of each monitor:

$$\begin{gathered} o_i = i \cdot 2 \cdot \arccos\left(\frac{d}{\sqrt{\left(\frac{b}{2}\right)^2 + d^2}}\right) \quad \text{with} \\ i = \begin{cases} \pm n \text{ and } n \in \mathbb{N}_0, n \leq \frac{M-1}{2}, & M \bmod 2 = 1 \\ \pm \frac{n}{2} \text{ and } n \in \mathbb{N}, n \leq \frac{M}{2}, & M \bmod 2 = 0 \end{cases} \end{gathered} \tag{2}$$

For example, three monitors result in $i = \{-1, 0, 1\}$. The position of the camera sensors is identical to the position of the driver's head in the vehicle coordinate system, as specified

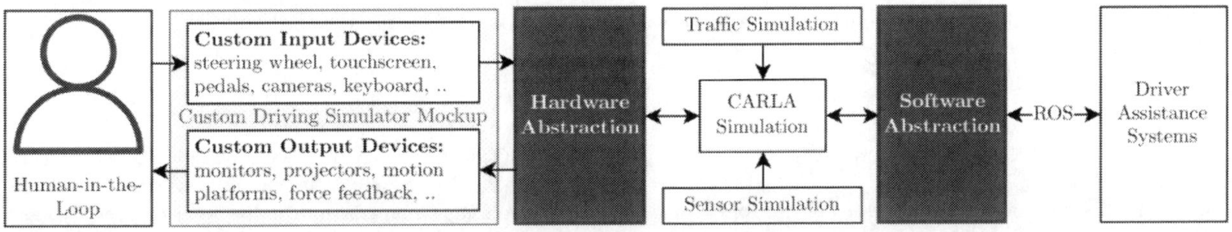

Figure 1. Abstract concept of the open simulation software for seamless and fast integration into custom driving simulators for HITL tests. The two abstraction modules are presented in this paper.

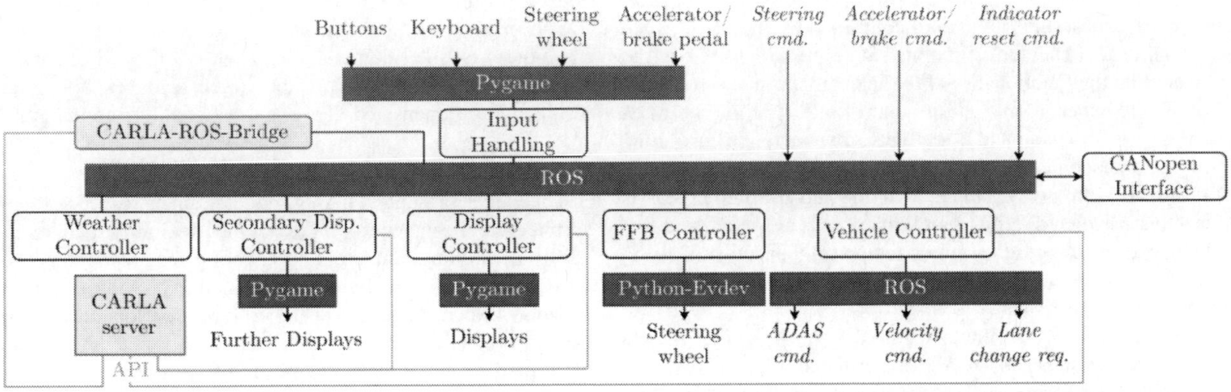

Figure 2. Integration of CARLA into a static driving simulator. Tasks are distributed across multiple ROS nodes (white) that communicate via ROS messages. Hardware interaction is facilitated by the use of the Pygame and Python-evdev libraries. All interfaces are shown in red.

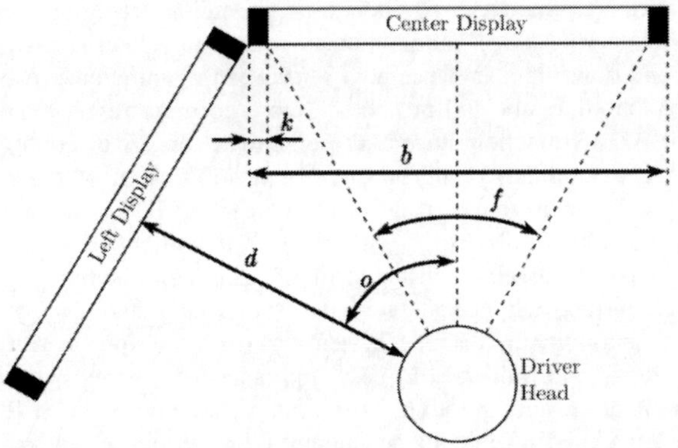

Figure 3. Geometrical description of the display setup of driving simulators with distance from driver head to display d, frame width k, display width b, horizontal field of view f and horizontal display rotation o.

in the configuration file. For reasons of runtime efficiency, the images from the camera sensors are not received from the server via ROS, but via API. They are then displayed side by side in a Pygame window with the total resolution of the screens as shown in Figure 4. Taking into account the monitor frames, rotations and distances, the image from the camera sensors will appear smooth and without shifting on the driver's monitor.

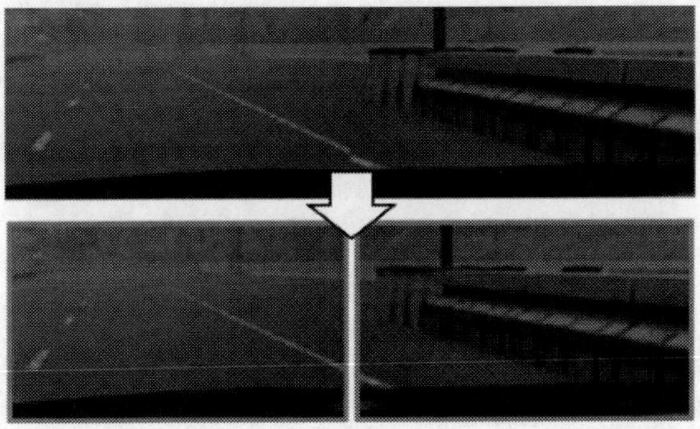

Figure 4. Example of offset compensation for simulators with displays. An automatically calulated offset based on the user-defined parameters resulting in a seamless image on the custom hardware setup.

A secondary display shows important information, such as current vehicle speed, vehicle lighting status, and current gear. The *Secondary Display Controller* can be used to integrate additional displays for mirrors and user interfaces.

D. Vehicle control

The *Vehicle Controller* node is responsible for controlling the simulated vehicle's steering, accelerator, brake, shift, and lighting functions. As given in the example programs including the values [22], the steering wheel angle is transmitted nonlinearly to the vehicle wheels (see (3)), with slight modifications to map the steering angle non-linear from -1 to 1. This results in less sensitive steering behavior at small steering angles, which helps prevent the vehicle's lateral dynamics from becoming unstable.

$$f(x) = 0.509 \cdot \tan(1.1x) \quad (3)$$

where x is the raw steering angle received from hardware steering wheel. A similar principle applies to the simulator's accelerator and brake pedals. Gears can be shifted manually by the driver or automatically. While brake lights and rear lights are activated and deactivated according to the vehicle's operating status, most other lights are controlled by the driver, such as high beams or interior lighting. State machines are used to ensure that the functionality of the indicators is consistent with real-world expectations, and to control the switching between parking, low beam, and fog lights. By way of illustration, the state machine for the indicators is shown in Figure 5. It can be seen, for example, that the left-hand indicator is deactivated when the right-hand indicator is activated, and that the hazard warning lights can be temporarily deactivated using the standard indicator switches, but are reactivated when the indicator is deactivated.

Six ROS topics facilitate external control of the vehicle by driver assistance systems, in particular CC, LKAS, and LCA. The node provides the necessary information on whether the driver has activated or deactivated the above systems and whether a lane change has been initiated by activating an indicator. In case of a successful lane change, the indicator can be reset via an external message. The node also provides the desired speed of the vehicle, which is the current speed of the vehicle when CC is engaged. This speed can be increased or decreased by the driver. The actual positions of the accelerator and brake pedals are then overwritten by the external values, except in cases where the driver applies more force to the accelerator than CC requires, such as when overtaking. CC is disengaged in the event of a collision or when the brake pedal is depressed. When LKAS is activated, the actual steering wheel angle is not overwritten by the external angle. Instead, the steering wheel is rotated to the correct position using force feedback effects as described in Subsection III-E. In the event of a collision, lane keeping is disabled.

E. Force feedback

The *FFB Controller* node has two tasks: generating force feedback and controlling the steering wheel angle when LKAS is enabled. These are achieved by using the Python-evdev library [23], which is based on the generic Linux input event interface evdev. This usually ensures compatibility with game controllers.

The inclined steering axis of a car results in steering resistance due to the centripetal force acting on the wheels. Without compensation, the wheels and steering wheel will automatically align in the center position [24]. The force, which is proportional to the square of the vehicle's velocity v, can be simulated with an autocentering effect. The strength s of the effect is calculated as follows

$$s = p \cdot v^2 \quad (4)$$

where p is a user defined constant.

Figure 6 shows the control loop required to turn the steering wheel to the desired angle. To avoid the nonlinearity inherent in the nonlinear transmission of the steering wheel angle y to the wheel angle y^*, the inverse nonlinearity is applied to w^* and the resulting steering wheel angle w is used as the setpoint. The controller output r is the strength of the constant effect. Note that this strength is not unlimited. It is reasonable to expect that small disturbances may occur in the motors or other components of the steering wheel, which are represented as z. When other force feedback effects are disabled or compensated, the wheel behaves like an integrator.

IV. Conclusion and Future Work

This paper presents a highly modular, open source software architecture designed to increase the flexibility and adaptability of driving simulators by enabling seamless integration of different hardware configurations and providing a plug-and-play experience for researchers and developers. By supporting the interchangeability of displays, input devices, and other peripheral components, the architecture promotes a user-centric approach that can accommodate different setups without requiring extensive reconfiguration. An additional feature of the proposed framework is its ability to replicate realistic steering wheel behavior during active Advanced Driver Assistance Systems (ADAS) operations, including scenarios where the steering wheel autonomously rotates to reflect real-world conditions. This enhancement improves the immersive quality of the simulator and provides a more accurate representation of ADAS functionalities and their impact on driver control.

The modularity and hardware-agnostic design of the proposed system makes it an ideal choice for HITL simulations where the flexibility to integrate different input and display devices is essential. This level of modularity supports different research needs, facilitates the testing and evaluation of autonomous driving systems across multiple hardware setups, and allows for easy upgrades or changes to the simulation configuration. Furthermore, integration with ROS allows driving data to be captured for further investigation in specific scenarios. The ScenarioRunner for CARLA [25] enables efficient, scenario-based testing using OpenDrive [26] and OpenScenario [27] data. By incorporating an architecture that is compatible with industry-standard hardware and adaptable to future advances, the framework provides a robust foundation for the continued development of HITL simulation environments and is used in our multi-simulator framework at the Karlsruhe University of Applied Sciences [28].

Future developments will focus on extending the capabilities of the system through full integration with the D-BOX motion platforms, providing enhanced physical feedback for even greater immersion. This addition will allow the simulator to

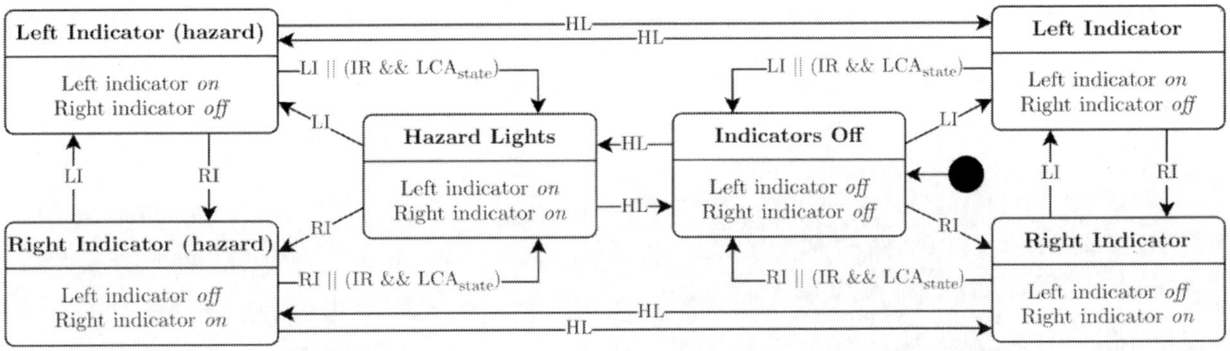

Figure 5. Indicator System State Machine. Events (rising edges): Hazard Light (HL), Left/Right Indicator (LI/RI), and Indicator Reset (IR). For IR to be effective, the state Lane Change Assist (LCA) must be active.

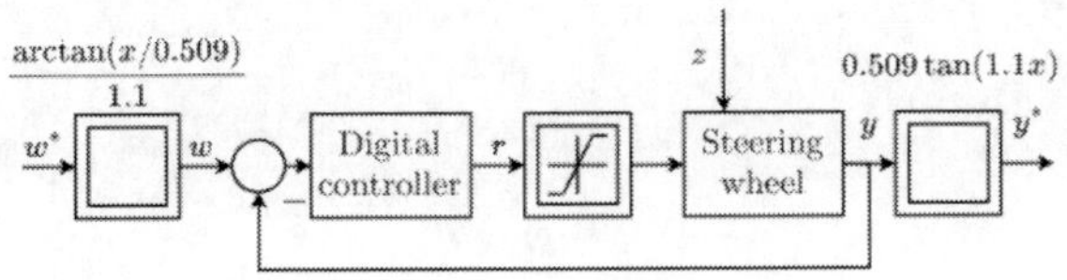

Figure 6. Control loop for steering angle x control according to external setpoints. The nonlinear steering transmission that would otherwise be present in the loop is avoided by using inverse nonlinearity.

convey realistic vehicle dynamics and road conditions to the user, increasing the fidelity of the simulation. In addition, we plan to develop an open interface to support custom motion platforms, allowing researchers and developers to use a variety of motion systems within the simulator framework. By enabling compatibility with a wide range of motion platforms, the simulator will offer increased adaptability, positioning it as a versatile tool for both research and industry applications in autonomous and assisted driving. Support for Windows devices is also provided by adding a DirectInput mode instead of the Linux-specific evdev library. The framework will be made publicly available at https://git.ieem-ka.de/public-repositories/carla-sim.

Acknowledgment

This work was developed in the project KIIWI (reference number: 16DHBKI060) which is funded by the German Federal Ministry of Research, Technology and Space (BMFTR).

References

[1] E. Musk, K. Swisher, and W. Mossberg, *Interview with Elon Musk at Code Conference 2016*, English, 2016. Accessed: Aug. 4, 2025. [Online]. Available: https://www.youtube.com/watch?v=wsixsRI-Sz4.

[2] K. Bimbraw, "Autonomous Cars: Past, Present and Future - A Review of the Developments in the Last Century, the Present Scenario and the Expected Future of Autonomous Vehicle Technology," *ICINCO 2015 - 12th International Conference on Informatics in Control, Automation and Robotics, Proceedings*, vol. 1, pp. 191–198, Jan. 2015. DOI: 10.5220/0005540501910198.

[3] B. Padmaja, C. V. K. N. S. N. Moorthy, N. Venkateswarulu, and M. M. Bala, "Exploration of issues, challenges and latest developments in autonomous cars," *Journal of Big Data*, vol. 10, no. 1, p. 61, May 2023, ISSN: 2196-1115. DOI: 10.1186/s40537-023-00701-y.

[4] S. Kelly, S.-A. Kaye, and O. Oviedo-Trespalacios, "What factors contribute to the acceptance of artificial intelligence? A systematic review," *Telematics and Informatics*, vol. 77, p. 101 925, Feb. 2023, ISSN: 07365853. DOI: 10.1016/j.tele.2022.101925.

[5] N. Gillespie, S. Lockey, C. Curtis, J. Pool, and Ali Akbari, "Trust in Artificial Intelligence: A global study," The University of Queensland; KPMG Australia, Brisbane, Australia, Tech. Rep., Feb. 2023. Accessed: Aug. 4, 2025. [Online]. Available: http://doi.org/10.14264/00d3c94.

[6] L. J. Molnar et al., "Understanding trust and acceptance of automated vehicles: An exploratory simulator study of transfer of control between automated and manual driving," *Transportation Research Part F: Traffic Psychology and Behaviour*, vol. 58, pp. 319–328, Oct. 2018, ISSN: 13698478. DOI: 10.1016/j.trf.2018.06.004.

[7] A. Dosovitskiy, G. Ros, F. Codevilla, A. Lopez, and V. Koltun, "CARLA: An Open Urban Driving Simulator," in *Proceedings of the 1st Annual Conference on Robot Learning*, S. Levine, V. Vanhoucke, and K. Goldberg, Eds., ser. Proceedings of Machine Learning Research, vol. 78, PMLR, 2017, pp. 1–16. Accessed: Aug. 4, 2025. [Online]. Available: https://proceedings.mlr.press/v78/dosovitskiy17a.html.

[8] A. J. Massa, "The Hardware Abstraction Layer," in *Embedded software development with e-Cos*, ser. Bruce Perens' Open source series, Upper Saddle River, NJ: Prentice Hall, 2003, ISBN: 978-0-13-035473-0.

[9] Y. Li, W. Li, and C. Jiang, "A Survey of Virtual Machine System: Current Technology and Future Trends," in *2010 Third International Symposium on Electronic Commerce and Security*, 2010, pp. 332–336. DOI: 10.1109/ISECS.2010.80.

[10] M. Quigley et al., "ROS: An open-source Robot Operating System," in *IEEE International Conference on Robotics and Automation*, vol. 3, Jan. 2009. Accessed: Aug. 4, 2025. [Online]. Available: https://api.semanticscholar.org/CorpusID:6324125.

[11] S. Voget, "AUTOSAR and the automotive tool chain," in *Proceedings of the Conference on Design, Automation and Test in Europe*, ser. DATE '10, event-place: Dresden, Germany, Leuven, BEL: European Design and Automation Association, 2010, pp. 259–262, ISBN: 978-3-9810801-6-2.

[12] G. Simmann, V. Veeranna, and R. Kriesten, "Design of an Alternative Hardware Abstraction Layer for Embedded Systems with Time-Controlled Hardware Access," English, SAE International, Jul. 2024. DOI: 10.4271/2024-01-2989.

[13] H. Krueger, M. Grein, A. Kaußner, and C. Mark, "SILAB—A Task Oriented Driving Simulation," 2005. Accessed: Aug. 4, 2025. [Online]. Available: https://api.semanticscholar.org/CorpusID:11019771.

[14] M. Cipelli, W. Schiehlen, and F. Cheli, "Driver-in-the-loop simulations with parametric car models," *Vehicle System Dynamics*, vol. 46, no. sup1, pp. 33–48, Sep. 2008, ISSN: 0042-3114. DOI: 10.1080/00423110701882280.

[15] M. Fischer et al., "Modular and Scalable Driving Simulator Hardware and Software for the Development of Future Driver Assistence and Automation Systems," de, in *New Developments in Driving Simulation Design and Experiments*, A. Kemeny, S. Espié, and F. Mérienne, Eds., ISSN: 0769-0266, Paris, Frankreich, Sep. 2014, pp. 223–229. Accessed: Aug. 4, 2025. [Online]. Available: https://elib.dlr.de/90638/.

[16] F. De Filippo, A. Stork, H. Schmedt, and F. Bruno, "A modular architecture for a driving simulator based on the FDMU approach," *International Journal on Interactive Design and Manufacturing (IJIDeM)*, vol. 8, no. 2, pp. 139–150, May 2014, ISSN: 1955-2513, 1955-2505. DOI: 10.1007/s12008-013-0182-3.

[17] R. Technologies, *RDS-Modular*, 2024. Accessed: Aug. 4, 2025. [Online]. Available: https://www.faac.com/realtime-technologies/.

[18] S. Kato et al., "Autoware on Board: Enabling Autonomous Vehicles with Embedded Systems," in *2018 ACM/IEEE 9th International Conference on Cyber-Physical Systems (ICCPS)*, Porto: IEEE, Apr. 2018, pp. 287–296, ISBN: 978-1-5386-5301-2. DOI: 10.1109/ICCPS.2018.00035.

[19] A.-M. Hellmund, S. Wirges, O. S. Tas, C. Bandera, and N. O. Salscheider, "Robot operating system: A modular software framework for automated driving," in *2016 IEEE 19th International Conference on Intelligent Transportation Systems (ITSC)*, Rio de Janeiro, Brazil: IEEE, Nov. 2016, pp. 1564–1570, ISBN: 978-1-5090-1889-5. DOI: 10.1109/ITSC.2016.7795766.

[20] M. Maarssoe et al., "ADORe: Unified Modular Framework for Vehicle and Infrastructure-Based System Level Automation:" in *Proceedings of the 11th International Conference on Vehicle Technology and Intelligent Transport Systems*, Porto, Portugal: SCITEPRESS - Science and Technology Publications, 2025, pp. 571–581, ISBN: 978-989-758-745-0. DOI: 10.5220/0013405200003941.

[21] P. Shinners, *Pygame*, 2000. Accessed: Aug. 4, 2025. [Online]. Available: https://www.pygame.org/.

[22] CARLA, *Python API examples manual_control_steeringwheel.py*, Nov. 2021. Accessed: Aug. 4, 2025. [Online]. Available: https://github.com/carla-simulator/carla/blob/master/PythonAPI/examples/manual_control_steeringwheel.py.

[23] G. Valkov, *Python-evdev Introduction*, 2022. Accessed: Aug. 4, 2025. [Online]. Available: https://python-evdev.readthedocs.io/en/latest/index.html.

[24] C. Smith, *Here's Why The Front Wheels Automatically Return To Center*, Jan. 2019. Accessed: Aug. 4, 2025. [Online]. Available: https://www.motor1.com/news/299470/why-front-wheels-return-center/.

[25] CARLA Team, *ScenarioRunner for CARLA*, 2024. [Online]. Available: https://github.com/carla-simulator/scenario_runner.

[26] Association for Standardization of Automation & Measuring Systems, *ASAM OpenDrive*, 2024. Accessed: Apr. 28, 2025. [Online]. Available: https://www.asam.net/standards/detail/opendrive/.

[27] Association for Standardization of Automation & Measuring Systems, *ASAM OpenSCENARIO XML*, 2024. Accessed: Apr. 28, 2025. [Online]. Available: https://www.asam.net/standards/detail/openscenario/.

[28] P. Rebling, R. Kriesten, and P. Nenninger, "Towards the Interpretation of Customizable Imitation Learning of Human Driving Behavior in Mixed Traffic Scenarios," Detroit, Michigan, United States, Apr. 2024, pp. 2024–01–2009. DOI: 10.4271/2024-01-2009.

Decision Modeling for Unmanned Swarm Suppression of Enemy Air Defenses Based on Deep Reinforcement Learning

Xiao Hu, Yonglin Lei, Fusong Luo, Hongfei Shi, Jiajun Zhu
College of Systems Engineering, National University of Defense Technology
Changsha 410003, China
email: huxiao14@nudt.edu.cn

Abstract—**The Suppression of Enemy Air Defense (SEAD) mission is a critical component of Unmanned Aerial Vehicle (UAV) swarm operations, presenting a complex challenge for modeling and simulation. Machine Learning (ML), particularly Deep Reinforcement Learning (DRL), offers a promising approach to enhance UAV swarm SEAD effectiveness through intelligent decision-making. This paper, therefore, explores a modeling and simulation approach to intelligent combat equipment decision-making based on deep DRL. We establish a DRL modeling framework grounded in combat simulation and specifically construct an intelligent decision-making framework for UAV Swarm SEAD. Focusing on the attack decision-making problem, we present a case study utilizing the Dueling Deep Q-Network (Dueling DQN) algorithm for intelligent combat decision modeling. Preliminary experimental results demonstrate that the ML-based intelligent decision-making model achieves superior combat effectiveness compared to traditional knowledge engineering-based models.**

Keywords- UAV swarm ;SEAD; decision-making modeling; combat simulation ; Dueling DQN.

I. INTRODUCTION

Traditional manned aircraft assault methods face significant challenges in ensuring the safety of personnel and platforms against the modern air defense system. With the rapid development of UAV technology, employing UAV swarms is poised to become the predominant approach for executing SEAD tasks in the future [1].

The core challenge in achieving autonomous mission execution for UAV swarms lies in solving the problem of intelligent combat decision-making for their operations. Conventional UAV swarm combat decision-making primarily relies on knowledge engineering techniques, such as production rules and expert database systems [2]. However, these methods exhibit limitations, including difficulty in enumerating the complexity of the situational space, challenges in handling the inherent uncertainties of complex scenarios, and a lack of adaptive evolution in combat decision algorithms. Concurrently, the increasing credibility of unmanned combat simulation systems enables the generation of vast amounts of offensive and defensive combat data. This data can not only be used to evaluate UAV swarm combat effectiveness but also serve as input samples for machine learning algorithms, supporting the reinforcement learning training of combat decision models. This development opens new avenues for significantly enhancing UAV swarm combat effectiveness.

In recent years, DRL has achieved remarkable breakthroughs in domains such as games, business, and control [3], often surpassing human performance and demonstrating substantial potential for intelligent decision-making applications. Within the military domain, research utilizing DRL is gaining traction: Reference [4] applied heuristic reinforcement learning to air combat intelligent decision-making; Reference [5] employed DRL to study aircraft air-to-ground combat decision-making; Reference [6] implemented cooperative maneuvering decision-making for multiple warheads during penetration using DRL, achieving superior results compared to rule-based methods in simulation; Reference [7] proposed a DRL-based decision-making process framework for multi-aircraft cooperative air combat and validated its feasibility and practicality on a wargaming platform.

This paper first proposes a general modeling methodology for intelligent combat equipment decision-making, integrating combat simulation with DRL. Building upon this, we establish an intelligent decision-making training and modeling framework utilizing the equipment combat simulation system WESS. Subsequently, the paper focuses on the specific problem of combat decision-making modeling for heterogeneous UAV swarm SEAD. We detail the design of an intelligent decision-making model framework, investigate suitable DRL algorithms, and present a case study on intelligent decision-making modeling. The effectiveness of the proposed method and algorithm is validated through experimental comparisons with traditional knowledge engineering-based decision models.

The remainder of this paper is organized as follows. Section II presents the conceptual framework for intelligent equipment combat decision-making modeling based on combat simulation and DRL, as well as the detailed training modeling framework. Section III is dedicated to the decision-making model framework for UAV Swarm SEAD operations, including the operational concept, decision network analysis, and the detailed design of the perception, jamming, and attack decision networks. Section IV describes the training process of the attack decision network based on the Dueling DQN algorithm, covering the algorithm summary, network structure, and reward design. Section V provides a case study to validate the proposed approach, detailing the problem setup, rule experiments, pre-training, iterative training, and intelligent testing results. Finally, Section VI concludes the paper and discusses future work.

II. Intelligent Equipment Combat Decision-Making Modeling Framework Based On Combat Simulation And DRL

A. Conceptual Framework of Intelligent Equipment Combat Decision-Making Model Based on Combat Simulation

Within the framework of combat simulation, the entire intelligent weapon equipment, including its combat decision-making algorithm, must be constructed as a combat simulation model. This enables its incorporation into the combat simulation environment for interactive exploration and learning evolution. The weapon equipment model supporting combat simulation can be divided into two modules based on the operational domain described: the equipment simulation model and the operational behavior model. The former primarily describes behavior within the physical information domain and is responsible for battlefield situation awareness and operational command execution. The latter primarily describes behavior within the cognitive organization domain. It is responsible for analyzing and processing battlefield situation information output by the equipment simulation model, generating action plans, making operational decisions, and passing the resulting commands to the equipment simulation model for execution.

The operational behavior within the cognitive organization domain can be further categorized into two types: pre-war planning behavior and real-time decision-making behavior. The former can be flexibly described using data or scripts and implemented as a scripted operational behavior model within the combat simulation system. The latter requires making ad hoc decisions based on real-time changes in the situation and can be described using various decision-making modeling methods. If knowledge engineering methods are employed for decision modeling, it can be flexibly implemented as a behavior script. If machine learning methods are used for modeling, it is typically implemented as a neural network for inference computation, with DRL used for training and modeling. Current neural network models are generally trained and inferenced using the Python scripting language, enabling their integration into the scripted description framework of combat behavior. During operational simulation, the operational behavior model obtains situation information from the equipment simulation model and generates operational commands based on this information. These commands then drive and control the execution of the equipment simulation model, as depicted in the simulation loop in Figure 1. The training loop shown in the bottom half of the figure indicates that combat simulation generates the training sample data required for DRL-based intelligent decision-making modeling. An updated intelligent decision-making network model is formed through DRL training. The generation of subsequent training sample data is influenced by this updated model rejoining the combat simulation loop, and this process iterates until convergence.

Reinforcement learning algorithms are categorized into two types based on whether the behavior policy and the target policy are identical: On-Policy and Off-Policy. In On-Policy training algorithms, the policy used to generate samples is the same as the policy being optimized. This requires the agent training to be executed synchronously with the combat simulation. Given the computational complexity of combat simulation, On-Policy algorithms are not well-suited for parallel execution of simulations. Conversely, Off-Policy algorithms represent a more suitable training approach. Off-Policy training allows the combat simulation and training processes to run in parallel. Training samples generated from each combat simulation run (termed a round) are written concurrently into the corresponding round's sample database.

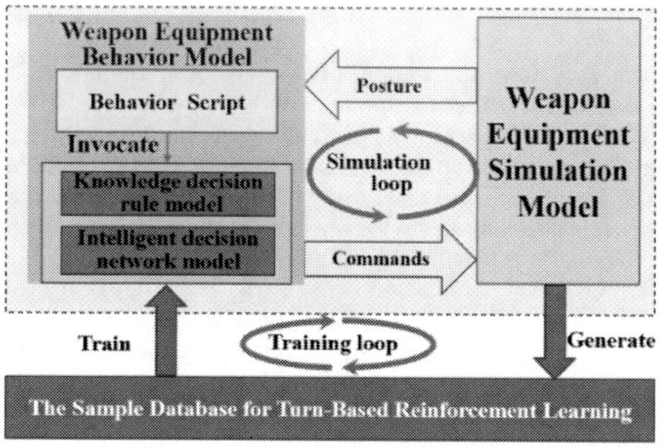

Figure 1. Conceptual framework of intelligent equipment operational decision-making mode

B. Intelligent Equipment Operational Decision-Making Training Modeling Framework Based on DRL.

1) Training modeling process: The process is divided into four stages as shown in Figure 2: rule experiment, pre-training, iterative training, and intelligent comparison test. Suppose there are m intelligent decision-making networks in UAV swarm.

a) The rule experiment: Aims to optimize the decision rules and prepare the pre-training data. By performing Monte Carlo experiments on all the rules of the decision problem in each training scenario space, a large number of rule experiment results data and reinforcement learning round sample data are obtained to evaluate the combat effectiveness of UAV swarm under each combination rule $\pi_R = (R_1, R_2, \ldots, R_m)$, and identifies the optimal rule to serve as the benchmark for subsequent intelligent test comparison.

b) The pre-training: Aims to provide an initial network for iterative training. By optimizing the round sample data obtained from the rule experiment, the data set with better combat effect of UAV swarm is obtained. On this basis, each decision network is trained offline to yield $\pi_N^0 = (N_1^0, N_2^0, \ldots, N_m^0)$. This stage utilizes the sample data generated by optimal rule experiments to avoid the "cold start" problem in iterative training and improve convergence efficiency.

c) Iterative training: Aims to accumulate experience and improve policy through continuous interaction between the agent and the training scene. On the basis of the pre-training, the network π_i is iteratively trained in turn, and the rest of the network is fixed in this process. Referring to the idea of policy improvement theorem [8], the policy improvement point is found in the single policy π_i, so that the joint policy π is improved. After all the policies are updated, the single round of policy iteration training is completed until the end conditions are met, such as achieving the desired operational effectiveness index or reaching the maximum number of iteration rounds, etc.The final optimized policy is denoted as $\pi'_N = (N'_1, N'_2, \ldots, N'_m)$.

d) The intelligent comparison test: Aims to verify the effectiveness of the single-strategy iteration training. Combat effectiveness evaluations are conducted for the UAV swarm in test scenarios using both the optimized policy π'_N and the baseline policy π_R . The experimental results are then compared to validate the efficacy of the intelligent decision-making approach.

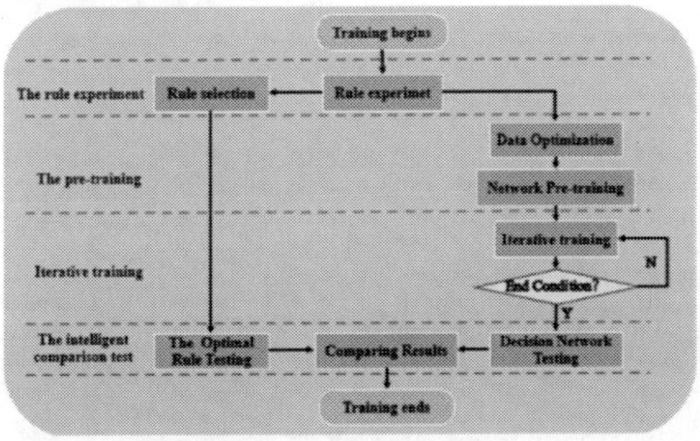

Figure 2. Policy iteration method

2) Training Support Environment : The reinforcement learning training support environment for intelligent decision-making based on combat simulation typically comprises four modules: combat scenario generation tool, combat simulation engine, parallel experiment and training management tool, and reinforcement learning training algorithm. The architecture of this training support environment is depicted in Figure 3.

a) Scenario generation module: Responsible for describing various scenarios that intelligent equipment may encounter in actual combat. It provides the diverse situational data sources required for decision-making model training.

b) Combat simulation engine module [9]*:* Responsible for simulating and executing numerous scenarios, generating both combat effectiveness data and the round sample dataset needed for training.

c) Parallel experiment and training management module: Responsible for managing large-scale parallel simulation experiments. It also orchestrates the synchronous scheduling of the DRL training algorithm and facilitates iterative updates to the decision model during experimentation.

d) Reinforcement learning training module: Responsible for implementing the reinforcement learning algorithm. It accepts scheduling directives from the parallel experiment and training management module and is specifically tasked with generating and updating the decision network model.

III. The Decision-Making Model Framework Of UAV Swarm SEAD Operation

A. Concept of UAV swarm SEAD operation

In SEAD missions, UAVs must perform reconnaissance, jamming/suppression, and strike tasks autonomously [10]. This enables the swarm to form a complete kill chain and achieve rapid "OODA" cycles. The UAV swarm composition typically includes: a reconnaissance aircraft equipped with radar pods, a jammer with electronic jamming pods, and an attack aircraft armed with multiple anti-radiation missiles.

The typical mission scenario involves: a number of mobile air defense positions (Blue Force) dispersed within a designated area. The Red Force organizes a UAV swarm to conduct SEAD operation against these positions. The attack aircraft form a low-altitude formation. After takeoff from the airfield, they proceed to the periphery of the operational area and enter a holding pattern. The jammer and reconnaissance aircraft form a high-altitude formation. They depart later than the low-altitude formation, flying at ultra-low altitude. At a predefined waypoint, they execute a pop-up maneuver to induce Blue Force air defense radars to activate and reveal their positions. The reconnaissance aircraft then detects and locates these targets, assigning them to the low-altitude attack formation. The primary actions of the attack aircraft (as depicted in Figure 4) are: selecting a launch point upon receiving assigned targets, proceeding to that location, launching missiles, and then entering a holding pattern while awaiting battle damage assessment (BDA) results from the reconnaissance aircraft to determine whether to conduct re-attack or proceed to the next target. The jammer continuously suppresses Blue Force air defense radars and jams incoming missile seekers, creating safer conditions for the low-altitude formation and reconnaissance aircraft. The mission concludes when: the reconnaissance aircraft is destroyed, all attack aircraft missiles are expended, all attack aircraft are destroyed, or all enemy targets are eliminated. Following mission completion, the surviving assets return to base. The objective is to destroy the maximum number of Blue Force air defense radars while sustaining minimum losses.

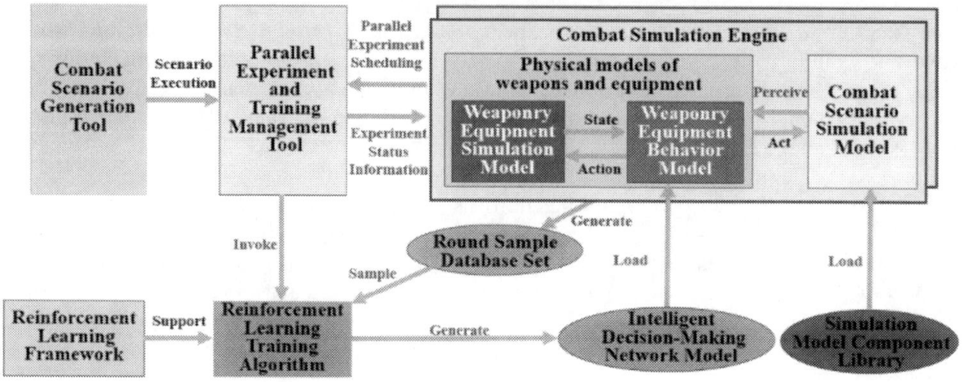

Figure 3. Reinforcement learning training supporting environment for intelligent decision making

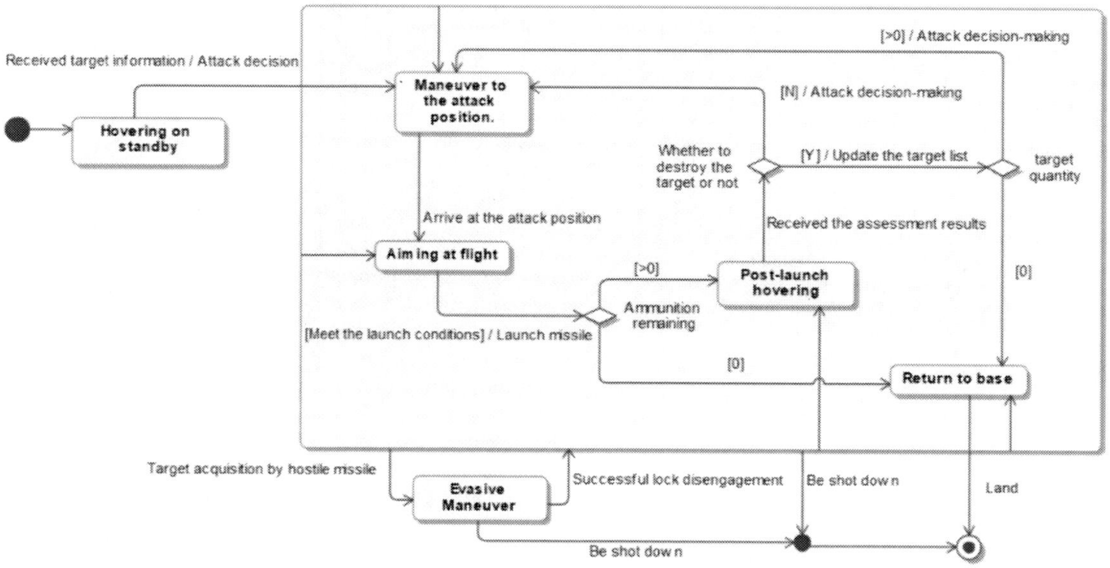

Figure 4. Attack behavior model of attack aircraft

B. *Analysis of UAV swarm SEAD operation decision network*

The SEAD mission encompasses multiple decision-making policies for the UAV swarm, such as formation flying, low-altitude penetration prior to engagement, electronic suppression, detection and perception, fire attack, and target assignment during engagement. Of these, the first three policies (pertaining to the pre-engagement phase) are particularly complex and challenging to describe using rules, and their decision outcomes significantly impact battle results. These decision problems exhibit the characteristics of a Markov decision process, making them suitable for description via neural networks and training using DRL. The remaining policies are directly modeled as rule-based scripts employing knowledge engineering methods. Figure 5 illustrates the composition structure of the entire UAV swarm SEAD operational decision-making model.

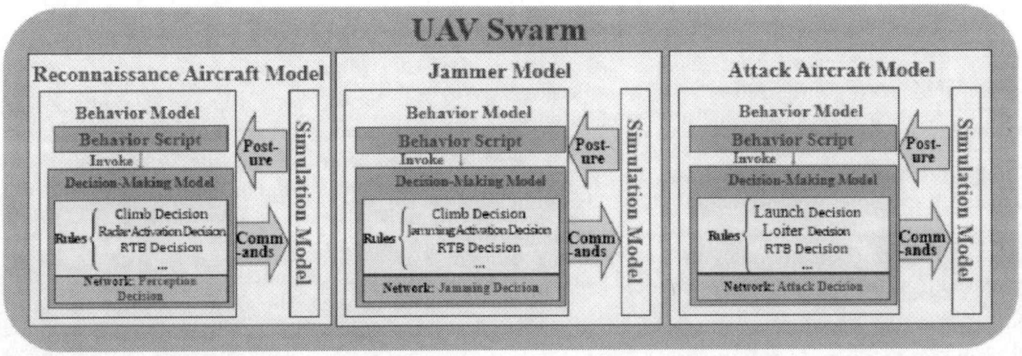

Figure 5. Operational decision-making structure of UAV swarm

C. UAV swarm SEAD operational decision-making network model framework

1) Perception and decision network

a) Input state space: The perception policy is designed to address the global situational awareness challenge for the reconnaissance aircraft, providing stable targeting information and fire damage assessment to the attack aircraft. It selects the following 4-dimensional inputs:

- Distance and bearing between the reconnaissance aircraft and the target group centroid.
- Distance and bearing between the reconnaissance aircraft and the nearest target.

Given the reconnaissance aircraft's position (x_0, y_0), the target group centroid (R_x, R_y) is defined as the weighted average of n targets' coordinates, with weights determined by target importance and threat level.

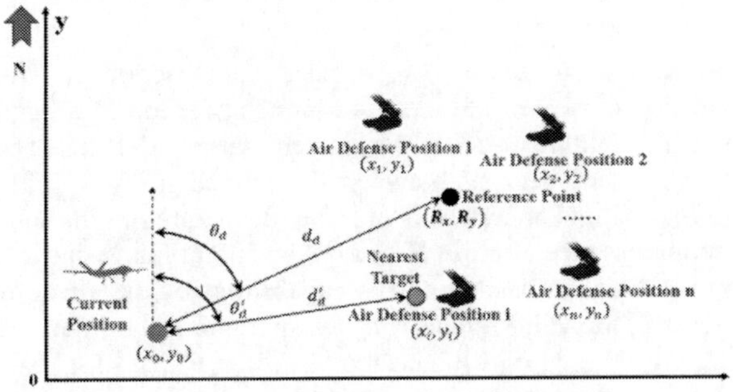

Figure 6. State space analysis of UAV

As illustrated in Figure 6, the distance and azimuth between UAV and the centroid of the target group are described by two parameters, d_d and θ_d, the nearest target is d'_d and θ'_d.Taking the former as an example, it is defined as (1).

$$\begin{cases} d_d = \sqrt{(R_x - x_0)^2 + \left(R_y - y_0\right)^2} \\ \theta_d = \tan^{-1}\frac{R_y - y_0}{R_x - x_0} \end{cases} \tag{1}$$

The input state space of the perception decision network can be specifically detailed in Table 1. In practical applications, data preprocessing is performed by taking the ratio of the azimuth value to π and the ratio of the distance value to the radar's maximum detection range (D_{dmax}) for a specific target type, serving normalization purposes.

TABLE I. INPUT STATE SPACE PERCEPTION DECISION NETWORK DESIGN

State variables	*Symbols*	*Data type*	*Preprocessing*
Centroid distance & bearing	d_d、θ_d	double	d/D_{dmax}
Nearest target distance & bearing	d'_d、θ'_d	double	$\theta/180^{\circ}$

b) Action space: In the process of fighting, the different array have different perception, interference effect, so the detection of perception and the output of electronic jamming decision network need to be able to reflect the correlation matrix of information, the concrete can be described as Figure 7.

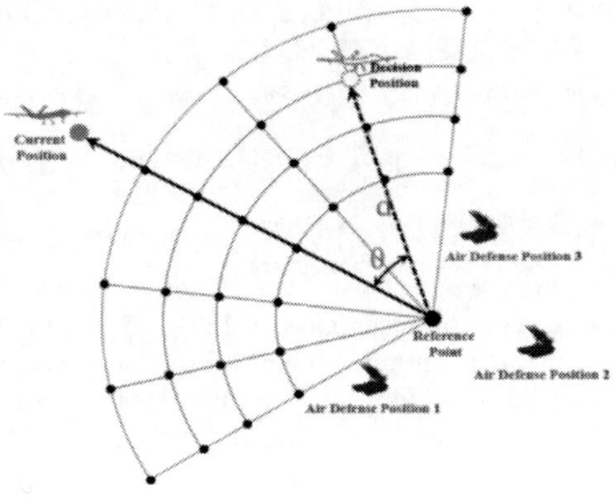

Figure 7. Action diagram of array position selection

Specifically, a polar coordinate system is established with the group centroid as the origin, the vector connecting the centroid to the current sensor array position as the zero-direction, and clockwise orientation as the positive direction; the decision network outputs two-dimensional coordinate information for the array configuration, which undergoes domain-specific processing in operational implementation—including parameter range bounding for direction θ and distance d and value discretization—according to equipment capabilities and mission requirements, for example constraining the operational distance range to 0.5 times D_{dmax} to 1 times D_{dmax} (where D_{dmax} denotes the reconnaissance aircraft's maximum effective detection range) in actual combat scenarios.

TABLE II. THE OUTPUT ACTION SPACE DESIGN OF THE PERCEPTION DECISION NETWORK

Decision-making action variable	*Range of values*	*Notes*
Array position Angle θ	$[-\theta_{max}, \theta_{max}]$	θ_{max} is the maximum Angle delimited
Array position distance d	$[0.5D_{dmax}, D_{dmax}]$	D_{dmax} is the maximum operating distance

c) Call time: The invocation opportunity is:

- When the precise coordinates of the enemy are obtained for the first time.
- When the enemy target is destroyed.
- Attack aircraft was shot down.

2) Interfere with the decision network

a) Interference decision network input state space: The jamming policy aims to solve the problem of enemy suppression and friendly support. The decision network accepts the following state inputs.

- Distance and bearing between the jammer and the centroid of the target cluster.
- Distance and bearing between the jammer and the centroid of the actively engaged target cluster.

The actively engaged target cluster refers to targets currently under attack by strike aircraft. All distance parameters are normalized against D_{jmax} (the jammer's maximum effective jamming range).

TABLE III. INPUT STATE SPACE DESIGN OF JAMMER DECISION NETWORK

State variables	*Symbols*	*Data type*	*Preprocessing*
Real-time attack target group centroid distance, bearing	d_j、θ_j	double	d/D_{jmax} $\theta/180^{\circ}$
Nearest target distance, bearing	d_j'、θ_j'	double	

b) Action space and call timing: During combat operations, both the reconnaissance aircraft and the jammer operate at high altitude. Their situational updates and decision-making actions are synchronized. Consequently, they share an identical action space definition and utilize the same set of call triggers for their respective decision networks.

3) decision network attack

The attack policy aims to solve the attack decision problem of each attack aircraft in the low-altitude formation. The decision network of each attack aircraft is isomorphic, but its execution is asynchronous.

a) Input state space: The attack decision network focuses on the selection of the anti-radiation missile launch position, and selects the following 9-dimensional state information as input (where D_{amax} is the maximum range of the anti-radiation missile and H is the current altitude of the attack aircraft):

- The distance, azimuth, and altitude difference between the current position of the attack aircraft and the target.
- The distance, azimuth, and elevation difference between the current position of the attack aircraft and the maximum threat target (the air defense position closest to the current attack target); the launch position should avoid this threat as much as possible.
- The distance and azimuth between the jammer and the attack target; the suppression effect of the jammer varies with its position.
- The current attack round count for the target and a flag indicating whether the first attack on this target was successful, reflecting the target's defensive capability strength or weakness.

All input data undergoes normalization.

TABLE IV. ATTACK DECISION NETWORK INPUT STATE SPACE DESIGN

State variables	*Symbols*	*Data type*	*Preprocessing*
Target distance, azimuth, elevation difference	$\boldsymbol{d_a}, \boldsymbol{\theta_a}, \boldsymbol{h_a}$	double	d/D_{amax} $\theta/180$ h/H
Maximum threat distance, bearing, altitude difference	d_a', θ_a', h_a'	double	
Jammer range, bearing	d_{aj}, θ_{aj}	double	
Current attack round	n	int	——

b) Output action space: The outcome of the attack decision network is the relative launch position of the attack aircraft with respect to the current target, defined by the distance and bearing between the launch position and the target. This concept mirrors the decision outputs of the reconnaissance aircraft. Based on the operational range of the anti-radiation missile and the capabilities of the air defense systems, the valid ranges for these parameters are defined as $[D_{amin}, D_{amax}]$ or distance and $[-\theta_{amax}, \theta_{amax}]$ for bearing. These ranges are discretized into $N_d + 1$ points (i.e., endpoints of N_d segments) for distance and $N_\theta + 1$ points (i.e., endpoints of N_θ segments) for bearing, forming a total of $N_{d\theta}$ discrete actions. The decision network evaluates the value of each discrete action and selects the one with the highest value as the optimal decision. This selected action is then converted into precise coordinates for the launch position. The attack aircraft maneuvers to this position to execute the strike.

TABLE V. ATTACK DECISION NETWORK OUTPUT SPACE DESIGN

Decision action variables	***Range of values***	***Action parsing***
Launch Position N	$\{0,1,\ldots,N_{d\theta}\}$	$d = \frac{(D_{amax} - D_{amin})}{N_d} \times \left\lfloor \frac{N}{(N_\theta + 1)} \right\rfloor + D_{amin}$ $\theta = \frac{2\theta_{amax}}{N_\theta} \times \left(N \bmod (N_\theta + 1)\right) - \theta_{amax}$

c) Call timing: The invocation of the attack decision network is centered on the attack target and requires the anti-radiation missile's passive seeker to lock onto a stable enemy radar beam to ensure attack accuracy. Therefore, subject to the preconditions of nonzero remaining ammunition and the reconnaissance aircraft being operational, the attack decision network is triggered under the following conditions:

- When the coordinates of the attack target are obtained for the first time.
- Upon attack failure.
- When successfully switching the attack target after a previous attack.
- Training the attack decision network based on Dueling DQN.

IV. Training The Attack Decision Network Based On Dueling DQN

To illustrate the training of the attack decision network as an example of intelligent decision-making, the remaining tactics employ the optimal rules.

A. Summary of Algorithm

Within the algorithm framework selection, the decision networks for each attack aircraft in the low-altitude formation are completely homogeneous; that is, they share identical state spaces, action spaces, and optimization objectives. This scenario can be simplified as a single-agent decision problem.

For the specific algorithm, addressing high-dimensional input, large action spaces, and the need to finely distinguish state and action values, the Dueling Deep Q-Network (Dueling DQN [11]) method demonstrates strong performance. As an improved algorithm over DQN [12], its core innovation is the decomposition of the traditional Q-value into two components: the state value $V(s)$ and the action advantage $A(s,a)$. A dual-branch neural network structure is employed to learn these two parts separately. The final action value $Q(s,a)$ is then calculated using the combination formula (2) (where $|\mathcal{A}|$ represents the size of the action space):

$$Q(s,a) = V(s) + \left(A(s,a) - \frac{1}{|\mathcal{A}|}\sum_{a' \in \mathcal{A}} A(s,a')\right) \quad (2)$$

This design enables the model to more effectively capture the relationship between state and action. It is particularly suitable for environments where the state value remains relatively stable while action advantages exhibit significant variation, thereby improving the algorithm's learning efficiency and stability.

B. Network Structure

The Dueling DQN algorithm is value-based. Its neural network architecture comprises two Q-networks with identical structures: a training network updated in real-time and a target network. The target network parameters are periodically synchronized with the training network parameters every fixed number of steps to enhance training stability. As shown in Figure 8, the Q-network utilizes a fully connected neural network that takes the 9-dimensional state vector as input and outputs Q-values for 35 discrete actions. Actions are selected according to a greedy policy, choosing the action with the maximum Q-value. This structure enables efficient feature sharing and effectively captures the dynamic advantages of different actions, making it particularly impactful in large-scale discrete action spaces and well-suited for the task.

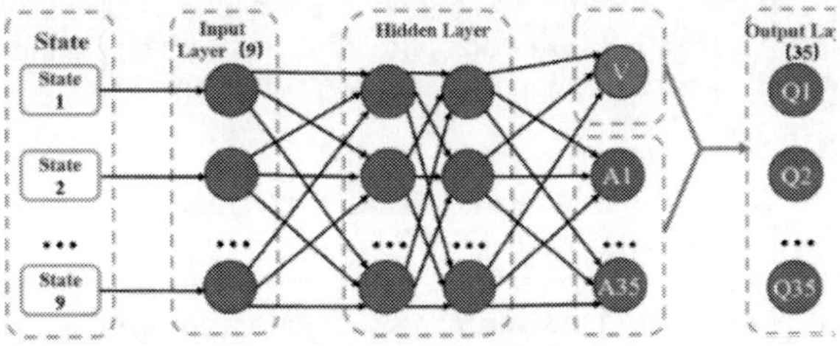

Figure 8. Dueling DQN decision network structure

C. Reward Design

The reward function plays a crucial role in guiding the iterative improvement of the decision-making network. Aligned with the objective of maximizing the exchange ratio and prioritizing the protection of the reconnaissance aircraft, the reward function evaluates operational actions based on the following dimensions: 1) reconnaissance aircraft survival status; 2) attack aircraft survival status. 3) successful missile launch; 4) successful missile hit on target. 16 distinct operational states are defined, encompassing nine feasible combinations of these dimensions. To differentiate between initial and supplementary attacks, a unique reward value is assigned to each state.

TABLE VI. REWARD DESIGN TABLE

No	State	Reward Value		No	State	Reward Value		No	State	Reward Value	
		Initial	*Follow-up*			*Initial*	*Follow-up*			*Initial*	*Follow-up*
1	[0,0,1,0]	-60	-65	4	[0,1,1,1]	-2	-4	7	[1,1,0,0]	0	0
2	[0,1,0,0]	-80	-90	5	[1,0,0,0]	-70	-75	8	[1,1,1,0]	20	10
3	[0,1,1,0]	-20	-40	6	[1,0,1,0]	-5	-10	9	[1,1,1,1]	90	50

TABLE VII. FORCES

Force	Units	Primary Mission Payload	Force	Units	Primary Mission Payload
Red Force	Reconnaissance Aircraft ×1	Radar Pod ×1	Blue Force	Early Warning Site ×1	Early Warning Radar ×1
	Jammer Aircraft ×1	Jamming Pod ×1		Air Defense Positions ×3	Fire Control Radar ×1
	Attack Aircraft ×2	Anti-Radiation Missiles ×2			Surface-to-Air Missiles ×24

The states [0,0,0,1], [0,1,0,1], [1,0,0,1], and [1,1,0,1] represent "missile launched but not hit" – these are impossible because if an attack aircraft is shot down after launch, the missile outcome becomes unknowable within the simulation. The states [1,0,1,1] and [0,0,1,1] are also impossible because the mission turn terminates immediately upon destruction of either the reconnaissance aircraft or an attack aircraft, precluding subsequent missile impact assessment. Additionally, the state [0,0,0,0] (indicating no launch and no hits) is impossible as it contradicts the context of evaluating attack actions.

V. SEAD UAV SWARM DECISION TRAINING MODEL

In the case study design and implementation, the training and verification environment was constructed using the WESS system developed by the research team [13].

A. Case Problem

The baseline forces for both Red and Blue sides are configured as detailed in TABLE VII. The lethality parameters are defined as follows: one anti-radiation missile is assumed to paralyze an air defense position, and one surface-to-air missile is assumed to shoot down one UAV.

For the Blue Force, early warning radars and air defense positions operate as an integrated system. In the absence of enemy threats, air defense radars remain silent to conceal their positions, while early warning radars—with longer detection ranges and wider scanning fields—perform aerial surveillance. Upon detecting incoming strikes, the early warning system relays target information to air defense positions in real time. When activated, air defense positions power on fire control radars for aerial search. After target lock is achieved and launch readiness confirmed, they intercept aerial targets (aircraft or missiles) using either autonomous or third-party guidance. If a target is destroyed and additional threats remain, engagement continues; if a missile misses, immediate re-engagement is initiated. Combat concludes when the position is destroyed or all airborne threats are neutralized.

Scenario generation involves six key variables defining the initial disposition of three enemy air defense positions. Each dimension (representing longitudinal or latitudinal coordinate offsets from actual deployment locations) has two discrete values, resulting in 64 distinct scenario configurations.

TABLE VIII. SCENARIO GENERATION COMBAT SCENARIO

Intelligence Position	Longitude Offset (minutes)	Latitude Offset (minutes)
Air Defense Company 1 (lon1, lat1)	{−1.58, 1.59}	{−2.04, 2.04}
Air Defense Company 2 (lon2, lat2)	{−1.87, 1.91}	{−1.94, 2.00}
Air Defense Company 3 (lon3, lat3)	{−1.95, 1.95}	{−2.27, 2.22}

B. Rule Experiments

The launch distance range [20,40] km was discretized into 5 values and the azimuth range [−30,30] degrees into 7 values, generating 35 candidate launch positions. Each position was evaluated across all 64 scenarios with 10 Monte Carlo repetitions per configuration. Combat effectiveness was quantified using the average exchange ratio per launch position over all experimental runs. This resulted in 35×64=2,240 scenario-position combinations and 22,400 total simulation runs. Key findings, visualized in the heat map of Figure 9, are summarized below:

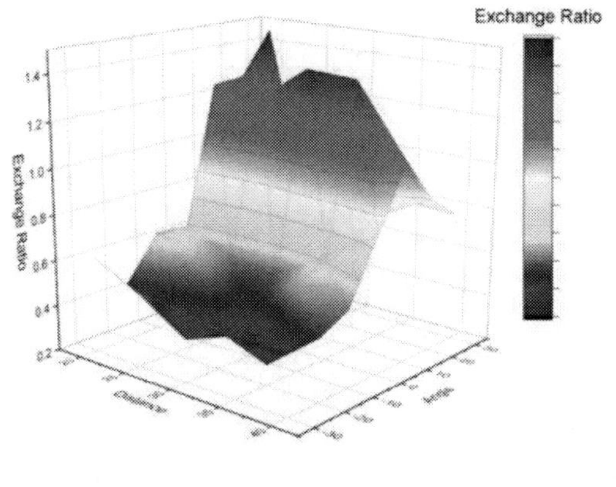

Figure 9. Specific heat map of regular experiment exchange

A The results demonstrate that selecting the launch position 20 km from the target at a 30° offset azimuth delivers optimal performance, achieving an average exchange ratio of 1.465.

C. Pre-training

1) Hyperparameter configuration : The value network was implemented using PyTorch. Core algorithm parameters include:

TABLE IX. DECISION NETWORK ATTACK DUELING DQN TRAINING PART PARAMETER CONFIGURATION

Hyperparameter	Value
Decision Network	2 hidden layers with 128 and 64 units
Discount Factor	0.99
Discount Factor	ReLU
Learning Rate	0.0001
Experience Replay Buffer Size	100000
Batch Size	256
Delayed Update Steps	200

2) Pre-train : Utilizing data samples where the reward value was non-negative, the neural network was trained for 100 rounds. Each round consisted of 200 training steps. Upon network convergence, the resulting model served as the initial decision model.

D. Iterative Training of Reinforcement Learning

he pre-trained attack decision-making model was loaded. For each training scenario, 10 simulation runs were executed, and the resulting experience data were stored in the database. The reinforcement learning algorithm then extracted batches of experience data from this database to train the decision network. After each training update, the updated decision network was loaded back into the simulation environment. This process—completing all scenario experiments—constituted one training round. The exploration rate was decayed by 0.01 per round. Training continued iteratively until the reward signal stabilized.

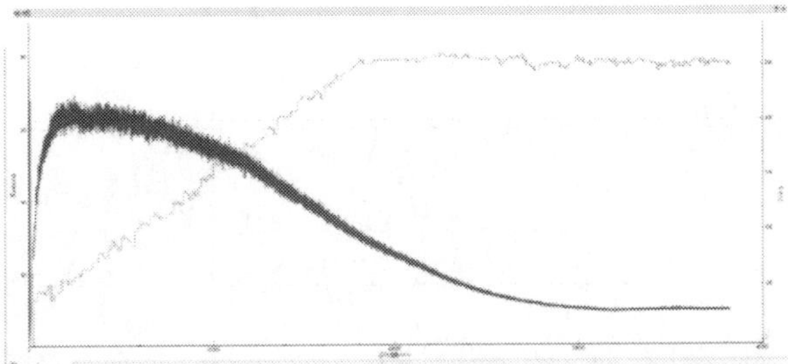

Figure 10. Schematic figure 10 reward (red curve) and loss (blue curve)

As shown in Figure 10, the average reward per round (calculated over 640 simulation runs) and the loss (mean squared error (MSE) between predicted and target Q-values) converged over the training process. After 38,235 training iterations spanning 200 rounds, the results stabilized: the average reward plateaued around 79. In the training scenarios, the attack aircraft demonstrated effective decision-making, achieving successful target hits both during initial engagements and follow-up attacks, while significantly improving the survival rate of the reconnaissance aircraft.

E. Intelligent Testing

The pre-trained attack decision-making model was loaded. For each training scenario, 10 simulation runs were executed, and the resulting experience data were stored in the database. The reinforcement learning algorithm then extracted batches of experience data from this database to train the decision network. After each training update, the updated decision network was reloaded into the simulation environment. This process—completing experiments across all scenarios—constituted one training round. The exploration rate was decayed by 0.01 per round. Training continued iteratively until the reward signal stabilized.

As shown in Figure 11, a total of five distinct test scenarios were constructed. The target locations of the three air-defense batteries remained consistent across scenarios. The actual deployment positions within each scenario corresponded to the vertices of the depicted rectangles. Brown markers represent training scenario positions, while other colors denote test scenario positions. To ensure simulation fidelity, each air-defense battery possessed four distinct disposition patterns. The combination of these patterns across the three batteries generated 64 unique Blue Force deployment configurations.

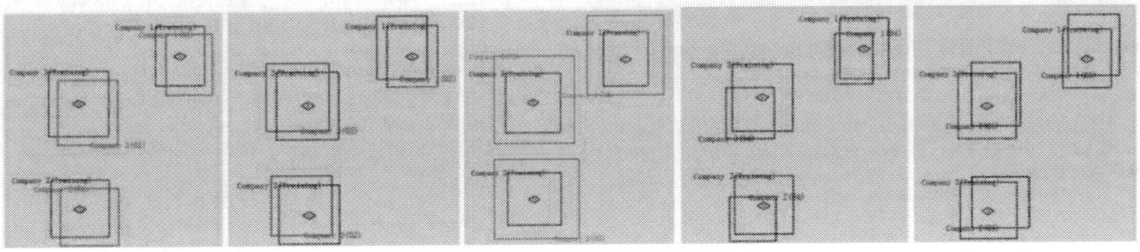

Figure 11. Intelligence test scenario 1-5

TABLE X. COMBAT SCENARIO TESTING SCENARIO GENERATION DESIGN

Scenario	Company 1		Company 2		Company 3	
	Longitude Offset	*Latitude Offset*	*Longitude Offset*	*Latitude Offset*	*Longitude Offset*	*Latitude Offset*
1	{−0.90,2.10}	{−2.70,1.50}	{−1.26,2.52}	{−2.54,1.40}	{−1.38,2.52}	{−2.87,1.63}
2	{−2.22,0.96}	{−1.50,2.70}	{−2.34,1.44}	{−1.34,2.60}	{−2.58,1.32}	{−1.67,2.83}
3	{−2.70,2.70}	{−2.70,3.30}	{−2.82,3.18}	{−3.00,3.00}	{−2.76,2.94}	{−3.06,3.54}
4	{−1.92,0.60}	{−2.40,1.02}	{−2.22,2.52}	{−2.40,0.60}	{−2.34,0.78}	{−2.76,0.66}
5	{−1.20,2.16}	{−1.20,3.06}	{−1.08,2.70}	{−1.20,2.34}	{−1.02,2.22}	{−1.38,3.00}

TABLE XI. STATISTICS OF STRIKE EFFECTS

Engagement Policy	Scenario 1	Scenario 2	Scenario 3	Scenario 4	Scenario 5
Optimal Rule-Based Policy	1.286765	1.102233	0.853608	1.276376	0.934328
Intelligent Decision Policy	1.503086	1.383281	1.039818	1.765705	1.19802
Performance Improvement	16.81%	25.50%	21.81%	38.34%	28.22%

For each of the 64 deployment configurations, 10 simulation runs were conducted. The resulting damage data for both Red and Blue forces across all 640 experiments were recorded and aggregated to calculate the exchange ratio.

As can be seen from the experimental results, in the new scenario, the exchange of the intelligent decision rules are better than decisions, verify the advantages of the intelligent decision.

VI. CONCLUSION

This paper addresses the intelligent decision-making problem for UAV Swarm SEAD missions. A decision modeling approach combining DRL with combat simulation is proposed, a corresponding modeling framework is constructed, and attack decision modeling based on the Dueling DQN algorithm is implemented. Leveraging the structured WESS system as a reinforcement learning training environment and designing a case study, experimental results verify that the DRL-based intelligent decision-making approach yields superior decision quality compared to traditional knowledge engineering-based methods.

For UAV Swarm SEAD tasks, this paper designs a comprehensive simulation scenario framework, successfully integrates the intelligent decision model, and demonstrates the feasibility of the DRL method. This work provides a training environment for subsequent intelligent decision-making research concerning reconnaissance and jammer aircraft within the swarm. Furthermore, it contributes to enhancing the overall intelligence level of UAV Swarms in SEAD missions and offers valuable insights for UAV Swarm decision modeling in other operational scenarios.

REFERENCES

[1] J. Tang, X. Li, and J. Dai, "Analysis on the application of U.S. UAV Air Defense Suppression Operations," *Aerodynamic Missile Journal*, 2020, no. 5, pp. 44-48.

[2] D. D. Diehl, *How to optimize joint theater ballistic missile defense*, M.S. thesis, Naval Postgraduate School, Monterey, CA, USA, 2018.

[3] S. Yang, Z. Shan, Y. Ding, and G. Li, "Survey of research on deep reinforcement learning," *Computer Engineering*, 2021, vol. 47, no. 12, pp. 19-29.

[4] J. L. Zuo, R. N. Yang, Y. Zhang, Z. Li, and M. Wu, "Intelligent decision-making in air combat maneuvering based on heuristic reinforcement learning," *Acta Aeronautica et Astronautica Sinica*, 2017, vol. 38, no. 10, p. 321168.

[5] L. Zhang, J. Xu, et al., "Air Dominance Through Machine Learning: A Preliminary Exploration of Artificial Intelligence - Assisted Mission Planning," RAND Corporation, 2020. [Online]. Available: https://doi.org/10.7249/RR4311 [retrieved: Sept, 2025].

[6] Y. Wang, Y. Lei, S. Lei, et al., "Research on multi-warhead Cooperative penetration Decision Modeling Based on Deep Reinforcement Learning," in *Proc. The Third Conference on Systems Engineering-Complex Systems and Systems Engineering Management*, 2021-04-16.

[7] W. Shi, Y. Feng, G. Cheng, H. Huang, J. Huang, Z. Liu, and W. He, "Research on multi-aircraft cooperative air combat method based on deep reinforcement learning," *Acta Automatica Sinica*, 2021, vol. 47, no. 7, pp. 1610-1623.

[8] R. S. Sutton and A. G. Barto, *Reinforcement Learning: An Introduction*, 2nd ed. Cambridge, MA, USA: MIT Press, 2018, ch. 4.2.

[9] F. Lu, X. Hu, B. Zhao, X. Jiang, D. Liu, J. Lai, and Z. Wang, "Review of the Research Progress in Combat Simulation Software," *Applied Sciences*, 2023, vol. 13, no. 9, p. 557.

[10] X. Wang, J. Cheng, Q. Guo, S. He, F. Guo, and Y. Chen, "Research on Intelligent Cooperative Combat System in Air Defense suppression Mission," *Unmanned System Technology*, 2020, vol. 3, no. 4, pp. 10-21.

[11] Z. Wang, T. Schaul, M. Hessel, H. van Hasselt, M. Lanctot, and N. de Freitas, "Dueling Network Architectures for Deep Reinforcement Learning," *arXiv preprint arXiv:1511.06581*, 2015. [Revised: Apr. 2016]. Available: https://arxiv.org/abs/1511.06581 [retrieved: Sept, 2025].

[12] V. Mnih, K. Kavukcuoglu, D. Silver, A. Graves, I. Antonoglou, D. Wierstra, and M. Riedmiller, "Playing Atari with Deep Reinforcement Learning," in *NIPS Deep Learning Workshop*, 2013. [Online]. Available: https://arxiv.org/abs/1312.5602 [retrieved: Sept, 2025].

[13] Y. Lei, J. Yao, N. Zhu, Y. Zhu, and W. Wang, "Weapon Equipment Combat Effectiveness Simulation System WESS," *Journal of System Simulation*, 2017, vol. 29, no. 6, pp. 1244-1252.

Algorithm for Predicting Radioactivity of Decommissioning Nuclear Power Plant

Changyeon Yoon
R&D Achievement Distribution Group
Korea Hydro & Nuclear Power CO., LTD.
Daejeon, South Korea
e-mail: changyeon.yoon@khnp.co.kr

Abstract— **In the decommissioning of nuclear power plants, it is often difficult to know the exact location and activity of radiation sources inside structures. For safe and efficient planning, it is important to estimate the radiation sources quantitatively using limited information. In this study, a numerical algorithm was developed to estimate the activity of radiation sources based on limited dose rate data and shielding structure information inside the plant. The proposed algorithm is based on the Electric Power Research Institute (EPRI) method, which traces source information from limited input, and uses both the Successive Over-Relaxation (SOR) method and the Gauss-Jordan Elimination to calculate the activity of the radiation sources. A virtual working scenario was created to test the algorithm, and both methods showed good accuracy, with error rate less than 10%. This result suggests that the proposed method can be used in real decommissioning sites to support source estimation and worker dose evaluation.**

Keywords-EPRI algorithm; SOR; Gauss-Jordan elimination;

I. Introduction

Nuclear power plants emit high radiation due to spent fuel and activated structures from long-term operation. Before decommissioning, it is necessary to estimate worker dose and get approval from regulatory authority. This helps ensure safe and efficient decommissioning and protects workers' health.

However, high-radiation areas are difficult to access, so direct measurement of source information is often not possible. This makes dose estimation less accurate, leading to either overly conservative protection or unexpected exposure risks. Therefore, a method that can estimate source characteristics with limited data is needed.

The EPRI algorithm is a well-known method for this purpose [1]. It uses simple calculations based on MicroShield, a deterministic radiation shielding code [2]–[4]. Therefore, the error can be larger compared to probabilistic methods. For example, when the amount of measurement data is small, the accuracy may be low.

To solve this issue, we developed a new numerical algorithm based on the EPRI method. Our method uses the SOR technique and Gauss-Jordan elimination to improve accuracy. It estimates radiation source activity using limited dose rate and shielding data. This paper explains the algorithm and tests its performance using a virtual scenario.

The algorithm developed in this study aims to estimate radioactivity with reasonable reliability using minimal information. To achieve this, multiple stages of calculations were performed, incorporating assumptions at a practical level. This approach was intended to obtain plausible results even with limited data. However, at the current stage of development, the error becomes significant when the geometry and worker pathways are highly complex. Therefore, this study focused on cases with relatively simple pathways and fewer shielding structures.

The Materials and Methods section describes the SOR iterative method used in this study, the Gauss-Jordan Elimination applied for its optimization, and the virtual work scenario designed to verify the developed algorithm. The Results and Conclusion sections present the evaluation of the algorithm's validity by examining the difference between the calculated results and the actual values.

II. Materials And Methods

This section presents the SOR iterative method and the Gauss-Jordan Elimination applied in the developed algorithm, as well as the virtual scenario used for its verification.

A. Background of iterative method application

In conventional dose estimation methods, direct solvers such as the Gauss Elimination method [5] are often used to solve systems of linear equations. However, these methods can be inefficient when the number of equations increases, as in complex decommissioning environments with multiple radiation sources and measurement points. In such cases, computational time increases, and accumulated numerical errors can reduce accuracy. Therefore, iterative methods are more effective for improving computational efficiency and maintaining solution stability while reducing the number of arithmetic operations.

B. Concept of iterative methods

The iterative method solves the linear system $Ax=b$ by starting from an initial guess $x^{(0)}$ and gradually improving the estimate through repeated correction. In each step, the solution is updated based on the residual error from the previous step. As the number of iterations increases, the solution converges to the exact value. The process stops when the error becomes smaller than a predefined threshold.

C. Successive Over-Relaxation (SOR) method [6]

The SOR method is an improved version of the Gauss-Seidel method. It adjusts the correction step by applying a relaxation factor w which affects the convergence speed. If $0<w<1$, it is called under-relaxation; if $w>1$, it is called over-relaxation. The value of w is chosen empirically. Since the convergence behavior strongly depends on the initial guess, selecting a proper initial value is critical. In this study, the initial value was calculated using the Gauss-Jordan Elimination [7] to ensure stability and faster convergence.

D. Use of Gauss-Jordan Elimination

The Gauss-Jordan Elimination is a direct method that solves systems of linear equations by transforming the matrix into a reduced row echelon form. Although computationally expensive, it can provide a useful initial estimate for iterative methods. In this study, it was used to calculate the initial solution for the SOR method. If the initial value is close to the exact solution, the number of iterations can be reduced, and the algorithm is less likely to diverge.

E. Virtual scenario for validation

Figure 1 shows the virtual workspace and worker pathway constructed to validate the developed algorithm.

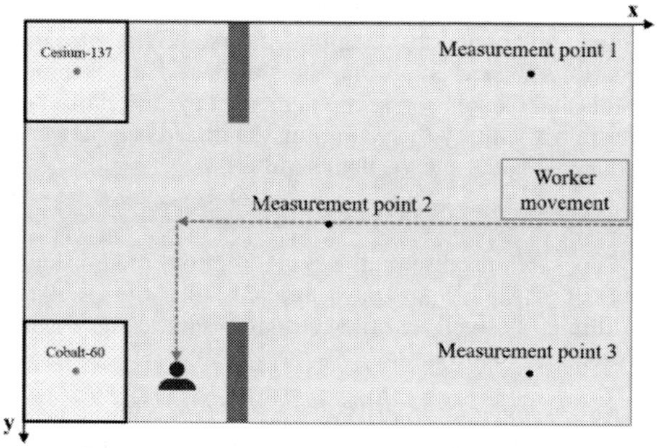

Figure 1. Virtual scenario for validating the algorithm

The worker enters an isotope storage room containing Cesium-137 (1,000 MBq) and Cobalt-60 (500 MBq) sources. The worker passes through a concrete shielding wall and performs a surface contamination measurement in front of the container that holds the Cobalt-60 source. After the measurement, the worker exits the room along the same path. The worker moves at a speed of approximately 2 meters per second and stays in front of the Cobalt-60 container for about 5 minutes during the task. In this scenario, both the Cesium-137 and Cobalt-60 sources are assumed to be located at the center of their storage containers and modeled as point sources.

III. RESULTS

In calculating radioactivity, iterative methods were used to overcome the drawbacks of direct methods for solving equations, such as long computation time and low accuracy. The SOR method was applied to reduce the computation time. In the SOR method, the solution may diverge, making it impossible to obtain exact or approximate values. However, by applying Gauss-Jordan Elimination, approximate solutions close to the exact values were always obtained. This approach minimized the number of iterations and also reduced the computation time.

Table I showed the estimated source activities using the SOR method.

TABLE I. ESTIMATED RADIOACTIVITY OF THE SOURCES USING THE SOR

Source	Estimated activity (MBq)	Real activity (MBq)	Difference (%)
Cesium-137	1,003	1,000	0.3
Cobalt-60	450	500	10

The activity of the Cesium-137 source was estimated to be 1,003 MBq, which is very close to the actual value of 1,000 MBq, with only a 0.3% error. For the Cobalt-60 source, the estimated activity was 450 MBq, resulting in an error of approximately 10%. These results show that the SOR method can provide reasonable accuracy, although its performance may vary depending on source characteristics and measurement conditions.

Table II summarizes the estimated radioactivity values of the sources calculated using the Gauss-Jordan Elimination method.

TABLE II. ESTIMATED RADIOACTIVITY OF THE SOURCES USING THE GAUSS-JORDAN ELIMINATION

Source	Estimated activity (MBq)	Real activity (MBq)	Difference (%)
Cesium-137	970	1,000	5
Cobalt-60	473	500	3

The result shows that the Cesium-137 source was estimated to be 970 MBq, which is about 5% lower than the actual value of 1,000 MBq. For the Cobalt-60 source, the estimated value was 473 MBq, indicating an error of approximately 3% from the actual 500 MBq.

These results suggest that both the SOR method and the Gauss-Jordan elimination method can provide reasonably accurate estimations. In particular, the proposed algorithm showed that it could offer a solution close to the true value even under conditions with limited input data. Furthermore, in situations similar to the test scenario, if the Gauss-Jordan method already produces sufficiently accurate results, further application of SOR may not be necessary. This indicates a potential advantage in terms of computational efficiency for practical use.

In addition, according to the EPRI algorithm, an uncertainty of 50–100% is considered a warning level, and over 100% is rejected. In this study, the maximum error of the proposed algorithm was about 10%, which shows that it can provide more accurate results than the EPRI method.

IV. Conclusion

In this study, a radiation source back-calculation algorithm was developed to accurately estimate worker dose prior to nuclear facility decommissioning. To improve upon the limitations of the existing EPRI-based method, the proposed algorithm integrates the SOR technique with Gauss-Jordan Elimination, enabling reliable source activity estimation even with limited dose rate and shielding data.

The algorithm was tested using a simplified virtual scenario involving two radiation sources (Cesium-137 and Cobalt-60). The results showed that while the SOR method exhibited a relatively large error (~10%) for the Cobalt-60 source, the Gauss-Jordan method produced estimates within 5% of the actual source strength for both isotopes. Notably, the Gauss-Jordan method alone yielded sufficiently accurate results, demonstrating its potential as a standalone solution.

These findings suggest that the proposed algorithm is applicable in real-world environments with limited input data and can be extended to more complex geometries and multi-source scenarios. Ultimately, this work is expected to contribute to improved radiation safety during decommissioning and provide a reliable basis for regulatory assessment. However, at the current stage, significant errors may occur when the workspace is complex, with many shielding structures or complicated worker pathways. Therefore, further studies are necessary to improve accuracy and optimization before the algorithm can be applied to various industries.

References

[1] EPRI, "3D Radiation Exposure Modeling Tool for ALARA Planning: Kewaunee Pilot", 2011

[2] ICRP 51, "Data for Use in Protection against External Radiation", 1987

[3] ANSI/ANS-6.4.3, "Gamma-Ray Attenuation Coefficiencts & Buildup Factors For Engineering Materials", 1991

[4] ICRP 38, "Radionuclide Transformations – Energy and Intensity of Emissions", 1931

[5] G. H. Golub and C. F. Van Loan, "Matrix Computations", Johns Hopkins University, 2013

[6] R. S. Varga, "Matrix Iterative Analysis", Springer, 2000

[7] R. L. Burden and J. D. Faires, "Numerical Analysis", Brooks/Cole, 2010

Feasibility Study of Simplification of Radiation Source Shape Using Monte Carlo N-Particle Transport(MCNP)

Changyeon Yoon
R&D Achievement Distribution Group
Korea Hydro & Nuclear Power CO., LTD.
Daejeon, South Korea
e-mail: changyeon.yoon@khnp.co.kr

Abstract—**In real radiation work environments, radiation sources can exist in various shapes (line, surface, or volume) and forms (gas or liquid). It is difficult to calculate the worker's exposure dose under all these conditions. Therefore, the source shape needs to be simplified. The Electric Power Research Institute (EPRI) algorithm suggests converting line or volume sources into point sources, and some studies report that this simplification is acceptable when the measurement point is far enough from the source. In this study, we analyzed the relative error in dose rate when a line source is simplified as a point source. Both theoretical methods and Monte Carlo N-Particle Transport (MCNP) simulations were used. Cesium was used as the source, and the dose rate was calculated at various positions. The results showed that the relative error was less than 10% when the distance was more than one source length, and less than 1% when the distance was more than twice the source length.**

Keywords-Source Simplification; Monte Carlo Simulation;

I. INTRODUCTION

Radiation sources can exist in various forms such as lines, surfaces, and volumes, and may also change in real time when in liquid or gas states. When theoretically calculating the dose received by radiation workers, it is not practical to consider all these complex source geometries. Therefore, simplifying the shape of the radiation source is necessary.

The EPRI developed an algorithm that estimates radiation dose by approximating extended sources (such as line or volume sources) as a series of point sources. The method recommends representing line and volume sources as multiple point sources spaced approximately 1 foot apart [1]. In addition, previous research has shown that when the measurement point is more than three times the length of a line source away, treating the source as a point source is acceptable without significant error [2].

In this study, we analyzed the relative error caused by this simplification process using both a theoretical approach and MCNP simulation. MCNP was developed at Los Alamos National Laboratory for radiation transport studies [3]. Its origin goes back to the late 1940s when the Monte Carlo method was first applied to nuclear research [4]. The code simulates the transport of neutrons, photons, and electrons by tracing random particle histories. At each step, interactions such as scattering, absorption, or collision are sampled statistically using random number [3]. This probabilistic approach allows accurate calculations even in complex geometries and material conditions. The relationship between the distance from the source and the resulting dose rate error was examined to evaluate the validity of approximating line sources as point sources in practical dose assessment scenarios.

In this study, both theoretical calculations and Monte Carlo simulations were used to evaluate the error introduced when a line source is approximated as a point source. This approach aimed to determine the distance from the line source at which the point source approximation becomes acceptable.

The Materials and Methods section explains the theoretical approach and the Monte Carlo simulation used to calculate the dose rate of an actual line source and approximated as a point source at various positions. The Results and Conclusion sections provide criteria for the distance at which a line source can be approximated as a point source.

II. MATERIALS AND METHODS

This section describes the theoretical methods for calculating the dose rate when a line source is approximated as a point source. It also presents the procedure of MCNP simulation under this assumption.

A. Theoretical Method [5]

The dose rate at different positions from a line source can be calculated using the following equation (1).

$$\text{Dose rate} = \Gamma(A / r^2) \qquad (1)$$

Γ is the gamma constant for Cesium, A represents the activity, and r is the distance between the source and the measurement point.

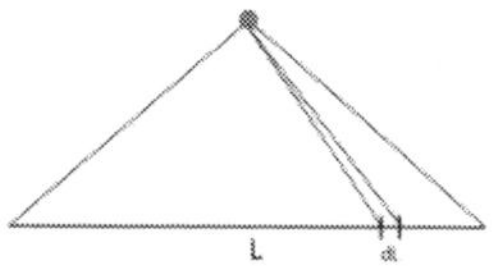

Figure 1. Radiation dose rate calculation from a linear source

A line source can be regarded as a collection of infinitely many point sources. Based on this logic, Figure 1 illustrates the method used to calculate the dose rate from a linear source.

A line source of length L can be divided into infinitesimal segments of length dL. The total dose rate from the entire source can be obtained by integrating the dose rate contributions from each segment (2).

$$\text{Dose rate} = \Gamma(A_l / h)(\theta_1 + \theta_2) \quad (2)$$

A_l is the total activity of the line source of length L, and h is the perpendicular distance from the line source to the measurement point. The angle θ is defined by the geometry formed by the measurement point, the foot of the perpendicular to the source, and both ends of the line source.

Using this equation, we calculated the dose rate under 4 different geometric conditions: (a) measurement point is perpendicular to the center of the source, (b) perpendicular to one end, (c) perpendicular to an off-center segment, (d) not perpendicular to any part of the source (Figure 2).

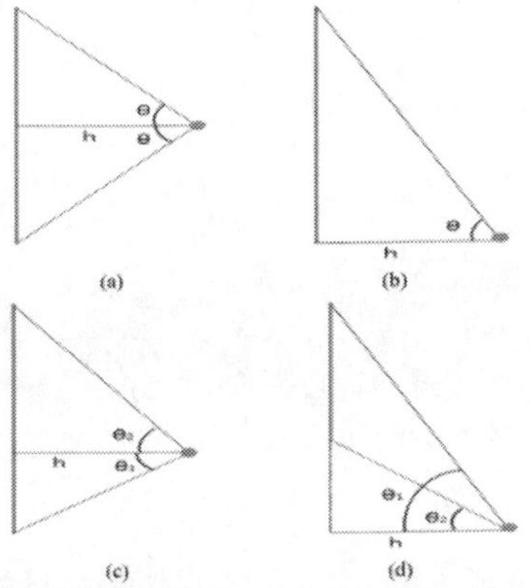

Figure 2. Dose rate calculation under four geometric conditions: (a) center, (b) end, (c) off-center, (d) non-perpendicular

B. Monte Carlo Simulation

The MCNP simulation was performed using a monoenergetic gamma source of 0.662 MeV, representing Cesium. The results of MCNP are presented with statistical uncertainties. When the number of particle simulations is small, the statistical error is large, while increasing the number of particles reduces the error. In this study, results were considered reliable when the statistical uncertainty was less than 10%. To achieve this, a total of 1,000,000 simulations were performed, where the number of simulations corresponds to the number of photons. The increase in dose at the measurement point due to scattered secondary gamma rays originating from the unscattered primary 0.662 MeV gamma rays is referred to as the build-up factor. This effect depends on factors such as the geometric structure of the source, the thickness and material of the shielding, and the energy of the gamma rays. In this study, the dose contribution from this effect was excluded; therefore, the attenuated dose rate was not considered. The simulation environment was set up on a 6 m × 6 m xy-plane, with the point source located at the origin. A 1-meter-long line source was placed along the y-axis, centered at the origin. Dose rates were calculated at intervals of 10 cm throughout the plane.

To convert photon fluence to ambient dose equivalent, the conversion coefficients from International Commission on Radiological Protection (ICRP) Publication 74 [H*(10)/Φ] were used. Figure 3 shows the MCNP simulation setup used for the dose rate calculation.

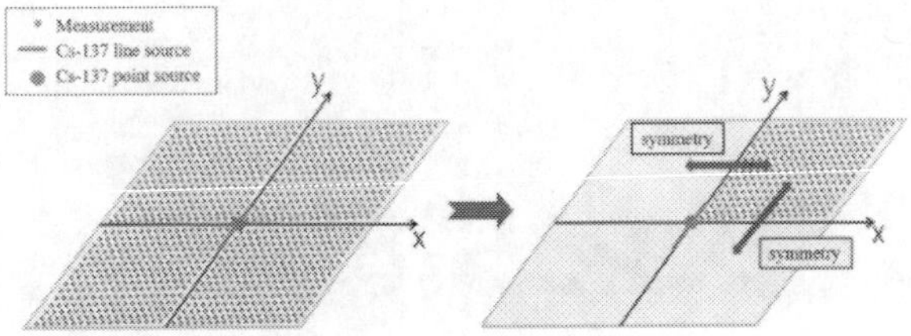

Figure 3. MCNP simulation setup for dose rate calculation

For each case, the relative error was calculated by comparing the result to the assumption that the line source is modeled as a single point source.

III. RESULTS

Table I shows the relative error at each measurement position calculated using the theoretical method.

TABLE I. RELATIVE ERROR BY POSITION (THEORETICAL CALCULATION)

Distance from source (multiples of source length)	Relative error (%)			
	(a)	(b)	(c)	(d)
0.1 times	264	74	48	61
0.2 times	110	50	12	46
0.3 times	62	31	4	32
0.4 times	40	18	10	21
0.5 times	27	10	11	13
0.6 times	20	5	10	8
0.7 times	15	1.4	9	4
0.8 times	12	0.3	8	2
0.9 times	10	1.3	7	0.7
1 times	8	2	6	0.3
3 times	0.9	0.8	0.9	0.7

In this study, relative error of 10% or less was considered a meaningful simplification, and an error below 1% was assumed to be practically error-free. Under condition (a) in Figure 2, the relative error was less than 10% when the measurement point was located at 0.9 times the source length from the source. For condition (b), the threshold was 0.5 times the source length, and for conditions (c) and (d), it was 0.6 times. Additionally, the relative error was below 1% when the distance was 3 times the source length for conditions (a) to (c), and 0.9 times for condition (d).

In the Monte Carlo simulation, the linear source was placed along the y-axis, and the point source was positioned at the origin. Since the dose distributions from both sources are symmetric with respect to the first quadrant of the xy-plane, the simulation focused on this region (Figure 4).

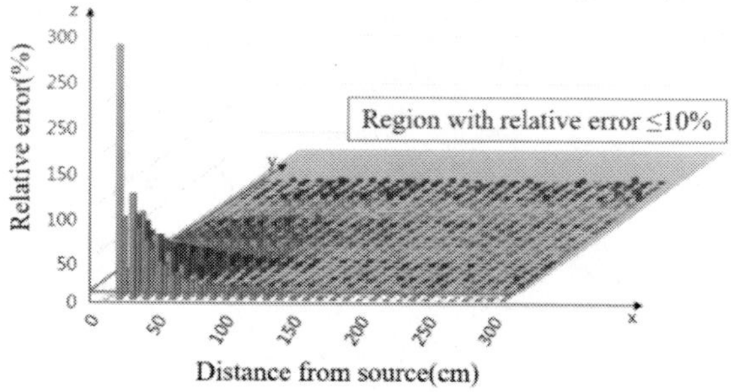

Figure 4. Relative error from approximating a line source as a point source

The results showed that the relative error was less than 10% at distances equal to the source length and less than 1% at twice the source length. These findings are consistent with the theoretical calculations.

IV. Conclusion

In this study, the relative dose rate error caused by approximating a line source as a point source was evaluated using both theoretical calculations and Monte Carlo transport simulations. The results showed that when the distance from the source exceeded the length of the line source, the relative error remained below 10%, and when the distance was more than twice the source length, the error was within 1%. This indicates that at distances of 2–3 times the source length, the line source can be reasonably simplified as a point source without significantly affecting the calculated worker dose. Based on these findings, users can construct an appropriate point source model depending on the allowable error margin in practical applications.

References

[1] EPRI, "Demonstration of Advanced 3D ALARA Planning Prototypes for Dose Reduction", Electric Power Research Institute, 2012

[2] J. J. Bevelacqua, "Contemporary Health Physics Problems and Solutions", Wiley, 2007

[3] C. J. Werner, "MCNP User's Manual(LA-UR-17-29981)", Los Alamos National Laboratory, 2017

[4] J. F. Briesmeister, "MCNP – A General Monte Carlo N-Particle Transport Code(LA-13709-M)", Los Alamos National Laboratory, 2000

[5] G. F. Knoll, "Radiation Detection and Measurement", Wiley, 2024

Maximizing Detection Efficiency of CZT and Scintillator Detectors - A Monte Carlo Study

Changyeon Yoon
R&D Achievement Distribution Group
Korea Hydro & Nuclear Power CO., LTD.
Daejeon, South Korea
e-mail: changyeon.yoon@khnp.co.kr

Abstract— **This study investigates the potential advantages of a Compton Positron Emission Tomography (PET) system utilizing Cadmium Zinc Telluride (CZT) detectors, in comparison with conventional PET systems based on scintillator materials such as Lutetium Yttrium Oxyortho-Silicate (LYSO) and Lutetium Gadolinium Oxyortho-Silicate (LGSO). The CZT-based system uses the detection of both photoelectric and Compton scattering events, leading to enhanced spatial resolution and more effective event utilization. Given that Compton scattering dominates at 511 keV, the system achieves a marked improvement in detection efficiency. Through Monte Carlo simulation studies using various detector materials, Compton PET demonstrated superior performance over traditional PET, with the CZT-based system exhibiting the highest spatial resolution and the LGSO-based system achieving the greatest detection efficiency.**

Keywords-CZT; LYSO; LGSO; Compton PET; GATE

I. Introduction

Monte Carlo simulation is a probabilistic method that uses random sampling to model physical processes. In radiation transport, it follows particle trajectories and their interactions with matter based on probability distributions. This allows accurate analysis even in complex geometries and diverse materials [1].

Genat4 Application for Tomographic Emission (GATE) is an open-source toolkit built on the Geant4 platform. It is widely used in nuclear medicine imaging such as PET and Single Photon Emission Computed Tomography (SPECT), as well as in radiotherapy [2], [3]. PET, in particular, is commonly applied in clinical practice for tumor detection, neurological disorder evaluation, and cardiovascular studies. GATE enables simulation of medical imaging systems and dynamic behavior of radiation sources, making it valuable for both research and clinical applications.

Most PET systems used in clinics today are based on lutetium-based scintillators, such as Lutetium Oxyortho-Silicate (LSO), LYSO, or LGSO. These materials have high atomic numbers and densities, which lead to good detection efficiency. However, in scintillator-based PET systems, the z-axis information of detected radiation cannot be distinguished. In addition, the resolution of these systems is limited by the size of the scintillator pixels and the connected photodetectors. This can reduce the accuracy of PET images, which is important for medical diagnosis. Although combining PET with high-resolution Computed Tomography (CT) or Magnetic Resonance Imaging (MRI) images can help provide better anatomical detail [4], improving the resolution of PET itself is still an important goal.

Semiconductor materials such as CZT show lower detection efficiency than scintillators but provide much higher resolution. They can also identify z-axis information accurately. As a result, Compton scattering events, which are regarded as invalid data, can be used as valid data and improve detection efficiency. In this study, a micro-PET system using pixelated CZT detectors was tested as an alternative. CZT has lower atomic number and density compared to common scintillators, so its basic detection efficiency is lower. However, it offers much better energy and position resolution. Also, pixelated CZT can detect both photoelectric and Compton scattering events by identifying the interaction point inside the detector. This makes it possible to improve overall detection efficiency [5]. Monte Carlo simulation results showed that the CZT-based Compton PET had about three times higher efficiency than a conventional PET with the same setup. The performance of this system was compared with LYSO and LGSO PET systems, focusing on detection efficiency and image quality.

The Materials and Methods section describes the scintillator PET and semiconductor PET systems simulated using GATE. The Results and Conclusion sections present the improved detection efficiency achieved through the use of Compton scattering and the resolution of the semiconductor PET system.

II. Materials And Methods

Monte Carlo simulations were conducted using GATE 9.0. LYSO and LGSO scintillators had compositions of $Lu_{0.4}Y_{1.6}SiO_5$ and $Lu_{1.9}Gd_{0.1}SiO_5$ respectively [6], and were voxelized into 7 mm × 1.5 mm × 1.5 mm elements. A cylindrical water phantom (radius: 10.39 mm, height: 1.5 mm) was placed at the center and surrounded by 40 scintillator detectors. For the CZT PET system, 100 detector modules (20 mm × 0.5 mm × 1 mm) were used, each consisting of 1 mm × 0.5 mm × 1 mm voxels (Figure 1).

Scintillators require photodetectors at the backend, which makes the detector size larger compared to CZT. In addition, since semiconductors can identify z-axis information, a single detector module was divided into several parts for the simulation.

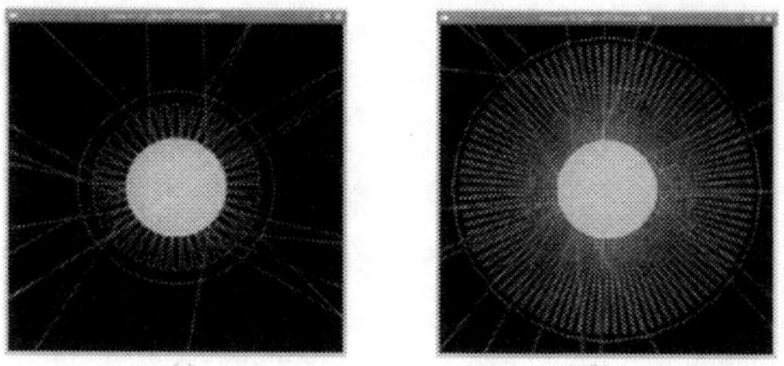

(a) (b)

Figure 1. Geometry of PET system (a) LYSO and LGSO PET (b) CZT PET

Eight disk-shaped positron sources with radii from 0.3 mm to 2.05 mm, in 0.25 mm steps, were simulated (Figure 2).

Figure 2. Position and size of positron sources

Image reconstruction was performed using the Filtered Back-Projection (FBP) method. Evaluations included: (1) comparison between images using photoelectric-only vs. photoelectric plus Compton events, (2) visual inspection based on varying source sizes, and (3) calculation of Relative Standard Deviation (RSD) for the largest sources to assess noise.

III. RESULTS

Table I showed the detected counts for LYSO, LGSO, CZT PET.

TABLE I. DETECTED COUNTS FOR EACH PET SYSTEM

	LYSO PET	LGSO PET	CZT PET
Photoelectric events only	311,078	1,499,760	311,325
Photoelectric and Compton scattering	354,345	1,665,079	369,375

More than 10% of detection efficiency increased in all PET systems when both photoelectric and Compton scattering events were considered in the reconstruction process. Among the three systems, LGSO PET showed the highest efficiency—approximately five times greater than the others—due to its high concentration of lutetium, which has the highest atomic number and density among the materials used. The lutetium content in LGSO is roughly four times that of LYSO, which explains the significant difference. In contrast, the efficiency of the CZT-based PET was comparable to that of LYSO. The gain from including Compton events in CZT PET was lower than reported in earlier studies [5], likely because the design used in this work had relatively large gaps between adjacent CZT detector modules.

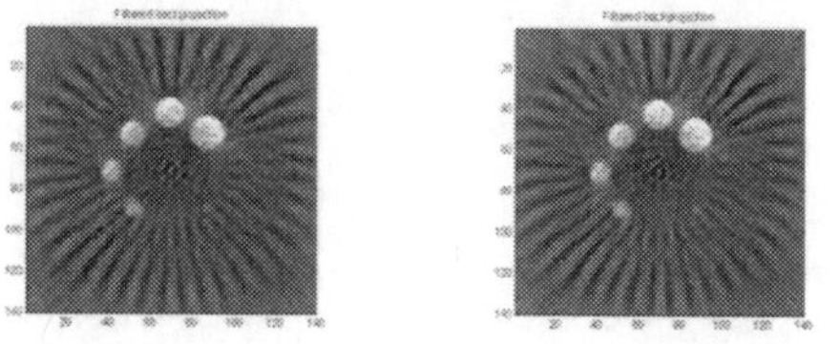

(a) (b)

Figure 3. Filtered backprcjection images for LYSO PET
(a) photoelectric events only (b) photoelectric and Compton scattering

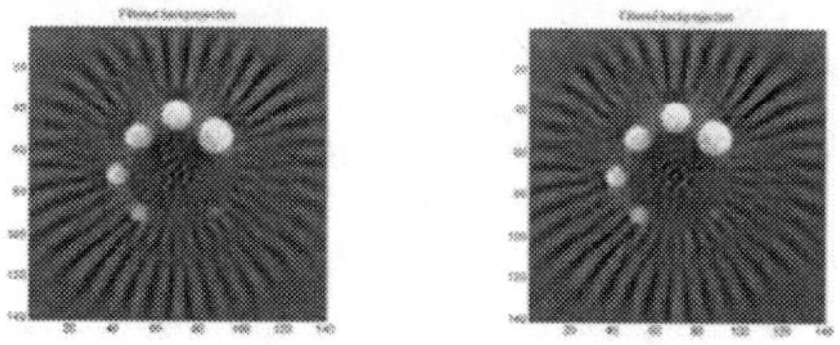

(a) (b)

Figure 4. Filtered backprcjection images for LGSO PET
(a) photoelectric events only (b) photoelectric and Compton scattering

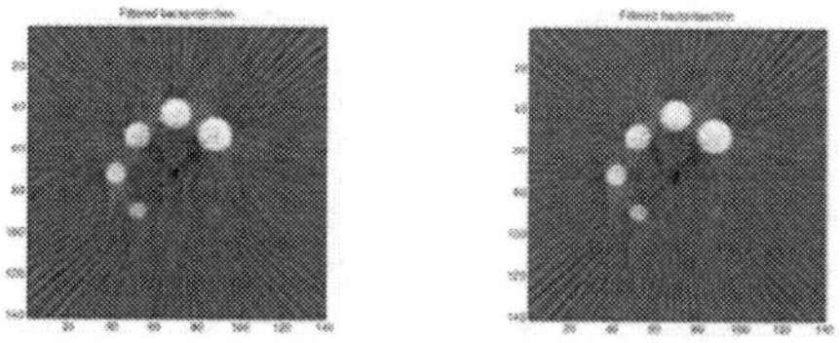

(a) (b)

Figure 5. Filtered backprcjection images for CZT PET
(a) photoelectric events only (b) photoelectric and Compton scattering

As shown in Figure 3-5, images reconstructed using both photoelectric and Compton events had lower noise than those using photoelectric events only, as expected. LGSO PET showed less noise compared to LYSO PET, which can be explained by its higher detection efficiency. In terms of spatial resolution, the CZT PET system successfully visualized all sources, including the smallest one, unlike the other systems. This result highlights the advantage of CZT in resolving fine details. However, the bottom source was not reconstructed by any of the PET systems, even though it was larger than some others. This may be due to limitations in the reconstruction algorithm.

TABLE II. RSD OF EACH PET SYSTEM

	LYSO PET	LGSO PET	CZT PET
Photoelectric events only	0.0687	0.0683	0.0706
Photoelectric and Compton scattering	0.0678	0.0677	0.0701

Table II shows the relative standard deviation (RSD) measured over a 10×10 pixel area for the largest source in each system. In all cases, the RSD values of Compton PET were lower than those of conventional PET. These findings indicate that Compton PET provides improved image quality compared to conventional PET systems.

IV. Conclusion

Three evaluation methods were applied to assess both Compton and conventional PET systems using LYSO, LGSO, and CZT detectors. In all cases, Compton PET showed higher detection efficiency than conventional PET, leading to improved image quality. Among the systems tested, CZT PET provided the highest spatial resolution, while LGSO PET achieved the best detection efficiency, resulting in the lowest image noise. Overall, Compton PET technology proved effective for all detector types. Most commercial PET systems currently in use are made only with scintillators. Since they treat only the photoelectric effect as valid data, a large amount of information is discarded. However, by applying the semiconductor-based Compton PET technology proposed in this study, both higher resolution and improved detection efficiency can be expected.

Future research will focus on developing methods to maximize the use of Compton scattering, which occurs more than three times as often as the photoelectric effect at 0.511MeV, as valid data. In addition, simulations with smaller sources will be conducted to analyze in greater detail the advantages of semiconductor detectors.

References

[1] D. P. Kooese, T. Brereton, T. Taimre and Z. I. Botev, "Why the Monte Carlo method is so impotant today", Wiley Interdisciplinary Reviews: Computational Statistics, Vol. 6, No. 6, pp. 386-392, 2014

[2] S. Jan et al., "GATE: a simulation toolkit for PET and SPECT", Physics in Medicine and Biology, Vol. 49, No. 19, pp. 4543-4561, 2004

[3] S. Jan et el., "GAET V6: a major enhancement of the GATE simulation platform enabling modeling of CT and radiotherapy", Physics in Medicine and Biology, Vol. 56, No. 4, pp. 881-901, 2011

[4] C. Go, "Nuclear medicine 3rd edition", Korea Medicine", Korea Medicine, 2008

[5] C. Yoon, W. Lee and T. Lee, "Simulation for CZT Compton PET - Maximization of the Efficiency for PET by Using Compton Event", Nucl. Instr. And Meth. A, Vol. 652, No. 1, pp. 713-716, 2011

[6] H. S. Yoon et al., "Initial Results of Simultaneous PET-MRI Experiments with an MRI-Compatible Silicon Photomultiplier PET Scanner", The Journal Of Nuclear Medicine, Vol. 53, No. 4, pp. 608-614, 2012

Airline Decision-Making in Sustainable Aviation Fuel Transition: A Hybrid Simulation Modeling Approach

Mohd Shoaib*, Fanny Camelia*, Ramona Bernhardt*, Ashraf Tantawy*, Yaseen Zaidi*, Ian Marr§
*Centre for Defence and Security Management and Informatics, Faculty of Engineering and Applied Sciences, Cranfield University
Defence Academy of the United Kingdom, Shrivenham, SN6 8LA UK
email:{mohammad.shoaib | fanny.camelia | ramona.bernhardt | ashraf.tantavy | yaseen.zaidi}@cranfield.ac.uk
§Airbus UK
e-mail: ian.marr@airbus.ac.uk

Abstract—**This study presents a hybrid simulation approach combining Agent-Based Modeling (ABM) and System Dynamics (SD) to capture the evolving system behavior through interacting stakeholders, including airlines, manufacturers, airports, and fuel suppliers, and to analyze how airlines adopt sustainable aviation fuels within the broader transition of the Air Transportation System (ATS). Because the existing models often overlook the interplay between micro- and macro-level dynamics, this study addresses that limitation by integrating both agent-level behaviors and broader systemic trends, such as passenger demand, Gross Domestic Product growth, and infrastructure constraints. SD captures the internal agent dynamics using stocks and flows, for example, passenger demand shaped by societal and economic trends. The ABM architecture represents each airline as an agent, modeled as a key decision-maker that monitors demand and capacity dynamics and makes strategic investment decisions in aircraft and fuel technologies. It is designed to represent how airlines implement and adjust their strategies in response to internal factors including various operational aspects and external factors including infrastructure support and sustainable fuel availability. Integrating ABM and SD enables concurrent simulation of agent-level behaviors and system-level feedback, providing a comprehensive view of the sociotechnical components in the ATS and their decision-making.**

Keywords-Air Transportation System; Hybrid Simulation; Sustainability; Agent-Based Modeling; System Dynamics.

I. INTRODUCTION

As climate change is becoming an emerging critical global challenge, the aviation industry has committed to achieving net zero CO_2 emissions by 2050 [1]. Achieving this goal requires various technical and operational measures within Air Transport Systems (ATS) [2], including the adoption of more sustainable fuels and advanced aircraft technologies compatible with these fuels with improved energy efficiency. Furthermore, enabling the transition from kerosene-based fuels to sustainable fuels involves the establishment of supporting energy infrastructure, including both the fuel technologies and the systems required for their deployment, production, storage, and distribution. To date, Sustainable Aviation Fuel (SAF), liquid hydrogen (LH_2), ammonia (NH_3), and methanol (CH_3OH) are considered as the potential sustainable fuel options for increased sustainability, each with its own characteristics in terms of technological maturity, scalability, environmental benefits, and transition challenges.

To understand the gradual transition of the ATS from keronese-based fuels to sustainability comprehensively, as characterized by the complex sociotechnical interactions and dynamic behaviors, it is important to adopt methodologies that can effectively capture inter-dependencies of different components within the system and their impacts on the overall system. Simulation-based methods, including Agent-Based Modeling (ABM) and System Dynamics (SD), are considered powerful tools for examining and explaining the key mechanisms and interactions within complex sociotechnical systems, to support the design and analysis of such systems [3]. ABM is used to simulate the behavior of the emerging system from the interactions of autonomous agents [4], while SD models the evolution of the system driven by feedback using causal loop diagrams and stock flow simulations [5]. Both are widely used for modeling complex, dynamic systems and support "what-if" analysis without real-world intervention [6].

The central objective of the present work is to study how airlines make strategic decisions about adopting more sustainable aviation fuels. Despite rising interest in sustainable transitions, hybrid simulations combining ABM and SD remain underexplored. Most existing studies either employ ABM or SD in isolation, and therefore miss the micromacro interplay which is important for fleet-transition planning that involves complex interactions among industry stakeholders, market forces, and policy measures [6][7]. To address this gap, this paper proposes a novel hybrid simulation approach that combines ABM and SD to model airline decision-making processes in sustainable aviation transitions.

The study aims to capture the complex interactions among technology, industry, markets, and society, and to simulate airline decision-making processes related to the acquisition of new sustainable aircraft. ABM and SD methods are complementary and can be integrated effectively; however, despite the feasibility, such integration remains rare and has limited application [7]. ABM uses a micro-modelling approach, focusing on the behavior of individual agents, while SD uses a macro-modeling approach, focusing on the aggregated stocks and flows that represent higher-level or broader population-level dynamics [7]. Both are relevant and valuable for analyzing the aviation transition to more sustainable fuels. The hybrid ABM and SD approach allows for a more comprehensive and realistic representation of the sociotechnical elements within the ATS, their interactions, and decision-making processes. It enables capturing relevant elements of individual heterogeneity and stochasticity of entities and processes [6], such as micro-level decision behaviors (e.g., individual airline strategies), while also providing a strategic overview [6] of macro-level system impacts (e.g., population and GDP trends) for estimating passenger demand, manufacturer capacity, government support, and infrastructure constraints. This study makes four key contributions. First, it introduces a conceptual architecture for a hybrid simulation of the ATS that unifies SD and ABM principles, providing a clear, holistic picture of how macro-level stocks-and-flows and micro-level agents interact in a single framework. Second, the paper specifies the SD side in-depth, elaborating the governing equations and feedback loops for core modules, such as fleet capacity, passenger demand, and environmental constraints, and showing how these modules shape aggregate system behavior over time. Third, it sets out a rigorous ABM methodology that captures the behavior of airlines, airports, regulators, and passengers. Special emphasis is placed on the airline decision logic for scheduling, pricing, and fleet deployment, thereby grounding the model in realistic operational choices. The work describes an explicit macro-to-micro coupling strategy that synchronizes SD state variables with ABM agent states, ensuring internal consistency and enabling the exploration of emergent phenomena across multiple temporal and organizational scales. Collectively, these advances deliver a reproducible blueprint for researchers who wish to combine SD and ABM when analyzing complex socio-technical systems, such as the ATS.

The paper is organized as follows. The overall framework is presented in Section II. Within this, the high-level SD modeling for *Society* and *Airlines* agents are outlined in Section II-A. The focus then shifts in Section II-B to the Agent-Based Modeling that governs airline decision-making. The paper concludes in Section III with a discussion of applications and future work.

II. Hybrid ABM-SD Conceptual Framework

The conceptual framework illustrating different sociotechnical elements considered in this study is shown via Figure 1. The figure provides a high-level view of interacting agent components of the ATS, including *Society, Airlines, Aircraft Manufacturer, Airport* and *Fuel Supplier*, and their underlying SD modules, forming the conceptual structure of the simulation model.

Within each agent's block are the names of the specific SD modules that represent that agent's internal dynamics. The agents are connected by arrows illustrating the key flows and dependencies and indicating how agents interact and influence each other. The framework highlights the holistic view of the system and shows how the interactions between various sociotechnical elements within the ATS together shape and drive the overall dynamics and evolution of the sustainable fuel transition. By modeling these key actors as interacting agents, the framework allows for capturing emergent system behaviors that arise from the bottom-up interactions of individual components, providing a powerful mechanism to analyze the complex pathways and challenges of aviation transition.

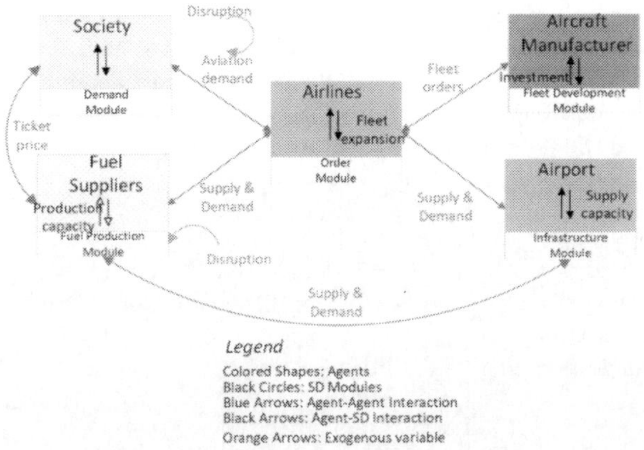

Figure 1. Hybrid ABM-SD conceptual framework of the ATS.

A. System Dynamics Modeling: Stock and Flow Diagrams for Society, Airlines, and Aircraft Manufacturers

The stock and flow diagrams were created to capture the feedback structure within the *Society, Airlines*, and *Aircraft Manufacturer* agents.

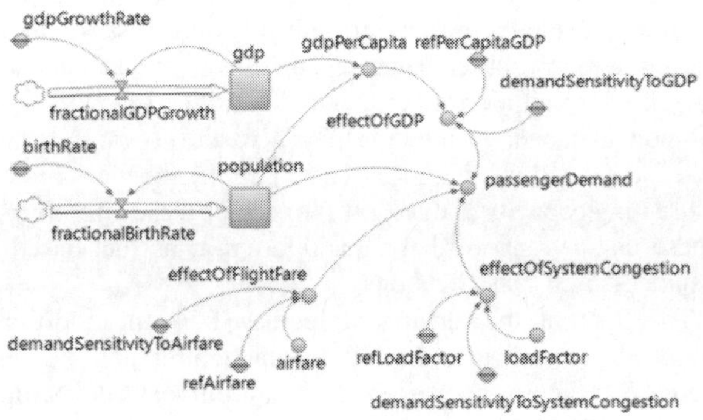

Figure 2. Stock and flow diagram of the *Society* agent

The stock and flow diagram shown in Figure 2 illustrates the core dynamics of the passenger demand module within the *Society* agent, which aims to simulate passenger demand and takes into account several key determinants of demand as contributing factors. Multiple factors have been identified in the literature that directly or indirectly influence aviation passenger demand; however, at a broad level, they can be differentiated into two categories: internal determinants and external determinants. The internal determinants of demand mostly cover the service level aspects of the service providers, including airlines and airports, and thus are related to passenger perception; whereas, the external determinants comprise demographic and geo-economic factors of a region [8][9]. Amongst all these, ticket prices, system congestion, population, and income of the population are selected as these have been considered important and utilized to estimate aviation demand in the literature [10]–[13]. To represent the effect of population income on demand, gross domestic product (GDP) per capita is employed as a common indicator of average income level within a population [14]. These dynamics are captured in the stock-and-flow structure, which includes two key stocks: the GDP stock representing GDP and influenced by the GDP growth rate; and the population stock, representing the total population of a region, which increases through the birth flow determined by the birth rate. The relationship is as follows:

$$p = K \times \gamma_{\text{gdp}} \times \gamma_{\text{sc}} \times \gamma_{\text{fare}} \tag{1}$$

where p denotes total aviation demand, K represents population size, and γ denotes effect of different factors. The relation used to estimate factors, such as the effect of GDP, system congestion, etc., is as follows:

$$\gamma_{\text{gdp}} = \left(\frac{A(t)}{A}\right)^{\alpha} \tag{2}$$

where the fraction represents the ratio of the current value (at time t) of the variable with respect to the reference value, and α denotes the sensitivity factor of the quantity at hand.

Figure 3 depicts the internal dynamic processes within the *Airlines* agent. The stock, represented by the 'operationalFleet' variable, represents the number of aircraft currently in service. Within this model, the overall fleet is divided into two subcategories based on the fuel type they may be able to utilize, *i.e.* the kerosene-based aircraft and the more sustainable fleet or non-kerosene-based aircraft. Moreover, within each category, the aircraft are further classified into the following types: 1) short distance, 2) medium distance, and 3) long distance, based on the flight haulage. The categorization is crucial as the seating capacity is different for each of these aircraft types. These distinctions are hereafter referred to as fuel-based and distance-based classifications.

The fleet of the airlines is increased by the addition of newer aircraft procured from the manufacturer, and the rate of increase is determined by the 'orderFulfillmentRate' variable. On the other hand, the 'operationalFleet' decreases due to aircraft 'retirement' flow, governed by the retirement rate (indicated by 'retirementRate' variable in Figure 3). Furthermore, as seen in the figure, Available Seat Kilometers (ASKs) and Revenue Passenger Kilometers (RPKs) are computed. Both these quantities are important metrics utilized by airlines to track their operational performance. ASKs are tracked by airlines to measure their total passenger carrying capacity, and RPKs are utilized to assess the volume of passengers carried by them [15]. These metrics are obtained by using the following relations:

$$\text{ASK}_d = n_d \times c_d \times s_d \tag{3}$$

$$\text{RPK}_d = p_d \times s_d \tag{4}$$

where d = {short, medium, long} and corresponds to different flight distance categories; n is the number of operational aircraft; c represents the capacity or the number of seats; s is the average flight distance; and p corresponds to the demand for the d type of aircraft, obtained by multiplying the proportion of demand for each flight category with the total demand.

Subsequently, ASKs and RPKs are used to generate the passenger load factor (PLF) which is defined as the proportion of available seats filled with passengers [15] and computed using the following relation:

$$\text{PLF}_d = \frac{\text{RPK}_d}{\text{ASK}_d} \tag{5}$$

This metric is subsequently utilized for the estimation of the total traffic intensity factor. Revenue is estimated as a function of traffic intensity, RPKs, and the average passenger yield is categorized according to flight distance. Profit is computed with revenue and costs as the contributing factors. The overall airline's costs are determined by the aggregation of various cost components, specifically fuel costs, operating costs, and penalty costs. Furthermore, a penalty is imposed as an external cost due to deviation from the sustainability target. In other words, airlines need to maintain a specific proportion of a more sustainable fleet, and when there is a shortfall in the target, a penalty is charged. Airline decision on new aircraft orders is governed by the interaction of variables representing fleet capacity and the target capacity. When the existing capacity falls below a pre-specified threshold level, orders are placed to the *Manufacturer* agent. This order management is handled by the agent architecture and is discussed in the next section.

The primary function of the SD module within the *Manufacturer* agent is to process orders and deliver fleet to the *Airlines* agent. As observed from Figure 4, there are two stocks in the figure: 'orderStock', which represents the backlog of aircraft orders received from the airlines and waiting to be manufactured. The production rate is controlled by the capacity variable. 'finishedOrders' stock variable accumulates the aircraft that have been manufactured and are ready for delivery. This information is then utilized to apprise the manufacturer about the delivery of aircraft. Conceptually, the figure outlines orders entering a backlog (orderStock), being processed through production (reducing order stock and increasing finished orders stock), and finally being delivered. The rates of production and delivery are constrained or influenced by the manufacturer's capacity.

B. Agent Based Modeling: Airlines Decision Making

Agent-based models are composed of individual agents, each with its own behavior, states, interaction protocols, and decision-making rules. Elements or components of the ATS are classified as passive agents and active agents. Both of these agent types share common features: they are autonomous, self-directed, interactive, and have explicit goals. Their key distinction lies in their decision-making ability; an active agent can learn and adapt its behavior in response to a change in the environment. Therefore, the *Society* agent can be categorized as a passive agent while the *Airlines* and *Manufacturer* agents are modeled as active agents.

As a passive agent, the primary purpose of the *Society* agent is to simulate the passenger demand which has been described in Section II-A; the generated demand is then communicated to the *Airlines* agent. Meanwhile, as an active agent, the *Airlines*

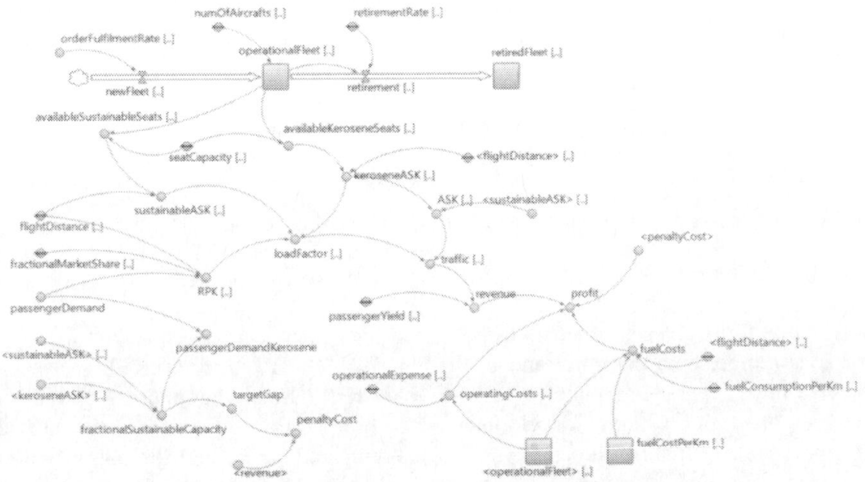

Figure 3. Stock and flow diagram of the *Airlines* agent.

agent compares the demand against the capacity. When the capacity-to-demand ratio reaches a specific threshold, a new order is placed.

The order-making process for selecting appropriate aircraft and fuel technology is grounded and structured on two key factors, including internal and external factors. The internal factors are those that pertain directly to the airlines' own operational context and priorities and reflect internal considerations. J is a set of different fuel technologies modeled in the paper, and $J=$ {Kerosene, SAF, NH_3, CH_3OH, H_2}, indicating different fuel technologies. Furthermore, internal factors are denoted using θ and external factors using ϕ notations, respectively. Also note that both, θ & $\phi \in [0,1]$. The internal factors, described in detail below, relate to variables intrinsic to the *Airlines* agent, reflecting operational or strategic considerations that influence decision-making.

1) Operational cost factor (θ^{oc}): This factor focuses on "per flight cost", encompassing both variable and fixed cost components of different aircraft types. The operational costs are represented with $C = \{c_j | j \in J\}$, and the operational cost factor for a flight of type j is computed using the relation:

$$\theta_j^{oc} = \frac{\min\{C\}}{c_j} \tag{6}$$

The aim is to select the aircraft with lower operational expenditures, therefore, the operational cost score is calculated to reflect this, where a higher score would typically be assigned to options with lower costs. The expression is used as it

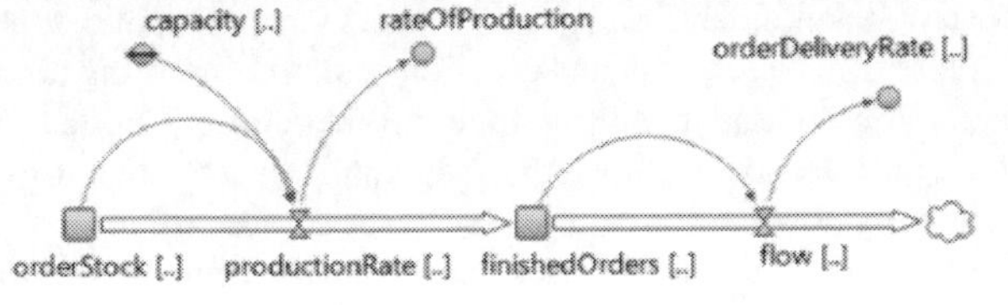

Figure 4. Stock and flow diagram of the *Manufacturer* agent

normalizes the cost of an option j against the minimum achievable cost, rewarding lower-cost options.

2) Operational life factor (θ^{ol}): Similar to the previous metric (discussed in section II-B1), this factor is used to capture the impact of the operational life of the aircraft. It is a relative score that is designed to assign a lower value to aircraft with shorter operational life and vice versa, as expressed below:

$$\theta_j^{ol} = \frac{\min\{L\}}{l_j} \tag{7}$$

where $L = \{l_j | j \in J\}$ representing life in years.

3) Sustainability gap factor (θ^{s}): A key consideration included in the decision-making process accounts for the airlines' performance against sustainable fleet targets. It specifically measures the gap between the actual proportion of sustainable fleet ASKs and the targeted proportion for a given period. It is to be noted that this factor adds extra weight to the score of non-kerosene-based aircraft. Thus, it is estimated using the relation:

$$\theta_j^{s} = \begin{cases} 0, & \text{if } j = \text{kerosene} \\ 1 - \min\left(\frac{f(t)}{f}, 1\right), & \text{otherwise} \end{cases} \tag{8}$$

where f stands for the sustainability target and $f(t)$ is a function of time and indicates the current proportion of non-kerosene-based aircraft.

These internal factors are then combined to calculate the total internal score for all the available aircraft options.

$$\theta_j = \theta_j^{s} + \theta_j^{ol} + \theta_j^{oc} \qquad \forall j \in J \tag{9}$$

The external factors are those which are external to the *Airlines* agent and concern the wider air transportation ecosystem. These factors, specifically, originate and depend on *Manufacturer*, *Airport*, and *Fuel Supplier* agents.

4) Order delivery factor (ϕ^M): This factor is specific to the *Manufacturer* agent. It assesses the manufacturing landscape by weighing in the expected delivery time of the aircraft order. The *Airlines* agent interacts with the *Manufacturer* agent to retrieve the order delivery time frame. A long order delivery time will translate to a lower value of the order delivery factor for that particular aircraft type. This factor is derived using the formula:

$$\phi_j^M = \frac{\min(T)}{t_j} \tag{10}$$

where $T = \{t_j | j \in J\}$ denotes time.

5) Infrastructure support factor (ϕ^{Infra}): The support infrastructure factor is available for a given fuel technology, in terms of fuel delivery and storage, both currently and in the future. The idea is to give more weight to technologies with better infrastructure with potential for future development. Consequently, this factor has two distinct components: 1) present (ϕ_p) and 2) future (ϕ_z), and is obtained using the relation:

$$\phi_j^{\text{Infra}} = w_1 \phi_j^p + w_2 \phi_j^z \tag{11}$$

where p and z denote present and future, respectively; and w_1 and w_2 are the weights that sum to 1 and denote the relative importance of these components. The score for the present state of the infrastructure support is calculated by considering the capacity utilization level, with a higher score assigned to lower capacity utilization values because of its capacity to accommodate more demand.

$$\phi_j^p = 1 - \rho_j \tag{12}$$

Where ρ_j indicates the utilization level of technology j. The future aspect is included to factor in the prospects of growth in a specific technology. For example, a higher relative investment in hydrogen technology signifies stronger future support and development, leading to a higher score.

$$\phi_j^z = \frac{Q_j}{\sum_j Q_j} \tag{13}$$

In this case, Q is the notation to indicate investment.

6) Fuel Supply Factor (ϕ^{FS}): This factor covers the supply side for different fuel types, considering the current availability and, the future growth prospects. This encompasses the assessment of how readily the fuel can be sourced now and the long-term outlook and the development of the fuel technology. Technologies that are relatively secure and scalable would be rated relatively favorably. Similar to the previous case, the fuel supply factor can be expressed as the weighted sum of the present availability (denoted as ϕ^{av}) and future growth potential (denoted as ϕ^{fp}), as presented:

$$\phi^{FS} = w_1 \phi_j^{av} + w_2 \phi_j^{fp} \qquad \forall j \tag{14}$$

where w_1 and w_2 are weights and sum to 1.

The current fuel availability is obtained by taking into account the fuel production capacities of all the different types of fuel. The following expression is used to obtain its value:

$$\phi_j^{av} = \frac{\kappa_j}{\max(\kappa)} \tag{15}$$

where κ indicates the current fuel production capacity.

Next, the prospect corresponds to the capital invested or the planned capital investment in the development of a technology. This factor is calculated by taking a ratio of capital invested in a specific technology and the total capital invested across all the technologies.

$$\phi_j^{fp} = \frac{I_j}{\sum_j I_j} \tag{16}$$

Here, the notation I is employed to refer to investment in fuel technologies. The external factors are then summed up to calculate the total external score for all the available aircraft options using the relation:

$$\phi_j = \phi_j^M + \phi_j^{\text{Infra}} + \phi_j^{FS} \qquad \forall j \tag{17}$$

After which, the internal and external factor scores are combined for different aircraft alternatives to estimate the aggregated score, and the option with the maximum score is selected. The entire decision-making procedure is explained using a pseudocode shown in Algorithm 1 via Figure 5. Furthermore, individual calculations of internal and external factor scores are implemented via functions which are presented using Algorithm 2 in Figure 6.

```
procedure AIRLINES AGENT AIRCRAFT TECHNOLOGY SELECTION PROCEDURE
    Determine the required aircraft category' (e.g., short, medium, long haul)
    Identify the set of fuel technologies (J) available for the required aircraft category
    Set 'bestSelectedTechnology' ← NULL
    Iterate and Evaluate Technologies:
    for j ∈ J do
        internalScore ← CALCULATEINTERNALSCORE(j)
        externalScore ← CALCULATEEXTERNALSCORE(j)
        aggregatedScore ← internalScore + externalScore
        'bestSelectedTechnology' ← max{internalScore + externalScore}   ▷ Identify the technology with the highest score and update.
    end for
    Decision and Action: Place an order for an aircraft of required aircraft category of the 'bestSelectedTechnology'type
end procedure
```

Figure 5. Algorithm 1: *Airlines* agent decision making procedure.

III. CONCLUSION AND FUTURE WORK

The hybrid ABM-SD frame provides a means to analyze how policy instruments or market shocks propagation through tightly coupled technical and behavioral system elements that ABM or SD alone can capture. The framework lays the analytical groundwork for rigorous, whole-system assessments of sustainable aviation strategies. It offers researchers, industry stakeholders, and policymakers an extensible tool to explore how heterogeneous decision-makers, emerging aircraft technologies, and evolving fuel infrastructures interact over the multi-decade horizon that separates todays fleet from a genuinely low-carbon future. By embedding explicit sustainability gap and penalty mechanisms, the framework offers a transparent way to test how airlines might schedule fleet

Input: $C \in$ {Cost}, $L \in$ {Operational Life}, $T \in$ {Order delivery time}, $\rho \in$ {Infrastructure capacity utilization}, $Q \in$ {Investment in infrastructure development}, $K \in$ {Fuel production capacity}, and $I \in$ {Investment in fuel technology development}, $f \in$ {Sustainability gap}, $w = \{w1, w2\}$, $w' = \{w'_1, w'_2\}$, and t represents simulation time.

function CALCULATEINTERNALSCORE(j)
  $\theta_j^{oc} \leftarrow \frac{\min\{C\}}{C[j]}$ ▷ Operational cost factor
  $\theta_j^{ol} \leftarrow \frac{\min\{L\}}{L[j]}$ ▷ Operational life factor
  θ_j^{s}
  if $j \equiv kerosene$ **then**
    $\theta_j^{s} \leftarrow 0$ ▷ Sustainability gap factor
  else
    $\theta_j^{s} \leftarrow 1 - min\left(\frac{f(t)}{f}, 1\right)$
  end if
return $\theta_j^{oc} + \theta_j^{ol} + \theta_j^{s}$ ▷ Return internal factor score
end function

function CALCULATEEXTERNALSCORE(j)
  Order delivery factor, $\phi_j^{M} \leftarrow \frac{min\{T\}}{T[j]}$
  $\phi_j^{p} \leftarrow 1 - \rho[j]$ ▷ Infrastructure level factor
  $\phi_j^{z} \leftarrow \frac{Q_j}{\sum Q}$ ▷ Infrastructure investment level factor
  $\phi_j^{\text{Infra}} \leftarrow w_1 \times \phi_j^{p} + w_2 \times \phi_j^{z}$ ▷ Infrastructure support factor
  $\phi_j^{av} \leftarrow \frac{\kappa}{\max(\kappa)}$ ▷ Fuel supply availability factor
  $\phi_j^{fp} \leftarrow \frac{I_j}{\sum_j I_j}$ ▷ Fuel supply investment factor
  $\phi_j^{FS} \leftarrow w'_1 \times \phi_j^{av} + w'_2 \times \phi_j^{fp}$ ▷ Fuel supply factor
return $\phi_j^{M} + \phi_j^{Infra} + \phi_j^{\text{FS}}$ ▷ Return the external factor score
end function

Figure 6. Algorithm 2: Functions for calculating *Airlines* agent internal and external factor scores for decision making.

renewal in response to decarbonization targets. The modular structure facilitates scenario experimentation, allowing researchers and practitioners to interchange empirically calibrated sub-models (e.g., refined fuel-supply curves or airport capacity modules) without re-engineering the whole system. The current implementation employs stylized parameters for infrastructure utilization, investment, and fuel production, and systematic calibration with historical airline, manufacturer, and energy-market data would strengthen predictive validity. The future work would aim to expand the models analytical boundaries by implementing active-agent logic for airports and fuel suppliers to enable the simulation of richer, co-dependent strategies, including the effects of slot constraints and supplier learning curves. Next, the model would be integrated with the wider energy infrastructure to simulate the cross-sectoral competition for key inputs, such as electricity and hydrogen, to identify potential risks and macroeconomic bottlenecks. Finally, coupling the model with optimization or reinforcement-learning techniques could support the design of adaptive policy portfolios that steer the ATS toward net-zero trajectories.

ACKNOWLEDGMENT

The authors would like to acknowledge support from Airbus Operations Ltd., Filton, UK. The views expressed in this article do not necessarily represent those of Airbus.
No new data were created or analyzed in this study. Data sharing is not applicable to this article.

REFERENCES

[1] ACARE, *Fly the Green Deal, Europes Vision for Sustainable Aviation*, 2022. Retrieved: April, 2025. [Online]. Available: https://www.acare4europe.org/acare-vision/..

[2] European Commission, *Reducing emissions from aviation*, Retrieved: May, 2025. [Online]. Available: https://climate.ec.europa.eu/eu-action/transport/reducing-emissions-aviation_en.

[3] L. J. Hettinger, A. Kirlik, Y. M. Goh, and P. Buckle, "Modelling and simulation of complex sociotechnical systems: envisioning and analysing work environments," *Ergonomics*, vol. 58, no. 4, pp. 600–614, Apr. 2015.

[4] N. Gilbert, *Agent-Based Models*, Second. SAGE, 2019.

[5] R. Coyle, *Management System Dynamics*. London: Wiley, 1977.

[6] G. D. C. N. Guerrero, P. Schwarz, and J. Slinger, "A recent overview of the integration of System Dynamics and Agent-based Modelling and Simulation," in *Proceedings of the 34th International Conference of the System Dynamics Society*, Delft, Netherlands, Jul. 2016.

[7] B. Callegari and C. Feder, "Integrating System Dynamics and Agent-Based Models for Enhanced Analysis in Sustainable Development," in *25th workshop "From Objects to Agents"*, Jul. 2022.

[8] T. Boonekamp, J. Zuidberg, and G. Burghouwt, "Determinants of air travel demand: The role of low-cost carriers, ethnic links and aviation-dependent employment," *Transportation Research Part A: Policy and Practice*, vol. 112, pp. 18–28, Jun. 2018.

[9] E. Suryani, S. Y. Chou, and C. H. Chen, "Air passenger demand forecasting and passenger terminal capacity expansion: A system dynamics framework," *Expert Systems with Applications*, vol. 37, no. 3, pp. 2324–2339, Mar. 2010.

[10] S. Y. Jung and K. E. Yoo, "Passenger airline choice behavior for domestic short-haul travel in South Korea," *Journal of Air Transport Management*, vol. 38, pp. 43–47, Jun. 2014.

[11] C. P. Milioti, M. G. Karlaftis, and E. Akkogiounoglou, "Traveler perceptions and airline choice: A multivariate probit approach," *Journal of Air Transport Management*, vol. 49, pp. 46–52, Oct. 2015.

[12] C. Thies, *SALSA - Simulation of Alternative Fuel Supply Chains for Sustainable Aviation*, 2024.

[13] K. Kieckhäfer *et al.*, "Simulation-Based Analysis of the Potential of Alternative Fuels towards Reducing CO2 Emissions from Aviation," *Energies 2018, Vol. 11, Page 186*, vol. 11, no. 1, p. 186, Jan. 2018.

[14] A. Cook, U. Kluge, A. Paul, and S. Cristobal, "Factors influencing European passenger demand for air transport: Westminster Research," in *Air Transport Research Society World Conference*, Antwerp, Belgium: Air Transport Research Society, Jul. 2017.

[15] IATA, "Demystifying Key Air Traffic Metrics: Understanding RPKs and ASKs," 2024. Retrieved: April, 2025, [Online]. Available: https://www.iata.org/en/publications/newsletters/iata-knowledge-hub/demystifying-key-air-traffic-metrics-understanding-rpks-and-asks/.

Introduction of Reinforcement Learning into Automatic Stacking of Wave-dissipating Blocks

Hao Min Chuah
Graduate School of Science and Technology
Niigata University
Niigata, Japan
e-mail: haominchuah01@gmail.com

Tatsuya Yamazaki
Faculty of Engineering
Niigata University
Niigata, Japan
e-mail: yamazaki.tatsuya@ie.niigata-u.ac.jp

***Abstract*—Accurate and strategic placement of wave-dissipating blocks is essential for effective coastal protection structures. Current supervised learning-based approaches have achieved precise single-block placement. However, they inherently suffer from significant limitations, such as a lack of adaptability to environmental and structural changes, an inability to optimize sequences of multiple-blocks, and a heavy reliance on extensive pre-generated labeled data. This paper identifies the key limitations inherent in supervised Convolutional Neural Network methods and proposes a novel reinforcement learning (RL)-based approach to address these issues. By illustrating how RL naturally provides adaptability, strategic multi-block placement, and reduced reliance on labeled data, this early-stage idea is expected to contribute to the integration of simulation methodologies and machine learning approaches.**

Keywords-wave-dissipating blocks; reinforcement learning; simulation; automatic stacking.

I. INTRODUCTION

Wave-dissipating blocks play a pivotal role in coastal engineering, protecting infrastructure by effectively dissipating wave energy. The optimal placement of these blocks significantly influences the overall stability, compactness, and performance of breakwater structures. However, the installation of wave-dissipating blocks still heavily depends on the empirical knowledge and experience of skilled workers. To overcome the limitations, Xu [1] achieved accurate single-block placements using supervised Convolutional Neural Network (CNN) methods. Albeit, his methods may suffer from inflexibility in adapting to structural changes and an inability to perform long-term optimization. In this paper, we explore an automatic stacking method for wave-dissipating blocks using Reinforcement Learning (RL) in our self-developed 3D-BW (3-Dimensional BreakWater Simulator) [2]. This RL-based method offers enhanced flexibility and adaptability, enabling the learning agent to optimize long-term structural integrity and dynamically adapt to changes in block types, structure geometry, and target goals.

In Section 2, we review related works, particularly focusing on supervised learning-based approaches for block placement and their limitations. In Section 3, we present our proposed methodology based on reinforcement learning, detailing the motivation, agent design, and inherent challenges. Finally, Section 4 concludes the paper by summarizing key contributions and outlining future directions for integrating reinforcement learning into coastal block placement simulations.

II. RELATED WORKS

Accurate placement of wave-dissipating blocks has been studied using several computational approaches, with supervised learning being one of the most explored methods. Xu [1] achieved accurate single-block placements using a supervised Convolutional Neural Network (CNN) trained on labeled data generated from a physics-based simulator.

A. *Xu's Supervised CNN Approach*

The process consisted of three phases.

1) Data Generation & Pose Labeling: A sliding window extracted 512 × 512 depth patches from the structure's surface. For each patch, 1000 simulated drops were tested at varying poses. Two criteria were evaluated:

- Compactness: measurement by comparing the placed block's position against the target height map, calculating insufficient volume (gap filling).
- Stability: horizontal displacement determination after settling (displacement ≤ 0.2m).

Then, the best performing pose becomes the ground-truth label for CNN training.

2) CNN Training: The network learned to predict optimal translation and rotation from depth patches, minimizing supervised loss between predictions and labels.

3) Real-Time Inference: The CNN predicted poses for each patch and placed blocks iteratively until the structure was completed.

This approach achieved high local accuracy and fast inference, making it suitable for controlled, static construction conditions. However, it has limitations:

- Dataset Dependence: Requires extensive pre-generated labeled data for each structural configuration.
- Lack of Adaptability: Cannot generalize new block types or changing conditions without retraining.
- Greedy Placement Strategy: Optimizes only immediate placement, ignoring long-term structural goals.

B. Other Relevant Approaches

Beyond CNN-based placement methods, other computational strategies have been explored for similar optimization problems. Physics-based heuristic approaches use deterministic rules to maximize local compactness and stability. However, their performance tends to degrade in dynamic or unpredictable environments. In the field of robotics, reinforcement learning has been successfully applied to adaptive planning tasks, such as object manipulation, grasping, and stacking under uncertainty [5][6]. Hybrid methods that combine CNN-based perception for accurate pose estimation with RL-based decision-making have also been proposed [7], enabling both precision and adaptability, although these approaches face scalability challenges when applied to large, irregular structures.

C. Summary of Achievements and Research Gap

Supervised CNN methods, such as that of Xu [1], have demonstrated high placement accuracy for static, controlled conditions, but their lack of adaptability and inability to perform strategic optimization over multiple steps remain significant drawbacks. In contrast, RL-based methods learn directly from interactions with the environment, removing the dependence on fixed datasets, and can evaluate the consequences of each placement in the context of a long-term construction sequence. They are also inherently more flexible, adapting to changes in block geometry, environmental constraints, and overall structural goals without the need for complete retraining. Nevertheless, Xu's dataset suffers from limited diversity, being tailored to specific block types and structural configurations. Incorporating data augmentation techniques, such as introducing synthetic noise, randomizing textures, and perturbing poses could improve the robustness of both supervised and RL-based methods, and in the RL case, could be integrated into pretraining phases, such as behavioral cloning to accelerate convergence.

III. Proposed Methodology: Reinforcement Learning (RL)-based Block Placement

To address the limitations identified in [1], we introduce a RL-based approach using Unity ML-Agents [3] and Proximal Policy Optimization (PPO). The method leverages the interaction-based learning paradigm inherent to RL to dynamically adapt and optimize the strategic placement of wave-dissipating blocks.

A. Motivation of Utilizing RL

RL allows a learning agent to iteratively obtain an optimal policy by interacting directly with its environment, receiving feedback through reward signals, and adapting actions accordingly. Unlike supervised methods that depend on extensive pre-labeled data, RL's ability to continuously refine its strategies based on outcomes makes it uniquely suited to scenarios that involve complex and dynamic decision-making, such as block stacking in coastal engineering. The primary reasons for employing RL in this research include:

- Adaptability: the RL agent dynamically adapts to structural or block-type changes.
- Strategic Long-Term Optimization: RL considers the implications of each block placement in a multi-block scenario, addressing global objectives, such as porosity reduction and structural stability.
- Reduced Data Dependency: the agent learns from interaction outcomes rather than extensive simulations, reducing the need for dataset preparation.

B. RL Agent Design

The RL agent operates within our self-developed 3D-BW environment, performing iterative block placements by observing the current structural state using data representations, such as gap maps and depth maps derived from discretized grid cells. Figure 1 illustrates a bird's-eye view visualization of a gap map. Based on these observations, the agent selects a discrete placement coordinate (x, z) and a rotation angle, then drops a block from a predetermined height.

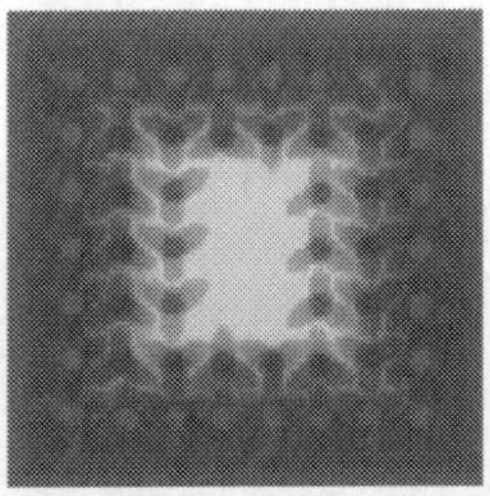

Figure 1. Visualization of gap map of breakwater structure from a bird-eye view

The agent aims to optimize multiple explicit and adaptable objectives, including compactness, stability, overflow penalty, and porosity. After multiple block placements, the Proximal Policy Optimization algorithm [4] updates the policy parameters based on the observed rewards and outcomes. Through iterative learning, the agent is expected to gradually improve its strategic placement capabilities.

C. Limitations

While RL offers significant potential advantages, several challenges must be acknowledged:

- Increased Training Complexity: potentially requires substantial computational resources and training time.
- Reward Function Sensitivity: strong dependency on effective reward design, potentially challenging to tune accurately.
- Exploration Efficiency: initial random placements may cause slow training convergence, necessitating strategies like curriculum learning or behavioral cloning to mitigate this issue.

IV. Conclusion

This idea contribution proposes an RL approach as an innovative, adaptive, and strategic method for optimizing the placement of wave-dissipating blocks. By leveraging Unity ML-agents, physics-based simulations, and well-designed reward functions, RL demonstrates significant potential to overcome the inherent limitations of supervised learning methods. Although challenges remain regarding computational resources and careful reward design, these issues may be mitigated by incorporating techniques, such as behavioral cloning. This approach lays the groundwork for more autonomous and efficient block placement strategies in future coastal engineering applications.

Acknowledgment

We extend our sincere gratitude to Honma Concrete Industry Co., Ltd. for generously providing the three-dimensional data essential to our research. We also wish to express our appreciation to Onogumi Co., Ltd. for their valuable guidance and insightful advice throughout the course of this research.

References

[1] Y. Xu, A study on stacked object recognition and stacking operation planning combining 3D point cloud representation, deep-learning and physics engine, M.Eng. thesis, Graduate School of Information Science and Technology, Hokkaido University, Sapporo, Japan, 2020, doi:10.14943/doctoral.k15552.

[2] H. M. Chuah, T. Yamazaki, R. Iwasawa, and T. Suto, "Development of wave-dissipating block installation simulation for inexperienced worker training," World Academy of Science, Engineering and Technology, International Journal of Computer and Systems Engineering, vol. 18, no. 9, pp. 611-618, 2024.

[3] Unity Technologies, "Unity ML-Agents Toolkit," GitHub repository, [Online]. Available: https://github.com/Unity-Technologies/ml-agents. [retrieved: July, 2025].

[4] J. Schulman, F. Wolski, P. Dhariwal, A. Radford, and O. Klimov, "Proximal policy optimization algorithms," arXiv preprint arXiv:1707.06347, 2017.

[5] S. Gu, E. Holly, T. Lillicrap, and S. Levine, "Deep reinforcement learning for robotic manipulation," in *Proceedings of the IEEE International Conference on Robotics and Automation (ICRA)*, pp. 3389-3396, 2017.

[6] D. Silver et al., "Deterministic policy gradient algorithms," in *Proceedings of the 31st International Conference on Machine Learning (ICML)*, pp. 387-395, 2014.

[7] K. He, X. Zhang, S. Ren, and J. Sun, "Deep residual learning for image recognition," in *Proceedings of the IEEE Conference on Computer Vision and Pattern Recognition (CVPR)*, pp. 770-778, 2016.

PAIRS: Physics-Enabled AI for Real-Time Simulations Surrogates

Zeinab Alfaytarouni and Hamza Ben Ammar
Capgemini Engineering
Toulouse, France
e-mail: {zeinab.alfaytarouni|hamza.ben-ammar}@capgemini.com

***Abstract*—The development and improvement of complex engineering systems increasingly depend on virtual and hybrid test benches for validating new designs or modifications to existing ones. Central to these test benches are simulation models, which are essential but time-consuming to develop due to their reliance on domain expertise. Full-fledged simulation models can also be slow, impeding the validation process that requires real-time simulation. Conversely, AI surrogate models, derived from sensor data, face constraints due to insufficient training data and potentially lacking physical sense. To address these challenges, we propose the use of physics-enabled AI models as surrogates, which strike a balance by integrating underlying physical laws through model equations, thereby requiring significantly less data for training. Once trained, these models operate in real-time, expediting the validation process. In this work, we introduce a Physics-enabled AI surrogate model development process that augments to the existing Machine Learning Operations (MLOps) workflow. Our approach employs an ontological framework to align user needs with a model template. We leverage Physics-Informed Neural Networks (PINNs) as the core building block for this template. Once a model structure is selected, the traditional MLOps process is applied to train and validate the AI surrogate. This methodology simplifies the model development process and hence accelerates the overall system development.**

Keywords-Physics-enabled AI; Physics-Informed Neural Networks; Ontology; Simulations.

I. Introduction

Advances in Artificial Intelligence (AI) have had a profound impact across numerous disciplines, including engineering. One particularly transformative development is surrogate modeling, especially approaches based on AI techniques [1]. Surrogate models offer simplified, fast, and reliable alternatives to complex, costly, and time-consuming multiphysics simulations or physical experiments.

The creation of an AI-based simulation model typically follows a common set of steps, regardless of the specific AI technique employed. The process begins with a clear definition of the problem that the model is intended to solve. This is followed by the acquisition of the necessary data, as well as the identification of performance requirements and constraints. The collected data must then be prepared, potentially merged if sourced from different origins, and cleaned to ensure quality and relevance. The next step involves selecting an appropriate model, designing its architecture, fine-tuning its parameters, and carrying out the training, validation, and testing phases. The process concludes with the deployment of the model in its target environment. Once deployed, the model can be monitored to assess its performance under real-world conditions and to detect any anomalies. One of the most complex tasks in this process is selecting the appropriate AI model. While data-driven Machine Learning (ML) algorithms have demonstrated success in many surrogate modeling tasks, they are often criticized for operating as "black boxes", their internal decision-making processes are difficult to interpret. This raises concerns about transparency and trust [2]. Additionally, such models tend to require large volumes of high-quality training data and significant computational resources, which may not be feasible in domains where data is scarce or expensive to acquire [3]. Furthermore, purely data-driven models can struggle to generalize beyond the specific conditions seen during training [2][3]. In response to these challenges, numerous studies have emphasized the importance of integrating domain-specific knowledge into machine learning [4] [5]. This integration improves interpretability, reduces data requirements, and increases consistency with known physical laws or constraints. This approach, which combines domain knowledge with data, is known as a hybrid approach and is gaining increasing popularity. Among these methods, Physics-Informed Neural Networks (PINNs) [6] [7] have recently attracted significant attention and have been applied to a wide range of applications across various fields. These models incorporate physical laws, typically in the form of differential equations, directly into the loss function during training. As a result, PINNs not only offer better generalization from limited data but also provide more transparent and physically consistent predictions.

Since the introduction of PINNs by Raissi et al. in 2019 [6], most studies have employed PINNs with feedforward neural network architectures. However, some researchers have explored alternative types of neural networks to assess their impact on overall model performance [8]–[14]. The effectiveness of a PINN architecture depends on both the data and the task at hand. This means that certain architectures are better suited to specific situations, depending on the characteristics of the data and the nature of the problem to be solved, while others may perform better in different contexts. Therefore, selecting a suitable architecture for a PINN is challenging due to the wide range of available options, from the type of neural network to various model parameter choices.

To simplify this task, we aim to develop an ontology-based Recommendation System (RS) to assist in selecting an appropriate PINN model. This work is part of a broader project that seeks to streamline and automate the entire process of developing physics-enabled AI surrogates designed to replace complex simulations. The primary goal of the project is to enable domain or simulation experts to build their AI Surrogate Models (SMs) without requiring extensive expertise in AI.

The remainder of this paper is organized as follows. In

Section II, we introduce the concept of Physics-Enabled AI, with a focus on PINNs. We present an analysis of the key parameters and structural choices that influence PINN's performance. Section III provides a literature review of existing PINN architectures across various applications and domains. In Section IV, we introduce the concept of ontology-based recommender systems. Section V details the development and implementation of our proposed ontology-driven recommendation system, including the ontology construction process and the recommender interface that suggests suitable PINN architectures based on user input. Finally, Section VI concludes the paper with a summary of our findings and directions for future work.

II. PHYSICS-ENABLED AI

A. Principle of Physics-Informed Neural Networks

PINNs [6] are a specialized category of deep learning algorithms designed to tackle both forward and inverse problems. Unlike traditional neural networks that rely solely on data, PINNs incorporate prior knowledge of the system, typically in the form of Partial Differential Equations, directly into the training process. This is achieved by embedding the governing equations into the network's loss function, effectively constraining the solution space and guiding the model toward physically consistent predictions. The primary motivation for developing these algorithms is that incorporating prior knowledge or physical constraints can lead to more interpretable machine learning models that require less data and remain robust in the presence of imperfect data.

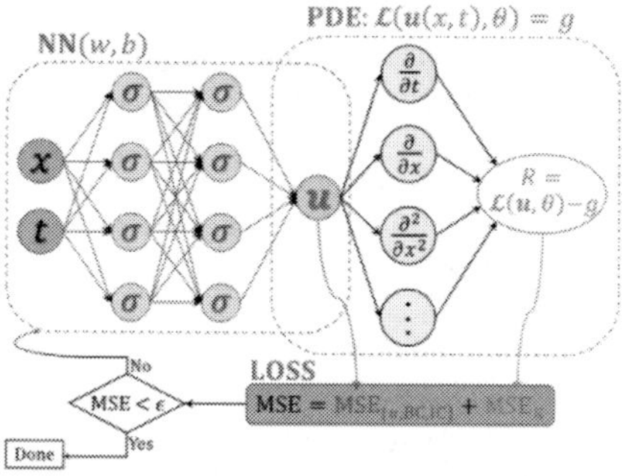

Figure 1. Principle of Physics-Informed Neural Networks [15].

As shown in Figure 1, a PINN consists of three main components:

- An approximation module: the neural network $NN(w, b)$, parameterized by weights w and biases b, takes as inputs x and t. Through nonlinear transformations governed by the activation function σ, the network outputs an approximation of the solution $u(x, t)$.
- A physics-informed module, where the predicted solution is inserted into the governing Partial Differential Equation (PDE), expressed as $\mathcal{L}(u(x, t), \theta) = g$. The derivatives of u with respect to t and x are computed automatically through differentiation of the neural network. These derivatives allow evaluation of the residual $R = \mathcal{L}(u, \theta) - g$, which measure the discrepancy between the network prediction and the governing equation.
- An optimization module, responsible for minimizing the loss and ensuring convergence toward a physically consistent solution. The loss is expressed as the Mean Squared Error (MSE), defined as: $MSE = MSE_{\{u,BC,IC\}} + MSE_R$. The term $MSE_{\{u,BC,IC\}}$ measures the discrepancy between the predicted solution and the available data, including Boundary Conditions (BC) and Initial Conditions (IC). The second term, MSE_R, evaluates the residual of the PDE. By combining both contributions, the optimization process balances fidelity to the observed data with consistency to the underlying physics, and training continues iteratively until the overall loss drops below a prescribed tolerance ϵ.

While this structure provides a powerful framework, choosing an appropriate NN architecture and parameters can be a significant challenge due to the vast number of available options. As highlighted in Section III, a wide variety of PINN architectures have been proposed across different industries and engineering domains. Without extensive experimentation, it is often difficult to determine the most effective configuration, making the process time-consuming. To address this, the present article explores various possible architectures to help guide the selection process based on the available data and input types.

B. Structure and Parameters

To select the most suitable PINN architecture for a given problem, several key aspects must be considered:

- Network Type: The architecture should match the task and the nature of the data.
- Depth and Width: The number of layers and neurons per layer, along with the choice of activation functions, significantly influence the model's ability to learn complex representations.
- Optimization Methods: The choice of optimizer and hyperparameters, such as the learning rate, plays a crucial role in the model's convergence.
- Batch Size and Regularization: Batch size, regularization strategies (e.g., dropout, L2 regularization), and data normalization are essential for efficient and stable training.
- Performance Enhancements: Techniques like data augmentation and early stopping can improve model performance and generalization.
- Hyperparameter Tuning: Methods such as Grid Search, Random Search, and Bayesian Optimization help in finding the optimal network configuration.
- Hardware Considerations: Available computational resources (e.g., GPUs, TPUs) and compatibility with deep learning frameworks like TensorFlow or PyTorch are important for scalability and efficiency.

In summary, designing an effective PINN architecture requires a strategic combination of these elements to ensure optimal performance.

III. Literature Review on Physics-Informed Neural Network Architectures

Several neural network architectures have been adapted for use in PINNs, including: Fully Connected Neural Networks (FCNNs) [16], Convolutional Neural Networks (CNNs) [8], Recurrent Neural Networks (RNNs) [13], Long Short-Term Memory networks (LSTMs) [12], Autoencoders (AEs) [17], Generative Adversarial Networks (GANs) [10], Bayesian Neural Networks (BNNs) [9], Graph Neural Networks (GNNs) [11], and Residual Networks (ResNets) [14], among others.

Among these, FCNNs are the most widely used. These networks are frequently employed to approximate solutions to scalar or vector-valued functions, such as PDEs and Ordinary Differential Equations (ODEs).

CNNs are designed to efficiently process grid-based data, such as images. They are widely used in tasks like image classification, object detection, and image segmentation, and are also applicable to problems involving spatially structured data, such as velocity fields in fluid mechanics or temperature distributions.

RNNs are a type of network where connections between nodes form directed cycles, allowing information to persist over time. This architecture is particularly well-suited for tasks involving sequential data, such as time series forecasting, natural language processing, and speech recognition. By retaining a form of memory, RNNs can use past information to influence current predictions, which is essential for understanding and generating sequences where context and order matter.

LSTMs, a specialized type of RNN, are designed to address the vanishing gradient problem in traditional RNNs. They incorporate gating mechanisms to better capture long-term dependencies in sequential data, making them especially effective for tasks such as speech recognition, machine translation, and sentiment analysis.

GNNs are designed to process data structured as graphs and are applied to systems where relationships between entities are important, such as transportation networks or molecular interactions.

Autoencoders are often used for dimensionality reduction and anomaly detection in complex physical systems, as well as for data denoising and generative modeling.

GANs are widely used to generate realistic images, videos, and other types of data, or to produce physically plausible solutions that respect physical constraints.

Bayesian Deep Learning (BDL) is an approach that integrates Bayesian methods into deep neural networks to quantify uncertainty in predictions. Unlike traditional neural networks, which provide deterministic predictions, Bayesian models generate probability distributions over model parameters, allowing the uncertainty associated with each prediction to be assessed. BDL is particularly useful in domains where decisions must be made cautiously and where prediction uncertainty can have significant consequences.

Finally, ResNets are used for tasks requiring very deep networks, enabling more stable training and improved performance through residual connections.

IV. Ontology-Based Recommender Systems

In an increasingly data-driven world, organizing knowledge in a structured and meaningful way is essential for understanding, sharing, and reusing information. Whether in science, business, or technology, we need systems that help us make sense of complex domains. To achieve this, various techniques have been developed to organize knowledge, each with different levels of complexity and expressiveness. These include taxonomies, ontologies, and knowledge graphs [18].

A taxonomy is the simplest form of knowledge organization. It arranges concepts in a hierarchical structure, typically from general to specific, using parent-child relationships [18]. Ontologies provide a more expressive and formal way to represent knowledge. They define concepts, properties, relationships, and rules within a domain, enabling both humans and machines to reason about the data. Ontologies are essential in fields like artificial intelligence, semantic web, and biomedical informatics [18]–[20]. Knowledge graphs extend ontologies by linking entities and their relationships in a graph structure [20].

For our project, we aim to develop an ontology-driven recommender system that suggests the most suitable Neural Network (NN) architecture based on the user's data type and task. This system combines a formally structured ontology, representing relationships between NN types, data modalities, and task categories, with a Python-based reasoning and querying engine. The ontology enables semantic inference, while the Python system handles user input, executes reasoning logic, and delivers recommendations.

Despite the growing interest in semantic technologies for intelligent systems, no published scientific work to date appears to directly implement an ontology-based recommender system specifically designed to suggest NN architectures based on the type of data and the task to be accomplished.

While there are ontologies that describe machine learning concepts, such as the Machine Learning Schema (MLS) [21], these are primarily intended for metadata annotation, experiment tracking, or model documentation. They do not aim to support reasoning or recommendation of neural network architectures based on task and data characteristics, which is the focus of our work.

V. Results

A. Guiding PINN Architecture Selection Through Input Analysis

The developed workflow, named PAIRS (for Physics-enabled AI for Real-time simulations Surrogates), allows users to input differential equations along with ICs and BCs, which can be integrated into the loss function. In addition, users provide data and specify the type of task to be accomplished.

Differential equations play a significant role in optimizing the learning process. However, the type of these equations (whether ODEs, PDEs, or Integro-Differential Equations (IDEs)) does not influence the choice of the PINN architecture. In contrast, the types and properties of the data, along with the tasks to be performed, play a crucial role in this choice.

Data can be classified into quantitative and qualitative types, as well as more advanced forms. Quantitative data refers to measurable information expressed numerically, such as discrete or continuous numerical data, and time series data (linear or nonlinear). Qualitative data includes descriptive information that cannot be measured numerically but can be categorized or described, such as categorical data, text, images, audio, and video. Sensor data may be either quantitative or qualitative, depending on what is being measured. Graph data is represented as graphs composed of nodes (or vertices) and edges (or links) connecting them. This format is particularly useful for representing complex relationships between entities.

These data types may exhibit various characteristics that influence their processing and analysis, such as:

- Temporal dependency (Dynamic Data): Data evolves over time, with short-term or long-term dependencies. This distinction is crucial for choosing between models like LSTM and RNN.
- Probabilistic nature: Data may contain uncertainty or variability.
- High dimensionality: Data with many features or variables, making processing more complex.
- Noise: Data may include errors, inconsistencies, or irrelevant information.
- Heterogeneity: Data from diverse sources and formats, requiring normalization for coherent analysis.
- Large volume: The data may be massive in scale.

PINNs are primarily applied to solving forward and inverse differential equations, including ODEs, PDEs, integro-differential, and stochastic equations, commonly encountered in physics and engineering. However, PINNs can also be applied to many other tasks. Some of these tasks influence the choice of the most appropriate PINN architecture, while others can be addressed with any architecture without a specific preference. Tasks that influence architecture choice include:

- Solving Differential Equations
- Inverse Problems:
  - Model Discovery: Identifying underlying models or physical laws from data
  - Parameter Estimation: Estimating unknown parameters in physical or statistical models from observed data
- Sequence Prediction: Forecasting future values or sequences based on time series or sequential data.
- Capturing Long-Term Dependencies: Modeling long-range dependencies in sequential or temporal data, important in time series forecasting or text analysis.
- Noise Reduction: Cleaning noisy data to recover the original signal, using techniques like autoencoders for image, audio, or other data types.
- Data Generation: Creating synthetic data from a learned model, especially when real data is scarce or expensive.
- Dimensionality Reduction: Reducing the number of variables while preserving important features
- Uncertainty Quantification: Estimating the uncertainty in model predictions.
- Preventing Degradation in Deep Neural Networks: Enhancing stability and performance in deep networks to avoid degradation during training, e.g., using ResNets to address vanishing gradients.

Other tasks, such as classification, predictive maintenance, and anomaly detection may also arise. For these, the choice of architecture primarily depends on the data type.

B. Ontology Development and Integration

Protégé [22], a free and open-source ontology editor, is used to develop the ontology. Created at Stanford University, Protégé is widely adopted in the semantic web community. It supports the creation and editing of ontologies in various formats, including RDF, RDFS, and OWL.

As shown in the Figure 2, in the first stage of ontology construction, we defined three main classes: Data, Task, and Neural Net Type. The Data class includes two subclasses: Type and Characteristics. The data types considered include: numerical data, sequences (e.g., time series), text, images, audio, video, and graphs. The characteristics include: temporal dependency, probabilistic nature, high dimensionality, heterogeneity, and data volume. For the Task class, only tasks that influence the choice of neural network architecture are considered. These include: solving differential equations and inverse problems, sequence prediction, capturing long-term dependencies, noise reduction, data generation, dimensionality reduction, uncertainty quantification, and preventing degradation in deep neural networks. This class represents the user's task preferences and requirements. The Neural Network class includes the architectures shown in Figure 2: FCNN, CNN, RNN, LSTM, AE, BNN, GAN, GNN, and ResNet. Each class is defined or described in detail using Annotations in Protégé. To establish relationships between these classes, four object properties were defined:

- areBestSuitedForData: Links a neural network type to data types or characteristics it is particularly well-suited for. For example, CNNs are best suited for image data, GNNs for graph-structured data, and RNNs for sequential data with temporal dependencies.
- canBeUsedForData: Also links neural networks to data types or characteristics they can be applied to, though not necessarily in an optimal way.
- areBestSuitedForTask: Indicates that a neural network is particularly well-suited for a specific task.
- canBeUsedForTask: Indicates that a neural network can be used for a given task.

The ontology is developed in OWL format, and the HermiT reasoner is used to validate its logical consistency by inferring implicit relationships and identifying contradictions. This involves checking that the defined classes, properties, and restrictions do not lead to inconsistencies in class hierarchies or instances. Queries are also executed using the DL Query tool in Protégé to ensure that the defined relationships and

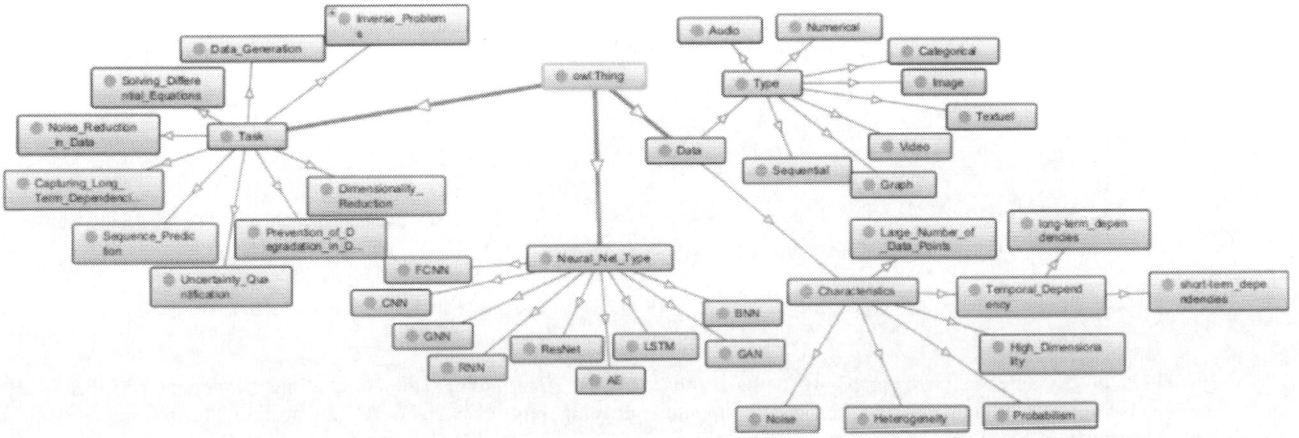

Figure 2. Ontology class diagram generated with OntoGraf, showing the main concepts: Data Types and Characteristics, Tasks, and Neural Network Types, along with their respective subclasses.

properties yield the expected results. An example of these queries is shown in Figure 3. All tests conducted during this phase confirmed that the ontology produces the expected results, both in terms of logical reasoning and query outcomes, reinforcing its reliability as the foundation for the recommendation system. Figure 4 illustrates the complexity of the ontology, with arrows indicating the links between classes based on the defined properties.

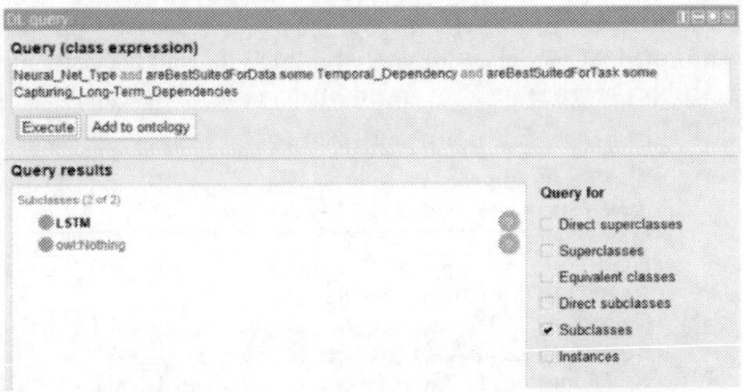

Figure 3. Example of DL queries used to test the ontology.

C. System Implementation and Recommender Workflow

To develop the recommendation system, user inputs are first connected to the ontology to extract relevant information. This linkage enables the system to derive meaningful insights and generate appropriate model recommendations. The implementation is carried out in Python, using the Owlready2 library to load and query the ontology.

The process begins with a user interface developed using Streamlit, which allows users to input their data, equations, IC, and BC. The interface also prompts users to specify the task they aim to accomplish by selecting from a set of predefined options.

Once the inputs are provided, the system analyzes the data to identify its type and specific characteristics. These are then mapped to corresponding concepts in the ontology. Based on this mapping and the selected task, the system generates a primary recommendation using the property areBestSuitedForData/Task, and suggests alternative models through the property canBeUsedForData/Task. Users can then select one of the recommended models that best fits their needs, guided by detailed descriptions that include relative levels of resource and time requirements.

After a model is selected, additional parameters—such as the number of layers, number of neurons, learning rate, and activation function—are either set to default values or defined as ranges for exploration through hyperparameter optimization techniques. The model is then implemented and trained using PyTorch. During training, validation, and testing, the user-provided equations and conditions (if available) are incorporated into the loss function alongside the data loss, ensuring that the model respects the underlying physics. These steps can follow a standard MLOps workflow. Once the model is trained and validated, it can be exported and deployed in its target environment for further testing and integration.

VI. Conclusion and Perspectives

This work presents a foundational version of an ontology designed to support the development of physics-informed AI surrogates, which aim to provide an alternative to complex, time-consuming simulations. While this initial version provides a structured framework, it remains a first iteration that will require further refinement. In particular, future enhancements should include the integration of additional types of hybrid models to better reflect the diversity of approaches in physics-enabled machine learning.

The ontology was constructed following an extensive literature review aimed at identifying the key factors influencing the selection of neural network architectures in PINNs. The

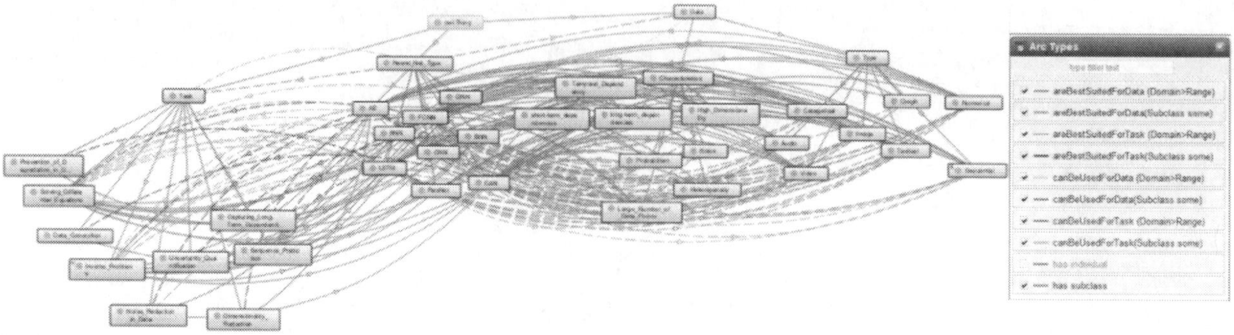

Figure 4. Diagram illustrating the complexity of the ontology, with arrows indicating the links between classes based on the defined properties.

review involved collecting and analyzing a wide range of studies that applied different architectures in various industrial and scientific contexts. Some of the relevant studies reviewed during this process are mentioned in Section III. Each study was examined based on architecture type, input/output structure, data characteristics, governing equations, task type, and application domain. Technical parameters such as activation functions, number of layers and neurons, optimization algorithms, learning rates, and performance metrics were also considered. This structured analysis enabled the classification of use cases and the identification of patterns linking specific architectures to particular contexts.

This study revealed that several aspects play a role in this decision, including the nature and characteristics of the data, the volume of available data, the complexity of relationships within the data (e.g., linear, nonlinear, or intricate patterns), the specific objectives of the modeling task, and the availability of computational resources and time constraints. The ontology serves as a structured framework that links the neural network, the data, and the task. Building on this foundation, a recommendation system suggests the most appropriate models to use, indicating the relative levels of resource and time requirements as well as the level of model complexity.

The ontology is currently in its first version and accessible only within our internal project environment. It is implemented in OWL format and can be edited using the Protégé tool, allowing for easy updates and integration with additional models and parameters. Although the development is ongoing and the full workflow is not yet complete, the ontology has been designed with extensibility in mind to support future enhancements and broader system integration. However, its current scope is limited to PINNs and does not yet cover the full spectrum of physics-informed machine learning models. Moreover, even within the PINNs domain, the rapid evolution of architectures presents a challenge for keeping the ontology up to date. Another challenge is integrating this approach into existing MLOps workflows, which can be complex due to the need to manage physics-based constraints and ensure alignment with the ontology.

This contribution is part of a broader initiative aimed at streamlining and automating the entire process of building physics-enabled AI surrogates. The primary goal is to empower domain experts, such as simulation engineers, to develop and deploy surrogate models without needing deep expertise in AI.

Several key directions are planned to extend this work:

- Automatic updating of the ontology using Generative AI (GenAI) to reflect evolving model types, as new models and approaches are constantly emerging in this rapidly evolving domain.
- Development of a database of pretrained models, facilitating reuse and accelerating deployment.
- Integration of GenAI and intelligent agents to assist users in model selection, configuration, and training.

These future developments aim to create a comprehensive, user-friendly ecosystem for building and managing physics-informed AI models, ultimately bridging the gap between simulation expertise and advanced machine learning capabilities.

REFERENCES

[1] S. Koziel and A. Pietrenko-Dąbrowska, "Basics of data-driven surrogate modeling," in *Performance-Driven Surrogate Modeling of High-Frequency Structures*. Springer International Publishing, 2020, pp. 23–58, ISBN: 978-3-030-38925-3. DOI: 10.1007/978-3-030-38926-0_2.

[2] G. Marcus, "Deep learning: A critical appraisal," Jan. 2018. DOI: 10.48550/arXiv.1801.00631. arXiv: 1801.00631.

[3] N. Thompson, K. Greenewald, K. Lee, and G. Manso, "The computational limits of deep learning," in *Ninth Computing within Limits 2023*, LIMITS, Jun. 2023. DOI: 10.21428/bf6fb269.1f033948.

[4] I. Pan, L. Mason, and O. Matar, "Data-centric engineering: Integrating simulation, machine learning and statistics. challenges and opportunities," *Chemical Engineering Science*, vol. 249, p. 117271, Nov. 2021. DOI: 10.1016/j.ces.2021.117271.

[5] G. Karniadakis *et al.*, "Physics-informed machine learning," *Nature Reviews Physics*, pp. 1–19, May 2021. DOI: 10.1038/s42254-021-00314-5.

[6] M. Raissi, P. Perdikaris, and G. E. Karniadakis, "Physics-informed neural networks: A deep learning framework for solving forward and inverse problems involving nonlinear partial differential equations," *Journal of Computational Physics*, vol. 378, pp. 686–707, Feb. 2019. DOI: 10.1016/j.jcp.2018.10.045.

[7] J. Pateras, P. Rana, and P. Ghosh, "A taxonomic survey of physics-informed machine learning," *Applied Sciences*, vol. 13, no. 12, 2023, ISSN: 2076-3417. DOI: 10.3390/app13126892.

[8] X. Zhao, Z. Gong, Y. Zhang, W. Yao, and X. Chen, "Physics-informed convolutional neural networks for temperature field prediction of heat source layout without labeled data," Sep. 2021. DOI: 10.48550/arXiv.2109.12482.

[9] L. Yang, X. Meng, and G. E. Karniadakis, "B-pinns: Bayesian physics-informed neural networks for forward and inverse pde problems with noisy data," *Journal of Computational Physics*, vol. 425, p. 109913, Jan. 2021, ISSN: 0021-9991. DOI: 10.1016/j.jcp.2020.109913.

[10] W. Li, C. Zhang, C. Wang, H. Guan, and D. Tao, *Revisiting pinns: Generative adversarial physics-informed neural networks and point-weighting method*, 2022. DOI: 10.48550/arXiv.2205.08754. arXiv: 2205.08754.

[11] D. Dalton, D. Husmeier, and H. Gao, "Physics-informed graph neural network emulation of soft-tissue mechanics," *Computer Methods in Applied Mechanics and Engineering*, vol. 417, p. 116351, Dec. 2023. DOI: 10.1016/j.cma.2023.116351.

[12] F. Liu, J. Li, and L. Wang, "Pi-lstm: Physics-informed long short-term memory network for structural response modeling," *Engineering Structures*, vol. 292, DOI: 10.1016/j.engstruct.2023.116500.

[13] Y. Zheng, C. Hu, X. Wang, and Z. Wu, "Physics-informed recurrent neural network modeling for predictive control of nonlinear processes," *Journal of Process Control*, vol. 128, p. 103005, 2023, ISSN: 0959-1524. DOI: https://doi.org/10.1016/j.jprocont.2023.103005.

[14] T. Shan *et al.*, "Physics-informed supervised residual learning for electromagnetic modeling," *IEEE Transactions on Antennas and Propagation*, vol. PP, pp. 1–1, Apr. 2023. DOI: 10.1109/TAP.2023.3245281.

[15] X. Meng, Z. Li, D. Zhang, and G. E. Karniadakis, "Ppinn: Parareal physics-informed neural network for time-dependent pdes," *Computer Methods in Applied Mechanics and Engineering*, vol. 370, p. 113250, Oct. 2020, ISSN: 0045-7825. DOI: 10.1016/j.cma.2020.113250.

[16] Z. Mao, A. D. Jagtap, and G. E. Karniadakis, "Physics-informed neural networks for high-speed flows," *Computer Methods in Applied Mechanics and Engineering*, vol. 360, p. 112789, Mar. 2020. DOI: 10.1016/j.cma.2019.112789.

[17] C. Tan, Y. Cai, H. Wang, X. Sun, and L. Chen, "Vehicle state estimation combining physics-informed neural network and unscented kalman filtering on manifolds," *Sensors*, vol. 23, no. 15, Jan. 2023. DOI: 10.3390/s23156665.

[18] T. Salatino A.and Aggarwal, A. Mannocci, F. Osborne, and E. Motta, "A survey of knowledge organization systems of research fields: Resources and challenges," *Quantitative Science Studies*, 2025. DOI: 10.1162/qss_a_00363.

[19] K. W. Fung and O. Bodenreider, "Knowledge representation and ontologies," *Clinical Research Informatics*, pp. 255–275, Jan. 2012. DOI: 10.1007/978-1-84882-448-5_14.

[20] Nature Research Intelligence, *Knowledge graphs and ontologies in semantic web applications*, https://www.nature.com/research-intelligence/nri-topic-summaries/knowledge-graphs-and-ontologies-in-semantic-web-applications-micro-92, Accessed: 2025-08-18.

[21] J. Braga, J. Dias, and F. Regateiro, *A machine learning ontology*, Oct. 2020. DOI: 10.31226/osf.io/rc954.

[22] M. A. Musen, "The protégé project: A look back and a look forward," *AI Matters*, vol. 1, no. 4, 2015. DOI: 10.1145/2557001.25757003.

Simulation Modeling of Multi-Agent Coordination in Maritime Emergency Response Systems

Jing Xu, Qingqing Yang*, Yingying Gao, Pengcheng Yang
College of System Engineering,
National University of Defense Technology
Changsha, China
Email: Jenniferxu98@163.com, yqq_1982@126.com, 15222638242@qq.com, yangpengcheng@nudt.edu.cn

***Abstract*—This research creates a multi-agent simulation model for the maritime emergency response system, integrating agent-based modeling with evolutionary game theory. The model captures strategic interactions among four key stakeholders, such as Maritime Administration, Ship Operators, Crew Members, and Insurance Companies—who adaptively adjust strategies under bounded rationality. Through replicator dynamics and stability analysis, we identify equilibrium conditions and optimal coordination mechanisms. Numerical simulations reveal critical thresholds for safety compliance and effective incentive structures. The framework bears the potential for action in maritime safety policy over the bottom-up modeling approaches to emergent complex system dynamics toward regulatory design applicable for safety-critical system domains.**

Keywords-Maritime emergency response; agent-based modeling; evolutionary game theory.

I. Introduction

Maritime emergency response faces critical coordination challenges, with inadequate stakeholder collaboration identified as a primary factor in accident escalation and delayed responses [1]. This real-world problem motivates our investigation into strategic interactions among regulatory authorities, ship operators, crew members, and insurance companies in emergency scenarios.

Traditional analytical methods struggle to capture the complex adaptive nature of maritime emergency systems, where multiple heterogeneous agents interact dynamically. Simulation modeling offers unique advantages in revealing emergent properties — how individual-level decisions generate system-level behaviors [2]. This study integrates agent-based modeling with evolutionary game theory to develop a multi-agent coordination model for maritime emergency response. Unlike conventional approaches, our model explicitly characterizes bounded rational agents who adaptively adjust strategies through environmental feedback and mutual observations.

Our contributions include: (1) developing a four-agent evolutionary game model tailored for maritime emergency scenarios; (2) systematically analyzing parameter impacts on system evolution through simulation experiments; (3) proposing validated mechanism design frameworks for enhanced coordination. These advances provide quantitative tools for maritime safety policy formulation.

This paper is organized as follows. Section II presents the model formulation, including agent definitions and game-theoretic framework. Section III provides the simulation experiments and analysis.

II. Model Formulation

This section presents the mathematical foundation of our multi-agent coordination model, establishing the game-theoretic framework and defining stakeholder interactions within the maritime emergency response system.

A. Game-Theoretic Distributed Auction with Spatial-Temporal Dynamics

Assumption 1: The evolutionary game involves four stakeholders, such as Maritime Administration (M), Ship Operators (O), Crew Members (C), and Insurance Companies (I)—all of whom are assumed to exhibit bounded rationality.

Assumption 2: Each stakeholder has two pure strategy choices [3][4]:

Maritime Administration (M) chooses between Strict Regulation (MS) and Lenient Regulation (ML);

Ship Operators (O) choose between High Safety Investment (OH) and Low Safety Investment (OL);

Crew Members (C) choose between Active Emergency Response (CA) and Passive Emergency Response (CP);

Insurance Companies (I) choose between Strict Review (IS) and Lenient Review (IL).

Assumption 3: The strategy choices of stakeholders are interdependent, and the probability of strategy adjustment is determined by payoff differences.

Table I presents the definitions of the relevant parameters.

B. Model Construction

One of the principal innovations of this model lies in its formulation of accident probability as a function of collective stakeholder actions. This mechanism can be intuitively conceptualized through a multi-layered risk mitigation framework.

TABLE I. PART OF FACTORS

Descriptions of Factors	Symbol	Description
Maritime Administration	C_M^S, C_M^L	Cost of strict or lenient regulation
	L_M	Social loss and liability cost in the event of an accident
	R_M	Social benefit from a good safety record
Ship Operators	C_O^H, C_O^L	Cost of high or low safety investment
	F_S, F_L	Fine for violation under strict or lenient regulation
	L_O	Direct economic loss from an accident
	R_O	Normal operational revenue
Crew Members	C_C^A, C_C^P	Cost of active or passive response
	B_C	Bonus for successful emergency response
	W_C	Base wage
Insurance Companies	C_I^S, C_I^L	Cost of strict or lenient review
	P_I	Insurance payout in case of accident
	R_I	Insurance premium revenue
Risk Parameters	P_B	The basic risk reflects the inherent risks of offshore operations
	$\alpha_M, \alpha_O, \alpha_C, \alpha_I$	Individually representing the risk reduction coefficient of safety measures for M, O, C, and I

Consider the safety measures adopted by each stakeholder as constituting an independent protective layer. The baseline risk, denoted as P_B, represents the intrinsic accident probability in the absence of any interventions. Each protective layer attenuates a portion of the aggregate risk:

$$P_{accident} = \begin{array}{l} P_B \cdot (1-\delta_M \cdot \alpha_M) \cdot (1-\delta_O \cdot \alpha_O) \\ \cdot (1-\delta_C \cdot \alpha_C) \cdot (1-\delta_I \cdot \alpha_I) \end{array} \quad (1)$$

Where:

δ_M=1 if M chooses Strict (MS), 0 if Lenient (ML);

δ_O=1 if O chooses High Safety Investment (OH), 0 if Low Safety Investment;

δ_C=1 if C chooses Active Emergency Response (CA), 0 if Passive Emergency Response (CP);

δ_I=1 if C chooses Strict (IS), 0 if Lenient (IL).

In the model, the maritime management administration, the ship operators, the crew members, and the insurance companies make their strategy choices based on their own will. According to the above assumptions, the partial payoff functions of the four-party game is shown in Table 2.

III. SIMULATION EXPERIMENTS AND ANALYSIS

We are implementing a three-phase experimental design using agent-based Monte Carlo simulations. Phase one establishes baseline dynamics with neutral parameters to observe natural system evolution without intervention. Phase two employs Latin Hypercube Sampling across 10,000 parameter combinations, systematically varying penalty ratios and risk reduction coefficients to identify critical control variables. Phase three tests policy interventions—pure economic incentives, combined strategies, and three temporal adjustment patterns—under crisis (high initial accident rate), stable, and chaotic initial conditions, ensuring robust policy recommendations across diverse real-world scenarios.

TABLE II. PART OF THE GAME PAYOFF FUNCTIONS

Stakeholder	Payoff Matrix
Maritime Administration	$R_M - C_M(\text{strategy}) - P_{accident} \cdot L_M$
Ship Operators	$R_O - C_O(\text{strategy}) - F(\text{regulation}) - P_{accident} \cdot L_O$
Crew Members	$W_C - C_C(\text{strategy}) + (1-P_{accident}) \cdot B_C \cdot \delta_C$
Insurance Companies	$R_I - C_I(\text{strategy}) - P_{accident} \cdot P_I$

IV. CONCLUSION

Looking forward, we are developing what we call an "adaptive policy framework" that learns from system feedback and adjusts parameters automatically. The ultimate vision is a living system that continuously optimizes itself, making maritime transport progressively safer while maintaining economic viability.

ACKNOWLEDGMENT

This research was supported by the National Natural Science Foundation of China (72374209).

REFERENCES

[1] L. Meng, K. Liu, J. He, C. Han, and P. Liu, "Carbon emission reduction behavior strategies in the shipping industry under government regulation: A tripartite evolutionary game analysis," Journal of Cleaner Production, vol. 378, pp. 134556, Dec. 10, 2022, doi: 10.1016/j.jclepro.2022.134556.

[2] S. Hacks and J. Pahl, " Cyber Security Assessment of An Interoperable Port Call and Voyage Optimization tool," Proc. 6th Int. Conf. on Maritime Autonomous Surface Ships and Int. Maritime Port Technology and Development Conf. (MTEC/ICMASS 2024), Journal of Physics: Conference Series, vol. 2867, pp. 012047, Trondheim, Norway, Oct. 29–30, 2024, doi: 10.1088/1742-6596/2867/1/012047.

[3] J. Solomonsz, J. Melbourne-Thomas, A. Constable, R. Trebilco, I. van Putten, and L. Goldsworthy, "Stakeholder Engagement in Decision Making and Pathways of Influence for Southern Ocean Ecosystem Services," Frontiers in Marine Science, vol. 8, p. 623733, 2021. DOI:10.3389/fmars.2021.623733.

[4] Y. Xi, S. Hu, Z. Yang, S. Fu, J. Weng, K. Li, and H. L. Mclaughlin, "Analysis of safety climate effect on individual safety consciousness creation and safety behaviour improvement in shipping operations," Maritime Policy and Management, vol. 50, no. 7-8, pp. 1050-1069, 2023. DOI:10.1080/03088839.2023.2172481.

Distributed Simulation of Multi-Agency Coordination in Maritime Emergencies

Qingqing Yang*, Jing Xu, Yingying Gao, Pengcheng Yang
College of System Engineering,
National University of Defense Technology
Changsha, China
Email: yqq_1982@126.com, Jenniferxu98@163.com, 15222638242@qq.com, yangpengcheng@nudt.edu.cn

***Abstract*—Maritime emergency response systems face unique challenges due to the need for cross-regional coordination, limited communication infrastructure, and the involvement of multiple international jurisdictions. This paper proposes a novel distributed simulation framework to enhance multi-agency collaboration in maritime emergencies, covering a comprehensive spectrum of hazards including vessel collisions, oil spills, search and rescue operations, piracy incidents, and extreme weather events. The framework leverages distributed simulation technologies to create an integrated method supporting real-time decision-making, resource optimization, and training for emergency responders.**

***Keywords*—Distributed Simulation Framework; Hybrid Modeling Approach; Maritime Emergency.**

I. INTRODUCTION

The 2021 Ever Given Suez Canal blockage exposed a fundamental architectural flaw in global maritime emergency response systems. Despite causing over $9 billion in daily economic losses, the incident's most significant revelation was not the scale of disruption, but rather the systemic failure of hierarchical command structures when confronted with multi-jurisdictional coordination requirements [1]. This catastrophic breakdown occurs precisely because maritime emergencies violate the core assumption underlying traditional response systems: that effective coordination requires centralized control. In reality, modern maritime operations span multiple sovereign territories, involve competing commercial interests, and engage diverse agencies.

Under operational realities, therefore, the complex interrelationships emergent from distributed optimization spread over three dimensions for responding to a maritime emergency. First, autonomy must be possessed by the actors who have to make choices about the allocation of resources that have to be made scarce without any capacity for global information or significantly centralized coordination. Then again, the decisions are nested in a three-dimensional critical environment, failing communications and incomplete data due to time-critical constraints that preclude centralized processing. Centralized architectures impede effective response when, for example, loss of connectivity in the command center results in network collapse-when local conditions call for immediate action; those approved by hierarchy may prove fatal-when agencies pursue conflicting objectives; centralized mediation becomes a bottleneck instead of a solution [2][3].

Our primary contribution is developing and proving convergence for three interconnected distributed algorithms specifically adapted to maritime emergency constraints. Section II presents our theoretical framework and problem formulation. Section III details the distributed optimization algorithms with convergence proofs. Section IV concludes with implications and future work.

II. PROBLEM FORMULATION AND THEORETICAL FRAMEWORK

Consider n maritime agencies responding to emergency scenarios with m shared resources. Each agency i controls decision variables $x_i \in \mathbb{R}^d$ representing resource requests and task assignments. The global optimization problem is:

$$\text{minimize} \sum_{i=1}^{n} f_i(\mathbf{x}_i) + g\left(\sum_{i=1}^{n} \mathbf{A}_i \mathbf{x}_i\right) \tag{1}$$

where f_i represents agency i's local cost (response time, fuel consumption), g enforces global resource constraints, and A_i are coupling matrices encoding resource sharing relationships.

III. DISTRIBUTED RESOURCE OPTIMIZATION ALGORITHMS

This section presents three distributed algorithms designed to address the unique coordination challenges in maritime emergency response.

A. Distributed Auction

Our distributed auction protocol extends classical market mechanisms by incorporating maritime-specific spatial-temporal constraints. Each resource j has time-varying availability $r_j(t)$ and position $p_j(t)$ following maritime navigation dynamics.

The iterative bidding rounds in the protocol allow agency i to build bids using marginal utility and spatial-temporal factors:

In Bid calculation, during round k, agency i's bid for resource j is expressed as:

$$b_{ij}(k)=u_{ij}(k)\cdot\varphi_{ij}(k)\cdot\psi_{ij}(k) \tag{2}$$

where $u_{ij}(k)$ is marginal utility, $\varphi_{ij}(k)$ is spatial accessibility, and $\psi_{ij}(k)$ is temporal urgency factor.

In Price dynamics, resource prices evolve through the following process:

$$p_j(k+1)=p_j(k)+\alpha(k)\cdot[D_j(k)-S_j(k)] \quad (3)$$

where $D_j(k)$ is aggregate demand, $S_j(k)$ is available supply, and $\alpha(k)$ is an adaptive learning rate ensuring convergence.

B. Dual-Decomposition for Collaborative Task Assignment

In tasks that involve collaboration among multiple agencies, such as area searching and pollution containment, we apply dual decomposition to the distribution of optimization while coupling constraints are retained [4].

The global maritime resource allocation problem can be formulated as a convex optimization problem:

$$\min_t \sum_{i=1}^{n} f_i(\mathbf{t}_i) \quad \text{subject to} \quad \mathbf{Ct}=\mathbf{b}, \quad \mathbf{t}_i \in \mathcal{T}_i \quad (4)$$

where $t=[t_1^T, t_2^T,..., t_n^T]$ represents the concatenated vector of all agencies' task assignments, $f_i(t_i)$ denotes agency i's local cost function, Ct=b represents the global coupling constraints to ensure resource conservation and task completion.

The dual variables are updated through a distributed consensus mechanism that preserves global consistency. Each agency i updates its local estimate of the dual variables according to:

$$\lambda_i(k+1)=\Sigma_j \in N_i\, w_{ij}[\lambda_j(k)+\rho(C_j t_j(k)-b_j/n)] \quad (5)$$

where weights w_{ij} form a doubly stochastic matrix ensuring $\Sigma_i\lambda_i(k) = n\lambda(k)$ is preserved.

C. Federated Q-Learning

Agencies learn the optimal resource pre-positioning both through distributed reinforcement learning and sharing, of course, without operational security risking.

States of the system are constructed as state space:

$$S = g \times R \times W \quad (6)$$

where g is discretized geographic grid, R is resource availability vector, and W encodes risk conditions. Action space A includes repositioning commands and readiness levels.

Each agency maintains Q_i: S × A → ℝ updated via:

$$Q_i(s,a) \leftarrow (1-\alpha)Q_i(s,a)+\alpha[r_i(s,a,s')+\gamma\cdot\max\ \bar{Q}(s',a')] \quad (7)$$

where $\bar{Q}$ is the federated average Q-function and r_i is agency-specific reward incorporating response time, coverage area, and operational costs.

To address non-stationary dynamics, we use experience replay with importance sampling to make sure agencies maintain prioritized replay buffers with importance weights:

$$w_e = \left(\frac{1}{N}\cdot\frac{1}{P(e)}\right)^{\beta} \quad (8)$$

where:

$$P(e) \propto |\delta_e| + \epsilon \quad (9)$$

where δ_e represents TD-error, ϵ represents a smoothing term.

IV. CONCLUSION

This paper presents a distributed simulation framework for multi-agency coordination in maritime emergencies. It can enhance emergency responses by reducing the impacts of disasters through a solid architectural underpinning concerning advanced simulation technologies considering the inherent complexity of managing maritime emergencies. A distributed architecture is in line with the operational reality of maritime environments and provides ample opportunity for the required coordination in effectively responding to maritime emergencies.

With increasing maritime traffic and new challenges, such as autonomous ships and climate change, the framework remains relevant in flexibility and extensibility. It is, therefore, a contribution toward building resilient maritime transportation systems to cope with various emergencies. This framework will be further developed and validated by the world's maritime agencies to provide a standard procedure for coordinating emergency preparedness and response.

ACKNOWLEDGMENT

This research was supported by the National Natural Science Foundation of China (72374209).

REFERENCES

[1] C. M. Lee, and E. Y. Wong, “Suez Canal blockage: an analysis of legal impact, risks and liabilities to the global supply chain,” in MATEC Web of Conferences, vol. 339, pp. 01019, 2021.

[2] Dinh, P. Yang, and J. Diesner, "From plan to practice: Interorganizational crisis response networks from governmental guidelines and real-world collaborations during hurricane events," Journal of Contingencies and Crisis Management, vol. 32, no. 3, pp. e12601, 2024.

[3] N. Andreassen, O. J. Borch, and A. K. Sydnes, "Information sharing and emergency response coordination," Safety Science, vol. 130, pp. 104895, 2020.

[4] S. Boyd, N. Parikh, E. Chu, B. Peleato, J. Eckstein, "Distributed optimization and statistical learning via the alternating direction method of multipliers," Foundations and Trends in Machine Learning, vol. 3, no. 1, pp. 1–122, 2011.

A Hybrid Modeling Framework for Airport Passenger Decision Making: A Markov Decision Process Approach

Ashraf Tantawy *, Fanny Camelia *, Ramona Bernhardt *, Mohd Shoaib *, Yaseen Zaidi *, Ian Marr §
*Centre for Defence and Security Management and Informatics, Faculty of Engineering and Applied Sciences, Cranfield University
Defence Academy of the United Kingdom, Shrivenham, SN6 8LA UK
e-mail: {ashraf.tantavy | fanny.camelia | ramona.bernhardt | mohammad.shoaib | yaseen.zaidi}@cranfield.ac.uk
§Airbus UK
e-mail: ian.marr@airbus.com

Abstract—**The end-to-end air passenger journey, from travel planning to arrival at the destination airport, encompasses a series of interdependent processes in which passenger behavior and airport infrastructure continuously influence one another. Passenger decision-making, such as arrival timing, use of services, and queue preferences, plays a central role in shaping these dynamics. Conversely, the design and efficiency of airport infrastructure can constrain or facilitate behavioral patterns, creating a feedback loop that is often overlooked in conventional modeling approaches. This study addresses the critical need to better understand the bidirectional relationship between passenger behavior and airport infrastructure. A hybrid modeling framework is developed, where Discrete Event Simulation (DES) for airport infrastructure is used to develop a passenger Agent-Based Model (ABM) via Markov Decision Process (MDP) formulation and optimal policy search. The model is informed by empirical data on passenger profiles, infrastructure configurations, and behavioral preferences. Preliminary analytical results highlight how small variations in passenger behavior can impact decision-making and infrastructure operation. The proposed framework will facilitate the design of behaviorally-informed, data-driven planning strategies for more resilient airport systems.**

Keywords-Markov Decision Process; Agent-Based Modeling; Airport infrastructure; Airport passenger; State machine; Decision-making; SysML; Discrete-Event Simulation; Dynamic Programming; Reinforcement Learning.

I. INTRODUCTION

The passenger journey in air travel encompasses a continuous sequence of phases, from initial planning and booking to airport arrival, check-in, security screening, boarding, and ultimately arrival at the destination. This journey represents a complex dynamic system where passenger decisions and airport infrastructure dynamically influence one another [1]. Central to this system are key airport infrastructure components, including check-in counters, security checkpoints, boarding gates, and waiting lounges, which play a critical role in determining the overall efficiency of airport operations [2][3]. However, airport infrastructure is increasingly challenged by systemic issues such as congestion, bottlenecks, and service delays, especially during peak periods. These challenges not only reduce operational performance and increase costs, but also have broader implications for airlines and aircraft manufacturers, impacting turnaround schedules and prompting new aircraft design considerations aimed at faster boarding [4]. On the other hand, passenger behavior acts as both a contributor to and a consequence of these challenges. Decisions about arrival times, use of on-site services, and queue selection can compound delays or alleviate pressure on infrastructure. For example, the tendency for last-minute queuing or congregation around certain kiosks can strain already-limited terminal resources [5]. These feedback dynamics and emergent behavioral patterns highlight the need to better understand the reciprocal relationship between passenger behavior and airport infrastructure capabilities.

Simulation-based approaches have emerged as important tools to enable a detailed yet scalable analysis of both behavioral and operational dynamics [6]. Formal methods, such as Markov Decision Processes (MDP), offer structured frameworks for modeling sequential decision-making in environments characterized by uncertainty and time constraints [7]. In addition, Agent-Based Modeling (ABM) provides a bottom-up approach by representing individual passenger agents and their interactions, while Discrete Event Simulation (DES) is adept at modeling process-driven phenomena such as service durations and queue dynamics. A hybrid approach combining these modeling paradigms enables the integration of behavioral insights with operational realism, thereby addressing both strategic and tactical dimensions of airport management [6].

Several studies have examined how passenger behavior and infrastructural design shape check-in performance. A simulation-based analysis of fifteen check-in configurations is conducted in [8], revealing that single-queue systems combined with variable counter allocation significantly reduced waiting times and operational costs. ABM is applied in [9] to investigate group travel dynamics, demonstrating that passengers traveling together often wait for one another, leading to longer dwell times and increased congestion. A mesoscopic simulation-optimization framework that incorporate infrastructure layout, stochastic passenger behavior, and resource constraints is proposed in [10] to minimize both staffing costs and passenger discomfort. Although these studies use modeling and simulation to explore passenger-infrastructure interactions, none integrate MDP within a hybrid ABM and DES framework. Without such integration, it is difficult to represent how individual passengers make decisions in complex, changing airport environments with diverse agent behaviors.

MDP is a powerful tool for modeling decision-making scenarios characterized by sequential actions and inherent uncertainty. It provides a systematic approach to describing how decision-makers, in this context, passengers, transition between various states through the selection of specific actions. It facilitates the derivation of optimal policies under uncertain conditions by accounting for both the immediate consequences of decisions and their long-term ramifications, effectively capturing the probabilistic transitions that define system performance. The intrinsic strength of an MDP-based approach lies in its capacity to encapsulate the sequential nature of decision-making throughout the entire journey, from the initial selection of a travel route to real-time adjustments in departure times. In modeling door-to-door transport scenarios, MDP systematically accounts for the full sequence of actions, including route selection, mode choice, and responses to unexpected delays, that collectively determine the efficiency of the travel experience. This modeling framework effectively captures uncertainties in passenger behavior, where the outcomes of individual decisions are contingent upon both personal choices and broader operational contexts [5].

This research is motivated by three central problems: (1) persistent airport inefficiencies due to passenger-induced bottlenecks and infrastructure limitations; (2) the absence of integrated models that consider feedback between infrastructure and behavior; and (3) the need for data-driven tools to inform decisions by airport planners and stakeholders. The primary objectives of the research are to better understand how passengers are influenced by airport infrastructure and to identify operational inefficiencies to improve passenger experience and airport performance. This paper addresses the need to understand the bidirectional relationships between passenger behavior and airport infrastructure by using a hybrid modeling and simulation approach.

The main contributions are summarized as follows: (1) a unified hybrid modeling framework is proposed to capture airport infrastructure-passenger interactions, (2) a methodology, through an example, is presented to transform the integrated passenger-infrastructure model into an MDP for optimal policy derivation, and (3) an approach is introduced to integrate the passenger profile into the decision-making reward system.The framework is illustrated using the passenger check-in system and supported with numerical calculations.

The rest of the paper is organized as follows: Section II defines the passenger profile that is used to drive passenger decision-making. Section III explains the airport infrastructure system and the overall modeling framework. Section IV describes a sample model for the check-in system. Section V explains the MDP formulation and its connection to the developed infrastructure model and passenger profile. Section VI illustrates the decision-making policy. A numerical example is given in Section VII. The work is concluded in Section VIII.

II. Passenger Profile

Airline passenger decision-making depends in part on passenger attributes, such as age, gender, and travel purpose. The passenger profile is defined as a set of key relevant features that could impact passenger decision-making. For rational agents, these features shape the reward function that drives the search for an optimal agent policy. Table I shows some of the relevant attributes of a passenger profile, including percentage values as per [2][11]. One-hot encoding is used with categorical data.

TABLE I. Passenger profile as a set of personal features [2][11]. One-hot encoding is used for categorical data. Only the features used in the paper are assigned symbols.

Feature	Symbol	Data type
Age	A	Int
Gender	G_M, G_F	Cat
Travel purpose	B, T	Cat
Household		Bool
Visa-free	V, V_F	Bool
Travel frequency		Int
Flight destination		Cat
Travel class		Cat

Symbols corresponding to features in Table I are used to shape the reward functions in Section V. The passenger feature vector is designated by $\theta_p = [\ A\ \ G_M\ \ G_F\ \ B\ \ T\ \ V\ \ V_F\ ]$.

III. Passenger-Infrastructure Interaction

Figure 1 shows a simplified block diagram for airport infrastructure from the passenger's perspective. The first stage is the check-in system, where available passenger choices are shopping, self-check-in, or manual check-in. The second stage is security check-in. Passengers have very limited choices at this stage, if any. However, passenger profile plays a role in the security check-in system dynamics, e.g., passengers who are more likely to carry forbidden articles will cause check-in delays. The third stage is the departure lounge, where passengers' choices are shopping or waiting. The fourth stage is the boarding gate area, where passengers have almost no choices. Airport infrastructure dynamics, particularly flight delays, play a key role in passenger satisfaction at this stage. The final stage is the runway. Passengers have no choice, but runway delays impact total passenger waiting time, hence passenger satisfaction as well. Note that the infrastructure is shown as a pipeline, as this is the passenger's perspective, given that the passenger cannot go back to an earlier system once passed through it, e.g., security check-in. However, infrastructure subsystems can interact in other configurations.

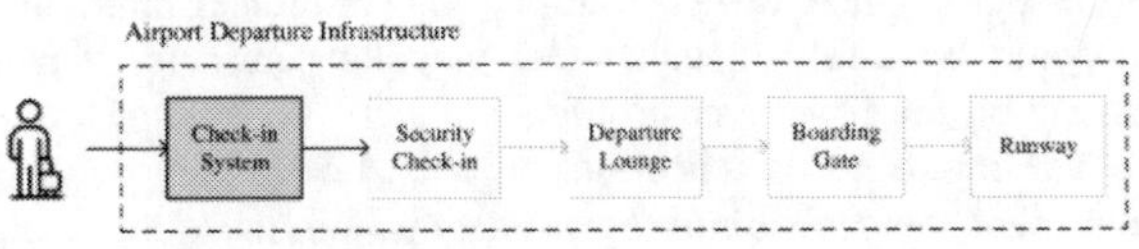

Figure 1. Airport infrastructure - Passenger's perspective

The modeling framework is summarized as follows: A DES model is developed for the airport infrastructure (Section IV). The DES model combined with the passenger profile is used to generate an MDP model (Section V). The MDP reward function is used to train the passenger agent (Section VI). The trained agent is finally represented in an ABM format.

IV. Airport Infrastructure Mathematical Model

This section presents a mathematical model for the check-in system that supports passenger decision-making. The rest of the infrastructure components in Figure 1 can be modeled very similarly and are not shown in the paper for brevity.

The check-in system is modeled as a DES, where state transitions occur at distinct points in time based on arrivals, service completions, and departures. The system includes one queue for manual check-in, a second queue for self check-in kiosks, and a third queue for baggage drop-off for passengers who checked in online. This follows recent airport organization, where each check-in system has a single queue that is served by multiple desks/kiosks. Figure 2 illustrates the check-in system architecture, and Table II summarizes the model parameters.

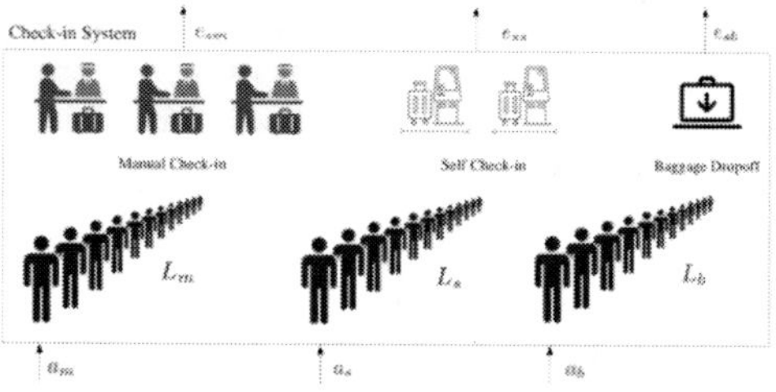

Figure 2. Airport check-in system

TABLE II. Check-in system model parameters

Parameter	Description
N_m	Number of serving desks for manual check-in
L_m	Queue length for manual check-in
N_s	Number of kiosks for self check-in
L_s	Queue length for self check-in
N_b	Number of serving desks for baggage drop-off
L_b	Queue length for baggage drop-off

The service time at each kiosk is modeled using an exponential distribution with rate parameter λ. This rate parameter depends mainly on the passenger profile, e.g., visa requirements, how many bags the passenger has, the number of family members checking in, or the fluency of using a computer system for self-check-in. For manual check-in, the rate parameter depends on the check-in agent's efficiency as well. For baggage drop-off, airline intervention is minimal, so it could be safely assumed that the rate parameter depends solely on the passenger profile.

The inputs to the check-in system, $A = [\ a_m \quad a_s \quad a_b\ ]$, represent the decision of a passenger to join/leave the manual check-in line, self check-in line, and baggage drop-off line, respectively. The state of the system is described by the length of each queue, $X = [\ L_m \quad L_s \quad L_b\ ]$, which is considered fully-observable by external agents. The output of the check-in system, $Y = [\ X \quad e_{sm} \quad e_{ss} \quad e_{sb}\ ]$, represents the events that a manual check-in customer, self check-in customer, and a baggage drop-off customer has been served, respectively. The service events are internal to the system, which impacts the number of passengers in each queue. As long as each queue length is observable by passengers, the system can be modeled with the state vector as the output. However, since the approach follows ABM, it is convenient to use these service events to simplify the queue position tracking performed by each passenger. For simulation, the passenger arrival rate is governed by passenger profiles instantiated according to profile population. To test the check-in system agent independently, a Poisson distribution could be assumed for passenger arrivals. Finally, a possible passenger action inside the system is to leave one queue and join another queue. This action could be achieved using the given action space by assigning two possible values to the input action, one for joining and another for leaving the queue, i.e., $a_m = 1$ to join the queue, and $a_m = -1$ for queue departure.

V. Passenger Agent and Decision-Making

To support passenger decision-making, an MDP is developed for the system [12]. The focus here is on the check-in system to present the technique, which could be extended easily to the rest of the infrastructure subsystems.

A. State Space

From the check-in perspective, two state variables could be identified for the passenger: the check-in status and the physical location in the check-in area. As per Section IV, the check-in system has three state variables representing the length of each queue. Also, the passenger may wish to track the length of the queue ahead of her position. Finally, a key factor impacting airline passenger decisions is the Time remaining To Departure (TTD). This variable is captured as a count-down timer that is represented as a global state variable T_d, allowing a compact representation of the state space. Table III summarizes the state variables and associated values.

TABLE III. Passenger decision-making - MDP States

State	Possible Values
Check-in status	{Online, !checked-in, Checked-in}
Location	{Lobby, Shopping, Check-in area}
Check-in area	{Waiting, Baggage, Self, Manual}
L_m, L_s, L_b, T_d	$\{x \in \mathbb{Z} \mid x \geq 0\}$
Queue position (P)	$\{x \in \mathbb{Z} \mid x \geq 0\}$

B. Action Space

While being in the check-in lobby, the passenger can decide to either go shopping or proceed to the check-in area. Once in the check-in area, the passenger has to choose between the different check-in queues. While standing in a queue, the passenger can also elect to switch queues.

C. Transition Function

Given the environment dynamics, a deterministic transition function is assumed, where $\forall(S, a)$ and a target state S':

$$P[S'|S, a] = 1, \quad P[S''|S, a] = 0 \quad \forall S'' \neq S' \tag{1}$$

D. Reward Function

To capture the influence of the passenger's profile on the decision-making process, the reward is designed to be a function of the passenger profile, as well as the current system state. For example, a business traveller could be more sensitive to time delays than a tourist, and a female traveller may select a shopping decision with higher probability. The following section defines the reward function for the shopping and queue selection decisions.

1) Shopping reward: Shopping reward comes from enjoying the experience, but the time spent during shopping, and the time remaining for boarding, play a role in the shopping decision. This could be captured given the following reward function:

$$R = \underbrace{G_M + 50G_F}_{\text{Pleasure}} - \underbrace{T_{sh}(\lambda_p)}_{\text{Shopping time}} - \underbrace{100(1 - \frac{T_d}{120})}_{\text{Time to board}} \tag{2}$$

where T_d is measured in minutes. T_{sh} is the shopping time, which is a random variable assumed here to have an exponential distribution with rate λ that depends on the passenger's gender [13][14], hence the reward is stochastic:

$$\frac{1}{\lambda_p} = 15G_M + 30G_F \quad \text{min} \tag{3}$$

2) Baggage Drop-off: This decision is driven by the time remaining to board as well as the baggage drop-off queue length. A longer queue urges the passenger to complete the check-in faster:

$$R = \underbrace{L_b T_s(\lambda_b)}_{\text{Queue time}} + \underbrace{100(1 - \frac{T_d}{120})}_{\text{Time to board}} \tag{4}$$

where the model assumes a constant service rate $1/\lambda_b = 3$ min, independent of the passenger profile.

3) Check-in and Security screening: These decisions are driven solely by the time remaining to boarding, assuming absence of additional information about queue lengths:

$$R = \underbrace{100(1 - \frac{T_d}{120})}_{\text{Time to board}} \tag{5}$$

4) Queue Selection: For manual check-in, the service time depends on both the passenger profile and the airport service rate. For self-check-in, the service time depends mainly on the passenger's profile. We model the service time with an exponential distribution as well. For the switching action, the same formulae below apply to the relevant queue, where the length of the queue reflects the current length at the switching time:

$$R = \begin{cases} -L_m T_s(\lambda_m) & \text{Manual check-in} \\ -L_s T_s(\lambda_s) & \text{Self check-in} \end{cases} \tag{6}$$

$$\frac{1}{\lambda_m} = 3G_M + 5G_F - B + 2V \text{ min} \tag{7}$$

$$\frac{1}{\lambda_s} = \begin{cases} 3 \text{ min} & 20 \leq \text{age} \leq 50 \\ 0.1A - 2 \text{ min} & \text{age} > 50 \end{cases} \tag{8}$$

For manual check-in, the service rate takes into account passenger gender (reflecting baggage need), a need for a visa (reflecting time to check the proper paperwork), and whether the passenger is a business traveler (reflecting light-weight travel). For self-check-in, the service rate reflects computer system fluency measured by age group.

Figure 3 is a state diagram representation of the MDP, where orthogonal region representation is used for the concurrent state variables `Check-in Status` and `Location`. The Check-in Area is a superstate that comprises four states representing the passenger location in the check-in area. The remaining Time to departure is initialized when entering the initial state, and globally decremented as the state diagram is executed. When a specific queue is served, an internal transition is triggered, and the passenger's position is updated. Reward functions are omitted to simplify the diagram. Dotted lines are used to distinguish actions due to environmental dynamics. For more details on SysML state diagram semantics, the reader is referred to [15].

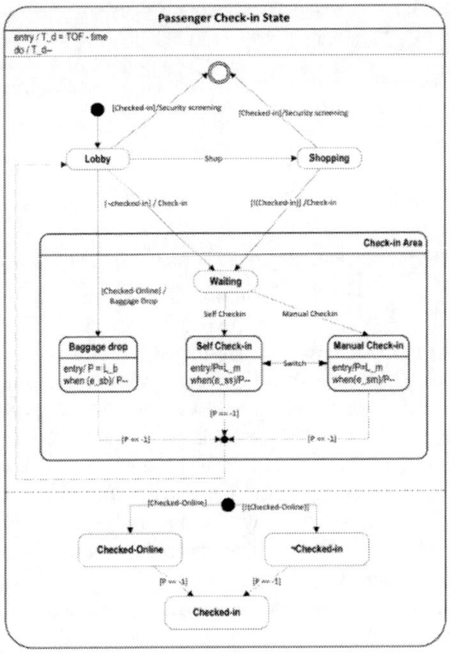

Figure 3. Check-in system state diagram. While waiting in a check-in queue, there is a decision at every time step whether to continue in the queue or switch queues. This loop-back transition is omitted to simplify the diagram.

VI. Decision-Making Policy

A rational agent maximizes the expected cumulative reward from the initial state (here airport check-in lobby) to final state (boarding) [12]:

$$v_\pi(s) = E_\pi \left[\sum_{k=0}^{n} \gamma^k R_i | S = s \right] \tag{9}$$

where n is the number of decisions the passenger takes from airport arrival to boarding, and γ is the reward discount factor. This is a classical dynamic programming problem that can be solved using a variety of algorithms [12]. In reality, passengers would take decisions to maximize the immediate reward due to the lack of information about subsequent infrastructure state, i.e., $\gamma = 0$, which simplifies the problem significantly, as the optimal action at each state is the one with the highest average immediate reward, producing a deterministic policy.

Figure 4 shows the decision tree for the system MDP that enumerates all possible decision paths, assuming no online check-in. Due to space limitations, the decision sub-tree following the initial shopping decision is omitted, as it is identical to the sub-tree with Waiting state as its root. Every edge is annotated with its expected reward. The cumulative reward is the sum of all rewards starting from the initial state to the final state. Numbers shown are related to the numerical example explained in the next section.

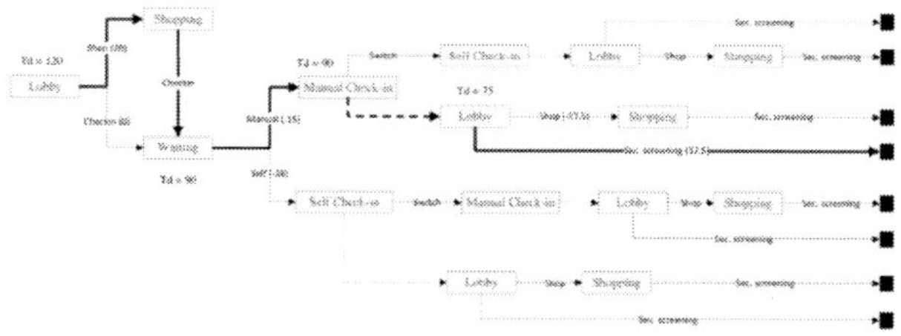

Figure 4. Decision tree for the airline passenger. Switching decision from Manual to self check-in and vice versa is not shown explicitly due to the compact representation of the state space. Dashed lines designate environmental actions not under the control of the passenger.

VII. Optimal Policy: A Numerical Example

Optimal policy of a cumulative reward system is often obtained using numerical algorithms along with interactions with the real system or a simulated version of it. An ABM approach guides the development of the airport infrastructure components. The trained agent with the optimal policy is then developed using ABM and integrated with the rest of the infrastructure environment. The presented work demonstrates the decision-making process using a numerical example and analytical techniques. This is mainly possible because of the assumption of immediate reward maximization, i.e., zero reward discount factor γ.

Assume a female, tourist, visa-free passenger profile, i.e., the feature vector is given by $\theta_p = [\,40 \;\; 0 \;\; 1 \;\; 0 \;\; 1 \;\; 0 \;\; 1\,]$. It is further assumed that the passenger arrives at the airport 2 hours before flight departure, i.e., initial $T_d = 120$ min. Furthermore, the queue lengths are $L_m = 3$ and $L_s = 6$ at the time of passenger arrival. The decision-making policy that maximizes the immediate reward results in the trajectory highlighted in bold in Figure 4, comprising Lobby $\rightarrow$ Shopping $\rightarrow$ Manual Check-in $\rightarrow$ Security screening. A passenger with the same profile who arrives 30 minutes late, encountering a longer manual check-in queue $L_m = 10$, even with matching self check-in queue length $L_s = 10$, will have the optimal path Lobby $\rightarrow$ Self check-in $\rightarrow$ Security screening.

This illustrative example highlights the benefits of a deeper understanding of passenger decision-making. Airport management can optimally allocate resources and redesign operational processes to minimize end-to-end travel time and passenger stress, ultimately enhancing overall satisfaction.

VIII. Conclusion and Future Work

This paper presents a framework that integrates ABM, DES, and MDP for studying decision-making for airline passengers. Different dynamic models can be transformed into an MDP that can be solved using a variety of dynamic programming and reinforcement learning algorithms to find the optimal policy for different discount factors. The framework facilitates the joint representation of individual decision-making and process-level system dynamics, which are often treated separately in existing studies. The contribution lies not only in the technical integration of modeling methods, but also in the application of this hybrid framework to analyze behavior-informed check-in processes under varying passenger conditions.

The analytical results demonstrate that even small variations in passenger decision-making, such as arrival time, queue preference, or check-in method, can lead to significant differences in airport performance. These decision patterns affect key metrics including queue lengths, waiting times, and passenger satisfaction. The hybrid framework, combining ABM and DES supported by MDP, provides an effective means of capturing both individual decision logic and operational flow dynamics. For airport operators, the model offers practical insights into how targeted, low-cost interventions, such as adaptive counter allocation or improved wayfinding systems, can reduce congestion as well as enhance service quality. Airlines benefit from increased predictability of passenger processing, which supports more efficient gate allocation and boarding schedules. Aircraft manufacturers may use this modeling approach to evaluate the likely impact of infrastructure-related delays on passenger behaviors and preferences.

Some simplifying assumptions are made in the presented model. Date and time of flight are important since they impact the number of passengers that are simultaneously at the airport, hence the passenger decision and experience. On the other hand, date & time also influence how the airport infrastructure functions, e.g., service rate. Moreover, flight delays and cancellations, and airport disruptions, are quite common and would significantly impact both the infrastructure dynamics and the passenger decision-making. Therefore, interfacing the developed model with external information sources, such as urban mobility networks and real-time flight scheduling, and capturing the impact in the system model are essential for realistic high-fidelity modeling and simulation. Also, we used the practical assumption that passengers seek to maximize the immediate reward, i.e., no look-ahead strategy. Lookahead strategy for decision-making would require algorithmic solutions, but may reveal counter-intuitive decisions that could be informative for both passengers and infrastructure operation. A service rate is also assumed to follow an exponential distribution, with arrival rate to follow a Poisson distribution. For a more sophisticated stochastic behaviour of the infrastructure obtained from available data, a high-fidelity simulation for the infrastructure combined with numerical algorithms would be needed to find the optimal policy, particularly for end-to-end policy optimization.

Several challenges represent the future work. First, the reward function formulation is challenging, particularly taking into account the passenger profile. Although the presented reward functions are intuitive from frequent travel experiences, tuning such reward functions is not an easy task. Available datasets could help, but there is no single integrated dataset that combines all the presented features; hence, data aggregation with practical assumptions is needed. Inverse reinforcement learning, where the reward is learned from observed behavior, is currently under investigation. Second, modeling decision-making for humans is a difficult task. Although the passenger profile presented can help significantly, modeling human behavior using a set of features may introduce bias and reduce the resulting accuracy. For example, assuming that all female passengers prefer shopping may be a biased assumption and inaccurate. Adding additional attributes may help, e.g., age and origin, but this complicates the problem due to the increased number of features that further require additional data. Finally, measuring passenger satisfaction is important for both airport operation and airline decision-making. Overall time from check-in to flying is one metric that is captured in the presented model. However, other factors can be considered, such as comfort and emotional stress, which are challenging to capture, yet significantly impact passenger behavior. Future research will aim to include the aforementioned modeling elements and to relax the simplifying assumptions for the complete airport infrastructure for wider model applicability. Also, available datasets will be used for model refinement and validation. Sensitivity analysis will be carried out to identify the most critical assumptions. Finally, the passenger agents will be explored to better understand the passenger-infrastructure interactions in modern airport systems.

ACKNOWLEDGEMENT

The authors would like to acknowledge support from Airbus Operations Ltd., Filton, UK. The views expressed in this article do not necessarily represent those of Airbus. No new data were created or analyzed in this study. Data sharing is not applicable to this article.

REFERENCES

[1] S. Kalakou and F. Moura, "Analyzing passenger behavior in airport terminals based on activity preferences," *Journal of Air Transport Management*, vol. 96, p. 102 110, 2021.

[2] D. Chonsalasin, S. Jomnonkwao, K. Chanpariyavatevong, W. Laphrom, and V. Ratanavaraha, "Modeling of airline passenger loyalty: A comparison of leisure and business travelers," *Research in Transportation Business and Management*, vol. 43, p. 100 735, 2022.

[3] M. Zargayouna, A. Othman, G. Scemama, and B. Zeddini, "Multiagent simulation of real-time passenger information on transit networks," *IEEE Intelligent Transportation Systems Magazine*, vol. 12, pp. 50–63, 2 2020.

[4] T. Rötger *et al.*, "Reduction of the environmental impact of aviation via optimisation of aircraft size/range and flight network," *IOP Conference Series: Materials Science and Engineering*, vol. 1226, p. 012 045, 1 Feb. 2022.

[5] K. Kölker, K. Lütjens, and V. Gollnick, "Analyzing global passenger flows based on choice modeling in the air transportation system," *Journal of Air Transport Management*, vol. 115, p. 102 530, Mar. 2024.

[6] R. Woltjer, B. J. Johansson, P. A. Oskarsson, P. Svenmarck, and B. Kirwan, "Air transport system agility: The agile response capability (arc) methodology for crisis preparedness," *Infrastructures*, vol. 7, no. 2, p. 11, 2 2022.

[7] F. Tavakoli, "Investigating the long-term impact of disruptions on passenger travel behavior using afc data a case study of washington d.c. metro network," Tech. Rep., 2024.

[8] A. T. Al-Sultan, "Simulation and optimization for modeling the passengers check-in system at airport terminal," *Review of Integrative Business and Economics Research*, vol. 7, p. 44, 2017, ISSN: 2414-6722.

[9] L. Cheng, V. Reddy, C. Fookes, and P. K. Yarlagadda, "Agent-based modelling simulation case study: Assessment of airport check-in and evacuation process by considering group travel behaviour of air passengers," in *Applied Mechanics and Materials*, vol. 568-570, Trans Tech Publications Ltd, 2014, pp. 1859–1864.

[10] L. Adacher and M. Flamini, "Optimizing airport land side operations: Check-in, passengers' migration, and security control processes," *Journal of Advanced Transportation*, vol. 2020, no. 1, p. 6 328 016, 2020.

[11] K. Boc, I. Štimac, J. Pivac, and M. Bračić, "An empirical investigation: Does new airport terminal infrastructure improve the customer experience?" *Sustainability (Switzerland)*, vol. 15, no. 17, p. 13 188, 17 Sep. 2023.

[12] R. S. Sutton and A. G. Barto, *Reinforcement learning: An introduction*. MIT press Cambridge, 2018, vol. 1.

[13] E. C. Rubiano Matulevich and M. Viollaz, "Gender differences in time use: Allocating time between the market and the household," The World Bank, Tech. Rep., 2019.

[14] K. Nair, S. Mundkur, and A. Tulshyan, "Difference in consumer shopping behaviour of men and women," *International Journal of*, vol. 12, no. 2, pp. 91–95, 2022.

[15] S. Friedenthal, A. Moore, and R. Steiner, *A practical guide to SysML: the systems modeling language*. Morgan Kaufmann, 2014.

Simulation-Based Evaluation of Autonomous Vehicle Penetration on Urban Traffic Efficiency and CO_2 Emissions via Integrated PTV VISSIM and Bosch ESTM

Melika Ansarinejad[1]
[1]Department of Civil, Construction and Environmental Engineering
North Dakota State University
Fargo; ND, USA
Email: melika.ansarinejad@ndsu.edu

Ying Huang[2]
[2]Department of Civil, Construction and Environmental Engineering
North Dakota State University
Fargo; ND, USA
Email: ying.huang@ndsu.edu

Pan Lu[3]
[3]Department of Transportation and Logistics
North Dakota State University
Fargo; ND, USA
Email: Pan.lu@ndsu.edu

Abstract: Carbon dioxide (CO_2) remains the leading contributor to greenhouse gas (GHG) emissions in the United States, with passenger vehicles playing a significant role. As emerging transportation technologies introduce Autonomous Vehicles (AVs) into the existing fleet, understanding their impact on urban traffic systems becomes increasingly important. This study presents a simulation-based analysis of the effects of AVs on urban mobility, fuel consumption, and CO_2 emissions under mixed traffic conditions. Utilizing the Planung Transport Verkehr(PTV) Verkehr In Städten - SIMulationsmodell (VISSIM) microscopic traffic simulation platform, integrated with the Bosch Environmentally Sensitive Traffic Management (ESTM) module; designed for high-resolution simulation of traffic-related emissions; vehicle behaviors and emissions at a representative U.S. urban signalized intersection is evaluated. The simulation framework models ten AV market penetration scenarios, ranging from 0% to 100% in 10% increments, and captures behavioral distinctions between Autonomous and Human-driven Vehicles through calibrated adjustments to the Wiedemann 99 car-following parameters and vehicle speed distributions. Results indicate that higher AV penetration leads to improved traffic flow and significant reductions in CO_2 emissions. This study highlights the power of high-fidelity, integrated simulation-based methods in assessing future transportation systems and informing sustainable urban mobility planning.

Keywords- Microsimulation; Autonomous Vehicles; Mixed Traffic Flow; Fuel Consumption; CO_2 Emission; VISSIM; Bosch; Driving Behavior

I. INTRODUCTION

Autonomous vehicles (AVs), also known as self-driving cars, are transforming transportation through advanced technologies that enable them to operate with minimal or no human intervention. It is anticipated that privately owned Level 4 AVs, which denote high automation will make up approximately 24.8% of vehicles on roadways in America by 2045 [1]. These vehicles utilize Artificial Intelligence (AI) and machine learning (ML) algorithms to perceive their environment and make informed driving decisions. Equipped with an array of sensors, such as cameras, radar, lidar, and ultrasonic devices, AVs continuously monitor their surroundings to detect objects, interpret traffic signals, and anticipate the actions of other road users. By processing real-time data, they can react faster than human drivers, making them less susceptible to errors caused by distraction, fatigue, or emotion. This technology is expected to enhance road safety, reduce collisions caused by human error, improve traffic flow, and offer greater mobility for individuals who are unable to drive due to age, disability, or other limitation [2].

There has been a growing emphasis on the impact of driving behavior on fuel efficiency and vehicular emissions in the literature investigating models and approaches for assessing the air quality, as well as the carbon footprint of transportation sector across different levels of analysis. These include microscopic levels [3], [4] [5], mesoscopic levels [6], [7], and macroscopic levels [8]- [10]. Aggressive driving is consistently linked to higher fuel consumption and pollutant emissions, while eco-driving improves energy efficiency and reduces CO_2 output [11], [12], [13], [14]. Alessandrini et al. [11] introduced the Eco Index, showing up to 30% CO_2 reduction at low speeds through eco-driving, though benefits diminish above 80–90 km/h. Szumska et al. [15] found urban aggressive driving increases emissions by around 40%. Miotti al.[13] highlighted the emission-reducing potential of manual and automated eco-driving. Suarez et al. [14] reported up to 5% more CO_2 from aggressive acceleration using Worldwide Harmonized Light Vehicles Test Procedure (WLTP), the European standard for measuring vehicle fuel consumption and CO_2 emissions and CO_2MPAS data (results from the European Commission's simulation tool that converts type-approval CO_2 values from the former NEDC test cycle into the WLTP framework).

As AVs are expected to play a central role in future urban transportation systems, recent research has shifted its focus from conventional traffic networks to mixed traffic flows, where AVs operate alongside human-driven vehicles in both freeway and urban environments. A common method in the literature for assessing the carbon footprint of such mixed traffic involves the integration of traffic simulation models with external emission calculation tools [16] [17]. These methods often require extensive data processing, and in cases involving tools like Motor Vehicle Emission Simulator (MOVES), the development of intermediary software is necessary to link mobility and emissions models effectively [5], [18]. Moreover, the process becomes increasingly complex when incorporating multiple simulation scenarios, such as different AV penetration rates or varying road and weather conditions; making it time-consuming, prone to error, and occasionally impractical depending on the software used.

Several studies have explored these integrated modeling approaches. Olia (2016) [19] utilized the PARAMICS microsimulation platform combined with the CMEM (Comprehensive Modal Emissions Model) to continuously estimate fuel consumption and pollutant emissions based on vehicle characteristics, such as type, age, fuel system, and emissions control technology. The study found that increasing the penetration of Connected Autonomous Vehicles (CAVs) leads to emission reductions, with the most substantial benefits occurring at around 50% CAV adoption. Later, Stogios et al. [20] employed the VISSIM microscopic traffic simulation tool integrated with the MOVES model to assess vehicular emissions under different traffic conditions and AV penetration levels. Their work incorporated eight car-following and two lane-changing parameters to simulate AV behavior, revealing that headway time had a significant impact on emissions. In the same year, Conlon et al. [21] used the SUMO traffic microsimulation framework together with the Newton-based Greenhouse Gas Model (NGM) to estimate CO_2 emissions in congested urban road networks. Their findings showed that emissions initially rose at low levels of AV penetration due to interaction inefficiencies between human drivers and AVs, but significant emission reductions emerged at higher penetration levels, eventually plateauing between 40% and 90% AV market share.

These studies collectively highlight the critical role of accurately integrating traffic flow simulation with emission modeling in understanding the environmental implications of AV deployment within mixed traffic ecosystems. They also emphasize the complexity involved in integrating multiple simulation tools, particularly when assessing emissions from modeled traffic flows under various AV penetration scenarios and dynamic traffic conditions, which requires substantial computational resources, data harmonization, and custom interfacing between platforms.

To tackle challenges of complex integration of traffic and external emission models, the extensive and error-prone data processing required, and the limited ability to evaluate CO_2 emissions across different AV penetration scenarios, this paper employs a new emission simulation tool in combination with an established traffic simulation platform. Specifically, this study utilizes the Bosch ESTM Module, which was developed in Germany through a collaboration between Robert Bosch GmbH and PTV Group [22], alongside VISSIM 2022 to investigate CO_2 emissions from light-duty passenger vehicles in mixed traffic flows, ranging from the early stages of AV deployment to a fully automated network. We hypothesize that autonomous vehicles (AVs), when introduced at varying penetration levels, will alter traffic flow efficiency and CO_2 emissions due to differences in car-following behavior, and that the integrated VISSIM–Bosch ESTM framework can provide accurate predictions of emissions and fuel consumption in parallel with mobility results. The model assumes Level 4 AVs operate under the "AV normal" profile calibrated from the CoExist project, balancing efficiency and caution in traffic flow.

The research focuses on the behavioral differences between human drivers and AVs and implements an integrated methodology for emissions estimation. To the best of the authors' knowledge, this study is among the few[16] that apply the Bosch ESTM module for project-level CO_2 emissions estimation in mixed traffic flows within an urban setting. This integration with VISSIM enables a detailed comparative analysis of how different AV penetration rates affect emissions and how these outcomes correspond with results from previous studies using alternative emission modelling tools. This study's methodology provides transportation professionals and urban planners with valuable insights into applying the Bosch ESTM module within the widely adopted VISSIM microsimulation platform. The consistency of the results with previous research; despite using different emission modeling tools; demonstrates the reliability of this integrated approach. Furthermore, the findings offer Infrastructure Owners and Operators (IOOs) a clearer understanding of how AV behavior can lower emissions besides contributing to the smooth urban traffic flow. These insights support the need for IOOs to begin preparing existing infrastructure to accommodate high AV penetration rates in the near future, given the significant potential benefits for both mobility and environmental sustainability.

To guide the reader through the remainder of this paper, the structure is organized as follows. Section II presents the methodology. Section III describes the simulation results, covering traffic mobility measures, fuel consumption, and CO_2 emissions. Section IV provides a detailed discussion of the findings, comparing AV and human-driven vehicles performance. Section V outlines potential directions for future work. Finally, Section VI concludes the paper with key insights and contributions of this study.

II. METHODOLOGY

This study employs an integrated simulation approach using PTV VISSIM 2022 and the Bosch Environmentally Sensitive Traffic Management (ESTM) module to assess traffic flow, fuel consumption, and CO_2 emissions at a congested signalized intersection in Saratoga Springs, Utah. The focus is a key intersection where two major five-lane arterials; Redwood Road (north-south) and Pioneer Crossing (east-west); converge. A detailed VISSIM model of the intersection and adjacent road segments was developed using links and connectors in Figure 1 to accurately represent the roadway network [23]. Traffic signals were modeled using a ring-and-barrier structure and in accordance with the Utah Department of Transportation's traffic signal timing guidelines [24].

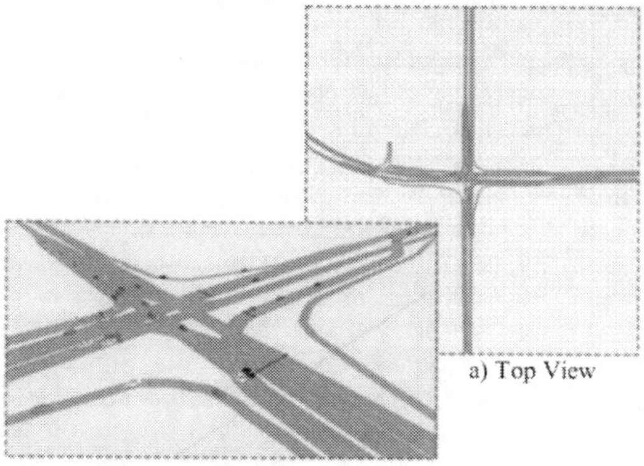

b) Perspective View

Fig.1. VISSIM Model of the Study Intersection: (a) Top View, (b) Perspective View

Real-world traffic volume data from UDOT's ATSPM system [25] was used to replicate 1.5 hour of weekday evening peak-hour conditions (4.00-5.30 pm). We modeled scenarios with AV penetration rates ranging from 0% to 100%, in 10% increments. Automated vehicles (AVs) and human-driven vehicles were simulated using distinct Wiedemann 99 car-following parameters. The AVs followed the "AV normal" profile, which represents automated vehicles with driving behavior comparable to human drivers. This profile incorporates standard car-following and lane-changing patterns, avoiding both excessive conservatism and aggressiveness. The parameters were adopted from the CoExist project [26], an EU Horizon 2020 initiative that developed simulation frameworks and guidelines to assess mixed traffic environments involving both conventional and automated vehicles. Human-driven vehicles used calibrated values from previous simulator-based research efforts [27]. Speed distributions were assigned based on naturalistic driving data for human-driven vehicles [28] and tightly constrained profiles for AVs [26]. Table 1 presents the categories and definition of each parameter, alongside the adopted values for the Wiedemann 99 car-following model for both AVs and Human-Driven Vehicles in the simulation model.

TABLE I: ADOPTED DRIVING PARAMETER VALUES FOR HUMAN-DRIVEN AND AVS

Parameter Category	**W99 Car following Parameter**	**Definition**	**AVs (normal)**	**Human-Driven Vehicle**
Thresholds for Safety Distance (Δx)	CC0 (m)	Standstill Distance	1.5	4.45
	CC1(s)	Headway Time	0.9	0.87
	CC2 (m)	Following Variation	0	5.28
	CC3 (s)	Threshold for Entering Following	-8	-7.92
Thresholds for Speed (Δv)	CC4 (m/s)	Negative Following Threshold	-0.1	-1.52
	CC5 (m/s)	Positive Following Threshold	0.1	1.52
	CC6 (-)	Speed Dependency of Oscillation	0	0.71
Acceleration Rates	CC7 (m/s^2)	Oscillation Acceleration	0.1	0.31
	CC8 (m/s^2)	Standstill Acceleration	3.5	1.03
	CC9 (m/s^2)	Acceleration at Speed of 80 km/h	1.5	0.33

The parameters are grouped into three main categories: thresholds for safety distance (Δx), thresholds for speed (Δv), and acceleration rates. Each scenario was simulated 10 times at 10 Hz resolution. Emissions were calculated through the Bosch ESTM cloud-based tool, which has a separate license to processes second-by-second vehicle trajectory data directly from VISSIM; eliminating the need for external data conversion [29][30]. Bosch provides VISSIM with a JSON file containing emission data for multiple vehicle classes. These classes are defined by six elements: Emission vehicle category, Emission vehicle class, Emission stage, Fuel type, Size class, and Use class, which differentiate vehicles based on their emission characteristics. During simulation, VISSIM generates a trajectory for each vehicle, which is then transferred to ESTM for emission calculation. The driving behavior element that most impacts emissions in Bosch ESTM is the dynamic profile of vehicle movement; particularly accelerations, decelerations, and stop-and-go patterns [29]. Bosch also offers lane-level visualization and real-time emission mapping across the network. For emission class distribution, the predefined MOVES-based 2022 profile for light-duty gas and diesel passenger vehicles was applied, representing U.S. fleet composition from 1992–2020. This approach ensures that emission outcomes isolate the effects of AV behavior and driving patterns, independent of variations in fuel or engine types.

III. SIMULATION RESULTS

For each scenario, 10 simulation repetitions were conducted following the recommendation in the VISSIM manual by MDOT [23]. This approach ensured that our results met established best practices and provided stable, representative averages. The results showed negligible variation across runs; therefore, the average values presented in Figures 2-5 are considered representative, with minimal variability observed across repetitions."

A. Mobility Results

As AV penetration increases, traffic performance improves across all metrics. According to Figure 2, the average number of stops shows an overall decline, with a slight increase at 10% AV, a significant reduction from 10% to 90%, and a minor uptick at 100% penetration. Average delay drops sharply from 440 seconds at 0% AV to a minimum of below 380 seconds at 50% penetration rate, then fluctuates slightly, stabilizing near 382 seconds at full penetration (Figure 3). Similarly, average speed increases from 62.38 km/h at 0% AV to 71.81 km/h at 50%, reaching a maximum of 73.92 km/h at 100% AV (Figure 4).

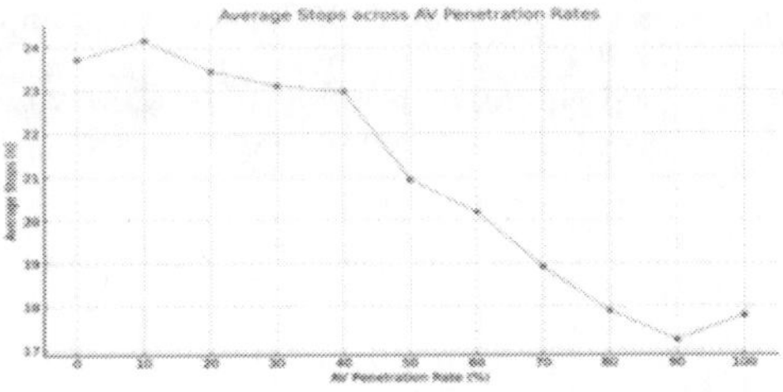

Fig.2. AV Penetration vs. Average Number of Stops (-)

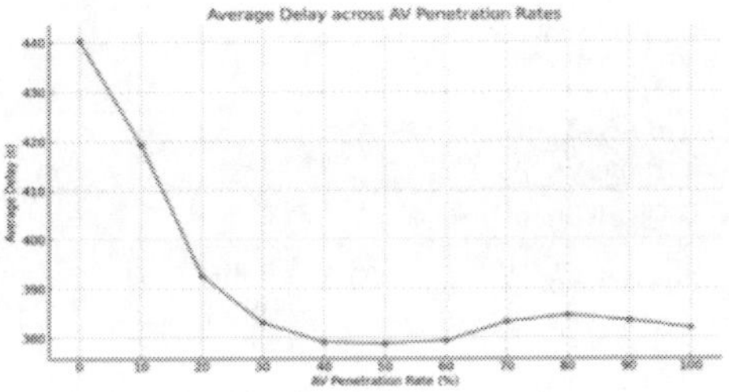

Fig.3. AV Penetration vs. Average Delay (s)

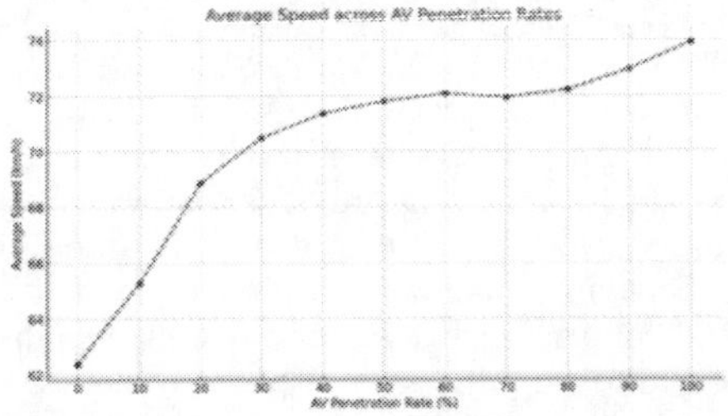

Fig.4. AV Penetration vs. Average Speed (km/h)

The mobility results of the baseline scenario (0% AVs) simulation were validated using Utah ATSPM peak-hour traffic data (4:00–5:30 PM). The recorded approach speed (38 mph/61 km/h), shown in Figure 5, closely matched the simulated average (38.7 mph/62.38 km/h), yielding 97.78% accuracy. Similarly, the average vehicle delays from simulation (38 s) aligned with ATSPM data (39 s), confirming the reliability of the results. This validated baseline therefore serves as the benchmark for evaluating the subsequent scenarios.

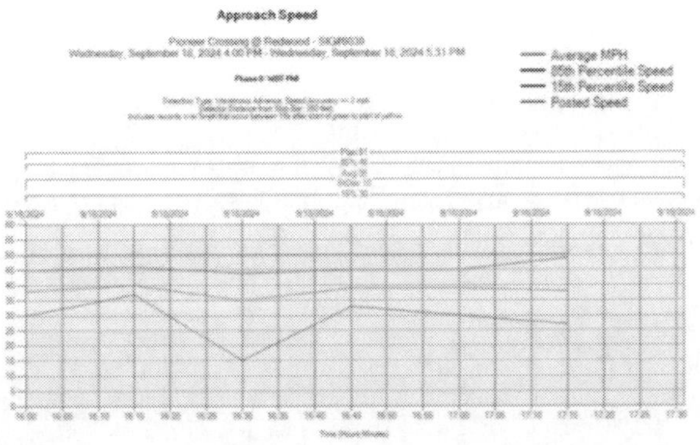

Fig.5. Chart of the Average Approach Speed of Vehicles During Peak Hour; Example of Westbound Through (WBT)- Utah ATSPM[25]

B. Fuel Consumption and CO_2 Emission Results

The emission results are not computed by VISSIM itself. VISSIM was used to simulate vehicle trajectories, and these outputs were then processed in the Bosch Environmentally Sensitive Traffic Management (ESTM). The Bosch ESTM applies vehicle-specific fuel consumption and emission models to the VISSIM trajectory data. The reported results represent aggregated outputs from Bosch ESTM, averaged over ten independent simulation runs of 1.5-hours (5400s) each per scenario and vehicle class. A warm-up period of 900s was applied at the beginning and the end of each simulation run, in accordance with the PTV VISSIM Manual, to ensure that the results capture stabilized traffic conditions [31].

Bosch results show a direct relationship between increasing AV penetration and decreasing fuel consumption and CO_2 emissions. As AV penetration rises from 0% to 100%, CO_2 emissions decrease by approximately 54.51%. However, the rate of reduction varies across different penetration levels. From 0% to 20% AV penetration, emissions drop by about 8%. Between 20% and 50%, emissions decline by around 12.5%. The most pronounced reduction occurs from 50% to 100%, with a drop of roughly 34%. A sharper decline is observed particularly between 70% and 100%, highlighting the potential for greater environmental gains as AV usage nears full saturation. The line chart in Figure 6 clearly illustrates CO_2 emission levels across different stages of AV penetration, from 0% to a fully autonomous network.

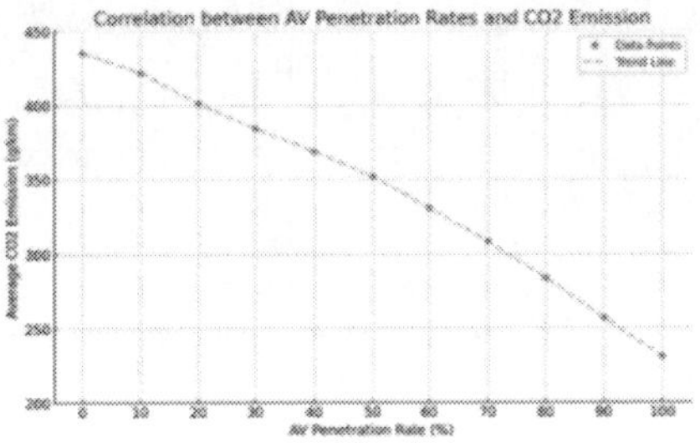

Fig.6. AV Penetration vs. Average CO_2 Emission (g/km)

As illustrated in the emission distribution maps generated within the VISSIM interface (Figure 7a–c), which use distinct color gradients to represent CO_2 emission levels across road segments, a 50% AV penetration leads to an approximate 25% reduction in emissions compared to the baseline scenario with 0% AVs. At 100% AV penetration (Figure 7c), emissions are reduced by approximately 55% relative to the mixed traffic scenario with equal shares of AVs and human-driven vehicles (HDVs) shown in Figure 7b.

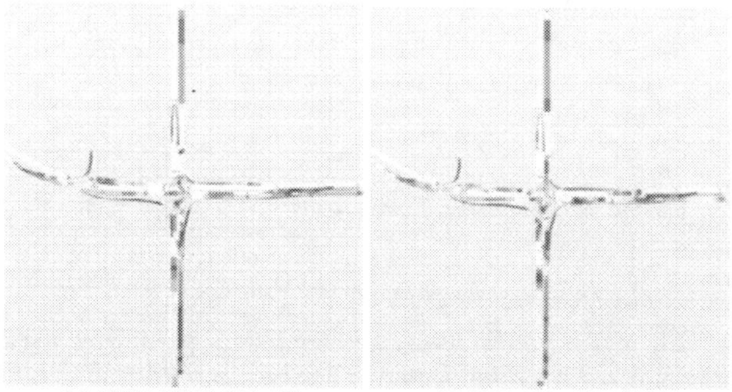

(a) 100% HDV, 0% AV (b) 50% AVs, 50% HDVs

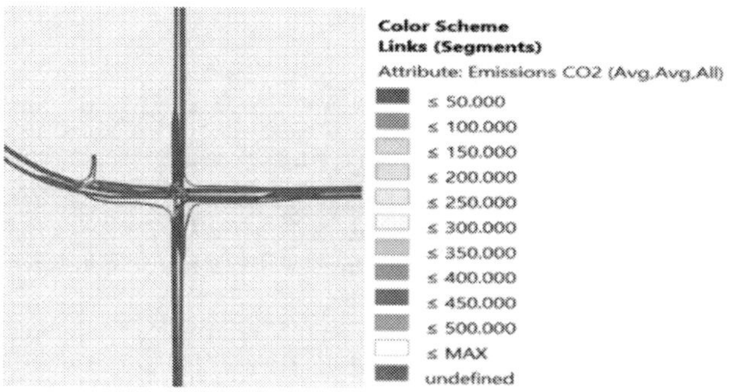

(c) 100% AVs, 0% HDV (d) Legend of CO_2 Distribution Map(g/km)

Fig. 7. CO_2 emission comparison at the intersection for three AV penetration rates: (a)100% Human-driven Vehicles (HDVs) ,0% AVs; (b)50% AVs,50%HDVs; (c)100% AVs,0%HDV

The findings of our study on CO_2 emissions and fuel consumption at signalized intersections align with previous literature. According to the U.S. Environmental Protection Agency [32], the average CO_2 emission from vehicles is 248.5 g per kilometer (approximately 400 g per mile). Our simulation results under the baseline scenario, showing a 43% increase compared to this benchmark, are validated by Szumska and Jurecki [12], who concluded that driving behavior near intersections can increase CO_2 emissions by 39–46% relative to calm driving. Furthermore, our results on emission patterns in the presence of Automated Vehicles are consistent with Tomas et al. [33], who found that automation at penetration rates of 30% or below yields only modest reductions. Similarly, the studies by Conlon et al. [21] and Rezaei et al. [34] demonstrated that the greatest fuel savings and CO_2 reductions occur within a fully autonomous network.

IV. Discussions

By examining the W99 car-following parameters and their influence on network performance in mixed traffic flow, this study reveals a dual impact of AV behavior at signalized intersections. AV behavior not only improves overall traffic flow but also significantly reduce CO_2 emission levels. Table 2 provides a comparison of driving behaviors for AVs and human-driven vehicles in car-following scenarios. It also presents comparative mobility and emission outcomes across two network types as an example: one composed solely of human-driven vehicles and another with mixed traffic. For each parameter, the greater absolute value; whether associated with AVs or human-driven vehicles; is highlighted in color, making performance contrasts visually clear. The table demonstrates that AVs consistently outperform human drivers across key behavioral metrics, resulting in smoother traffic dynamics which resulted in reduced CO_2 Emission.

TABLE II. COMPARISON OF DRIVING BEHAVIOR, MOBILITY, AND EMISSIONS IN AV AND HUMAN-DRIVEN TRAFFIC SCENARIOS

Parameters	**AVs**	**Human-Driven Vehicles**
Level of Caution (CC0, CC1, CC2)		
Level of Perception-Reaction (CC3)		
Level of Sensitivity to the Dec/Acc (CC4, CC5)		
Level of Acceleration Oscillation (CC7)		
Level of Standstill acceleration (CC8)		
Speed Distribution		
Mobility Measures	**Mixed Traffic Flow**	**Traditional Network**
Average Speed (km/h)		
Average Stops (-)		
Average Delay(s)		
Bosch Emission Measures		
CO_2 Emission		
Fuel Consumption		

The analysis of car-following behavior differences between human drivers and AVs across (CC0–CC9) parameters in Table 2, also provides a clearer understanding of the observed results. Human drivers tend to exhibit more cautious behavior, maintaining higher standstill distances (CC0) and longer headway times (CC1), which results in larger safe following distances. They also require more extra distance (CC2) before moving closer to a lead vehicle, whereas AVs typically operate with a CC2 value close to zero. In terms of perception and reaction, AVs demonstrate quicker responsiveness, indicated by lower CC3 values, while human drivers generally respond more slowly, contributing to frequent stops and delays. Human drivers also display greater sensitivity to the acceleration and deceleration of leading vehicles, reflected in higher absolute values of CC4 and CC5. This heightened sensitivity causes frequent fluctuations in speed, reducing traffic flow efficiency. In contrast, AVs respond more smoothly, which helps maintain steady traffic movement. During stop-and-go scenarios, human drivers tend to accelerate more aggressively (higher CC7), leading to erratic driving patterns, whereas AVs show much lower acceleration oscillations, resulting in smoother motion. Additionally, AVs exhibit stronger acceleration capabilities both from a standstill (CC8) and at higher speeds, 80 km/h (CC9), further contributing to consistent and efficient driving behavior.

These behavioral differences have direct implications for traffic flow and environmental impact. Human-driven traffic is characterized by frequent stop-and-go movements, abrupt accelerations, and longer delays, all of which lead to higher fuel consumption and CO_2 emissions. Simulation results from Bosch confirm that such inconsistent driving behavior significantly increases emissions and energy use in networks dominated by human drivers. In contrast, traffic scenarios incorporating AVs demonstrate improved mobility, greater energy efficiency, and lower environmental impact. The higher the proportion of AVs in the urban network, the more pronounced the reductions in fuel consumption and emissions. In fully autonomous networks, the most substantial benefits are observed, with CO_2 emissions and fuel usage reduced by over 50%. These improvements are largely due to the smoother, more homogenous, and consistent traffic flow facilitated by AVs. However, these results reflect the assumption that AVs operate with "normal" driving behavior, balancing efficiency and caution. What if the AV fleet exhibited heterogeneous driving styles, with some vehicles programmed conservatively and others more aggressively? This indicates that fleetwide behavioral programming should be studied as a critical determinant of outcomes. Furthermore, the present analysis assumed AVs were not connected to infrastructure. If AVs were integrated with adaptive signal control in a fully automated network, vehicle-to-infrastructure (V2I) connectivity could enable smoother progression through intersections, further reducing unnecessary stops and acceleration spikes, and potentially amplifying emission reductions beyond the levels observed here Another consideration is the infrastructure readiness at lower penetration levels. What if modest AV adoption (e.g., 30-40%) were paired with adaptive infrastructure? Could such a scenario achieve mobility and emission outcomes comparable to, or even surpassing those of a fully automated network operating without infrastructure modifications? This possibility indicates that investing in infrastructure to support AVs during transitional phases may be as important as advancing the vehicle technology itself in realizing sustainable benefits.

V. Conclusion and Furure Work

This study applied an integrated VISSIM–Bosch ESTM framework to evaluate the impacts of Level 4 automated vehicles (AVs) on traffic performance, CO_2 emissions, and fuel consumption at a congested urban intersection. The results confirmed substantial environmental benefits, with emissions reduced by more than 50% at full AV adoption. Improvements were modest at low penetration rates, while the steepest benefits occurred between 70% and 100% adoption. At 100% AV penetration, a slight increase in vehicle stops was observed, suggesting potential operational challenges in fully autonomous environments. This indicates that the full benefits of AV technology depend not only on high adoption rates but also on supportive infrastructure, realistic driving profiles, and well-designed policy frameworks. Low levels of AV integration may yield only incremental improvements, while complete automation could introduce new challenges, particularly if overly cautious driving behaviors or induced demand leads to increased travel. These findings highlight the importance of coordinated planning, where technological advances in automation are integrated with traffic management strategies, upgrades to both physical and digital infrastructure and built environment, and policies that prevent rebound effects. Furthermore, the consistency of Bosch ESTM emission estimates in AV-integrated networks with previous studies; reporting similar reductions on both congested and uncongested roadways using alternative simulation models[34], [35]; underscores the reliability of Bosch ESTM. This provides a robust foundation for future research to apply and extend this approach in broader contexts.

Future work will extend the analysis to multiple intersections and scenarios and will include comparisons of Bosch ESTM+VISSIM with alternative tools, such as VISSIM+MOVES to provide insights. Furthermore, future research will develop a digital twin of the modeled intersection to enhance validation. Although current low AV market penetration limits direct validation at higher adoption levels, this approach will improve calibration of baseline and early-stage scenarios, strengthening the reliability of projected mobility and emission results. Future work should also evaluate human comfort in relation to the AV calibration used in this study. As a complement to Winkel et al. [36], real-world experiments or simulators with larger motion envelopes are needed to capture a wider range of motion pulses, including abrupt braking and acceleration events. This would overcome the limitations of restricted simulators and allow refinement of AV calibration parameters to balance traffic efficiency with passenger comfort.

Acknowledgment

This work was supported in part by the National Science Foundation (NSF) EPSCoR RII Track-2 Program under Grant No. OIA-2119691, and in part by the U.S. Department of Transportation through a University Transportation Center for multi-modal mobility in urban, rural, and tribal areas. The authors thank the PTV Group for providing technical support with the VISSIM and BOSCH License used in this study.

Reference

[1] P. Bansal and K. M. Kockelman, "Forecasting Americans' long-term adoption of connected and autonomous vehicle technologies," *Transp Res Part A Policy Pract*, vol. 95, pp. 49–63, Jan. 2017, doi: 10.1016/j.tra.2016.10.013.

[2] M. Ansarinejad, K. Ansarinejad, P. Lu, Y. Huang, and D. Tolliver, "Autonomous Vehicles in Rural Areas: A Review of Challenges, Opportunities, and Solutions," *Applied Sciences*, vol. 15, no. 8, p. 4195, Apr. 2025, doi: 10.3390/app15084195.

[3] K. Zhang, S. Batterman, and F. Dion, "Vehicle emissions in congestion: Comparison of work zone, rush hour and free-flow conditions," *Atmos Environ*, vol. 45, no. 11, pp. 1929–1939, Apr. 2011, doi: 10.1016/J.ATMOSENV.2011.01.030.

[4] H. Abou-Senna, E. Radwan, K. Westerlund, and C. D. Cooper, "Using a traffic simulation model (VISSIM) with an emissions model (MOVES) to predict emissions from vehicles on a limited-access highway," *J Air Waste Manage Assoc*, vol. 63, no. 7, pp. 819–831, 2013, doi: 10.1080/10962247.2013.795918.

[5] X. Xu *et al.*, "Estimating project-level vehicle emissions with Vissim and MOVES-Matrix," *Transp Res Rec*, vol. 2570, pp. 107–117, 2016, doi: 10.3141/2570-12.

[6] A. Papson, S. Hartley, and K. L. Kuo, "Analysis of emissions at congested and uncongested intersections with motor vehicle emission simulation 2010," *Transp Res Rec*, no. 2270, pp. 124–131, Jan. 2012, doi: 10.3141/2270-15.

[7] K. Kutlimuratov, S. Khakimov, A. Mukhitdinov, and R. Samatov, "Modelling traffic flow emissions at signalized intersection with PTV vissim," *E3S Web of Conferences*, vol. 264, pp. 2–9, Jun. 2021, doi: 10.1051/E3SCONF/202126402051.

[8] H. C. Chu and M. D. Meyer, "Methodology for assessing emission reduction of truck-only toll lanes," *Energy Policy*, vol. 37, no. 8, pp. 3287–3294, Aug. 2009, doi: 10.1016/J.ENPOL.2009.03.058.

[9] D. Choi, M. Beardsley, D. Brzezinski, J. Koupal, and J. Warila, "MOVES Sensitivity Analysis: The Impacts of Temperature and Humidity on Emissions," *U.S. Environmental Protection Agency*, 2011.

[10] Y. Xu *et al.*, "Clearer skies in Beijing-revealing the impacts of traffic on the modeling of air quality," *HuMNet Lab*, pp. 4–6, Jan. 2016, Accessed: Aug. 17, 2025. [Online]. Available: http://humnetlab.berkeley.edu/wp-content/uploads/2020/02/air-quality-trd.pdf

[11] A. Alessandrini, A. Cattivera, F. Filippi, and F. Ortenzi, "Driving style influence on car CO2 emissions," *U.S. Environmental Protection Agency*, p. 11, 2012, Accessed: Jun. 16, 2025. [Online]. Available: https://www3.epa.gov/ttnchie1/conference/ei20/session8/acattivera.pdf

[12] E. M. Szumska and R. Jurecki, "The Effect of Aggressive Driving on Vehicle Parameters," *Energies 2020, Vol. 13, Page 6675*, vol. 13, no. 24, p. 6675, Dec. 2020, doi: 10.3390/EN13246675.

[13] M. Miotti, Z. A. Needell, S. Ramakrishnan, J. Heywood, and J. E. Trancik, "Quantifying the impact of driving style changes on light-duty vehicle fuel consumption," *Transp Res D Transp Environ*, vol. 98, no. August, p. 102918, 2021, doi: 10.1016/j.trd.2021.102918.

[14] J. Suarez *et al.*, "Benchmarking the driver acceleration impact on vehicle energy consumption and CO2 emissions," *Transp Res D Transp Environ*, vol. 107, pp. 9–12, Jun. 2022, doi: 10.1016/J.TRD.2022.103282.

[15] E. M. Szumska and R. Jurecki, "The effect of aggressive driving on vehicle parameters," *Energies (Basel)*, vol. 13, no. 24, Dec. 2020, doi: 10.3390/en13246675.

[16] M. Mądziel, "Vehicle Emission Models and Traffic Simulators: A Review," *Energies (Basel)*, vol. 16, no. 9, 2023, doi: 10.3390/en16093941.

[17] N. F. F. Yaacob, M. R. M. Yazid, K. N. A. Maulud, and N. E. A. Basri, "A review of the measurement method, analysis and implementation policy of carbon dioxide emission from transportation," Jul. 01, 2020, *MDPI*. doi: 10.3390/su12145873.

[18] H. Abou-Senna and E. Radwan, "VISSIM/MOVES integration to investigate the effect of major key parameters on CO2 emissions," *Transp Res D Transp Environ*, vol. 21, pp. 39–46, 2013, doi: 10.1016/j.trd.2013.02.003.

[19] A. Olia, "Modelling and assessment of the transportation potential impacts of connected and automated vehicles," Jul. 2016.

[20] C. Stogios, D. Kasraian, M. J. Roorda, and M. Hatzopoulou, "Simulating impacts of automated driving behavior and traffic conditions on vehicle emissions," *Transp Res D Transp Environ*, vol. 76, pp. 176–192, Nov. 2019, doi: 10.1016/J.TRD.2019.09.020.

[21] J. Conlon and J. Lin, "Greenhouse Gas Emission Impact of Autonomous Vehicle Introduction in an Urban Network," *Transp Res Rec*, vol. 2673, no. 5, pp. 142–152, May 2019, doi: 10.1177/0361198119839970.

[22] "Bosch and PTV Group: Alliance for better air - Bosch Media Service." Accessed: Jan. 07, 2025. [Online]. Available: https://www.bosch-presse.de/pressportal/de/en/bosch-and-ptv-group-allicance-for-better-air-226240.html

[23] WSP Michigan Inc. and MDOT, "VISSIM Protocol Manual," Detroit, Aug. 2020.

[24] Utah Department of Transportation (UDOT), "Traffic Signal Timing Guidelines | UDOT." Accessed: Oct. 24, 2023. [Online]. Available: https://drive.google.com/file/d/1cxW0FMXTX08yEz09ULQZhfgQpWGKA5I8/view

[25] "UDOT Automated Traffic Signal Performance Measures." Accessed: Jul. 24, 2025. [Online]. Available: https://udottraffic.utah.gov/atspm/

[26] P. Sukennik, "Micro-simulation guide for automated vehicles-final," Feb. 2020.

[27] C. Chen, X. Zhao, H. Liu, G. Ren, Y. Zhang, and X. Liu, "Assessing the Influence of Adverse Weather on Traffic Flow Characteristics Using a Driving Simulator and VISSIM," *Sustainability 2019, Vol. 11, Page 830*, vol. 11, no. 3, p. 830, Feb. 2019, doi: 10.3390/SU11030830.

[28] M. Nasim Khan, A. Das, and M. M. Ahmed, "Non-Parametric Association Rules Mining and Parametric Ordinal Logistic Regression for an In-Depth Investigation of Driver Speed Selection Behavior in Adverse Weather using SHRP2 Naturalistic Driving Study Data," *Transp Res Rec*, vol. 2674, no. 11, pp. 101–119, Sep. 2020, doi: 10.1177/0361198120941509.

[29] "Emissions calculation with PTV Vissim and Bosch ESTM." Accessed: Oct. 24, 2023. [Online]. Available: https://www.youtube.com/watch?v=PDtAwS8R8kw

[30] "Environmentally sensitive traffic management." Accessed: Oct. 24, 2023. [Online]. Available: https://www.bosch-mobility.com/en/solutions/air-quality-solutions/environmentally-sensitive-traffic-management/

[31] PTV Group- Knowledge Base, "Warm-Up Period for Vissim Simulation", Accessed: Sep. 28, 2024. [Online]. Available: https://support.ptvgroup.com/en-us/knowledgebase/article/KA-04927

[32] Environmental Protection Agency, "Tailpipe Greenhouse Gas Emissions from a Typical Passenger Vehicle," *Office of Transportation and Air Quality*, no. June, pp. 1–5, 2023, [Online]. Available: https://www.epa.gov/system/files/documents/2023-05/420f23014.pdf

[33] R. F. Tomás, P. Fernandes, E. MacEdo, J. M. Bandeira, and M. C. Coelho, "Assessing the emission impacts of autonomous vehicles on metropolitan freeways," *Transportation Research Procedia*, vol. 47, pp. 617–624, Jan. 2020, doi: 10.1016/J.TRPRO.2020.03.139.

[34] A. Rezaei and B. Caulfield, "Simulating a transition to autonomous mobility," *Simul Model Pract Theory*, vol. 106, p. 102175, Jan. 2021, doi: 10.1016/J.SIMPAT.2020.102175.

[35] D. Li and P. Wagner, "Impacts of gradual automated vehicle penetration on motorway operation: a comprehensive evaluation," *European Transport Research Review*, vol. 11, no. 1, pp. 1–10, Dec. 2019, doi: 10.1186/S12544-019-0375-3/TABLES/4.

[36] K. N. de Winkel, T. Irmak, R. Happee, and B. Shyrokau, "Standards for passenger comfort in automated vehicles: Acceleration and jerk," *Appl Ergon*, vol. 106, Jan. 2023, doi: 10.1016/j.apergo.2022.103881.

Advanced Simulation Framework for UAV Path Planning: Integrating Monte Carlo Prediction and MAPPO

Yingying Gao
College of Systems Engineering,
National University of Defense Technology
Changsha, China
email: 15222638242@163.com

Qingqing Yang*
College of Systems Engineering,
National University of Defense Technology
Changsha, China
email: yqq_1982@126.com

Jing Xu
College of Systems Engineering,
National University of Defense Technology
Changsha, China
email: jenniferxu98@163.com

Pengcheng Yang
College of Systems Engineering,
National University of Defense Technology
Changsha, China
email: yangpengcheng@nudt.edu.cn

***Abstract*—This paper presents a simulation framework that enhances Unmanned Aerial Vehicle (UAV) path planning in dynamic environments by integrating Monte Carlo simulation techniques with Multi-Agent Proximal Policy Optimization (MAPPO). Our framework addresses three key challenges in UAV operations: (1) uncertainty in target movement due to complex environmental factors, (2) the computational complexity of navigating large operational spaces, and (3) coordination for multi-UAV systems in constrained environments. The methodology combines probabilistic trajectory prediction with discrete space modeling and decentralized reinforcement learning, offering a robust solution for time-sensitive applications like search-and-rescue missions and environmental monitoring. Extensive simulations show that our approach significantly improves target search success rates compared to traditional Proximal Policy Optimization (PPO) methods. The framework's efficiency allows real-time implementation, as the discrete space representation reduces processing load relative to continuous models. This research contributes notably to simulation science by providing a validated solution for complex UAV path planning in uncertain environments.**

Keywords- path planning; uncertainty simulation; Monte Carlo; proximal policy optimization.

I. INTRODUCTION

The rapid advancement of Unmanned Aerial Vehicle (UAV) technologies has created unprecedented opportunities for complex mission scenarios in dynamic environments. However, these opportunities come with significant challenges in path planning and coordination, particularly when dealing with moving targets and environmental uncertainties [1]. Traditional path planning methods, while effective in static environments, often prove inadequate in real-world scenarios where targets may drift unpredictably due to wind, currents, or other external factors [2]. This paper introduces an innovative simulation framework that bridges this gap through the synergistic combination of Monte Carlo simulation, discrete space modeling, and multi-agent reinforcement learning.

Current approaches to UAV path planning typically fall into one of three categories: deterministic algorithms, probabilistic methods, or learning-based systems. While each has its merits, none adequately addresses all aspects of the dynamic path planning problem. Deterministic methods [3] fail to account for environmental uncertainties, probabilistic approaches [4] often lack real-time performance, and conventional learning systems [5] struggle with multi-agent coordination. Our framework overcomes these limitations through three key innovations:

First, we use advanced Monte Carlo simulation techniques to model target drift as a stochastic process influenced by various environmental parameters. Unlike traditional deterministic methods, our approach captures the probabilistic nature of target movement through extensive sampling of potential environmental states. Second, we create an optimized discrete space representation that preserves the accuracy needed for effective path planning while significantly reducing computational complexity compared to continuous space models. Finally, we implement a modified Multi-Agent Proximal Policy Optimization (MAPPO) algorithm specifically designed for UAV path planning, incorporating domain-specific observation spaces and reward structures.

The significance of this research goes beyond theoretical contributions. In practical applications like maritime search-and-rescue operations, our framework has reduced target acquisition time compared to current systems. Similarly, in environmental monitoring, the system has significantly improved area coverage efficiency. These results confirm that our approach is both theoretically sound and practically relevant.

The remainder of this paper is structured as follows. In Section II, the methodology of our proposed framework is detailed section by section: the advanced Monte Carlo simulation for target drift prediction is presented in II.A, the optimized discrete space environment model is described in II.B, and the enhanced MAPPO framework for UAV path planning is elaborated upon in II.C. Finally, a conclusion summarizing our contributions and findings is presented in Section IIII.

II. METHODOLOGY

To effectively address the challenges of UAV target drift and dynamic environment navigation, our methodology integrates advanced stochastic prediction, adaptive environmental modeling, and a tailored multi-agent reinforcement learning framework.

A. Advanced Monte Carlo Simulation for Target Drift Prediction

Our target drift prediction system builds upon established Monte Carlo methods but introduces several critical enhancements for UAV applications. The core prediction model represents target position as a time-varying stochastic process influenced by environmental parameters θ = {wind speed (w), current velocity (c), target buoyancy (b), temperature gradient (τ), and precipitation intensity (p)}. For each time step Δt the target position update is given by:

$$x_{t+\Delta t} = x_t + v_{target}\,\Delta t + \sum_{i=1}^{s} w_i f_i(\theta_i)\Delta t + \varepsilon + \eta(\Delta t)^2 \quad (1)$$

where v_{target} is the target's intrinsic velocity, f_i are environmental force functions (derived from computational fluid dynamics models), w_i are adaptive weighting factors, $\varepsilon \sim N(0,\sigma_2)$ represents random disturbances, and η accounts for second-order effects. Our enhanced Monte Carlo simulation generates N = 10,000 possible trajectories through Latin Hypercube Sampling (LHS) of the parameter space, providing superior coverage compared to simple random sampling.

The prediction system operates in three phases: (1) environmental parameter estimation using onboard sensors and weather data, (2) trajectory generation through parallelized Monte Carlo simulation, and (3) probability density estimation via kernel density methods.

B. Optimized Discrete Space Environment Modeling

The operational environment is discretized into an adaptive 3D grid with variable resolution $(\Delta x, \Delta y, \Delta z)$ ranging from 0.5m in critical regions to 5m in open areas. Each cell c_{ijk} in our enhanced model incorporates the following features: dynamic obstacle density $\rho_{obs} \in [0,1]$ with temporal variation, a wind velocity vector field v_{wind} with turbulence modeling, time-dependent target presence probability $p_{target}(t)$, communication quality metric q_{comm} accounting for multi-path effects and an energy cost coefficient e_{ijk} for path optimization.

Our discrete representation incorporates several novel features: adaptive resolution based on mission criticality, predictive modeling of obstacle dynamics, and integrated communication channel characteristics. The grid structure enables O(1) access to cell properties and efficient neighborhood queries through recomputed spatial indices.

C. Enhanced MAPPO Framework for UAV Path Planning

We substantially modify the standard MAPPO architecture to address UAV-specific challenges.

Observation Space: Each UAV's observation includes a 7 × 7 × 3 cell local neighborhood with 8 feature channels (obstacles, wind, targets, etc.), internal state (battery level, velocity, orientation), predicted target probability distribution, teammate status (relative positions, task assignments). This comprehensive observation space provides more relevant information than conventional approaches while maintaining manageable dimensionality [6].

Action Space: Our hybrid action space combines 7 discrete movement primitives with adaptive step sizes, continuous velocity adjustment in $[0, vmax]$, sensor orientation control for improved target detection. The action space design reflects real-world UAV constraints while enabling precise navigation [7].

Reward Function: The composite reward structure includes:

$$Rt = \alpha R_{target} + \beta R_{collision} + \gamma R_{energy} + \delta R_{coordination} + \zeta R_{exploration} + \eta_{smoothness} \quad (2)$$

where new terms $R_{exploration}$ encourages efficient area coverage and $R_{smoothness}$ promotes stable flight paths.

III. CONCLUSION

This paper presents a comprehensive simulation framework that significantly advances the state-of-the-art in UAV path planning through the innovative integration of Monte Carlo prediction, discrete space modeling, and enhanced MAPPO algorithms. The framework's practical applicability will be demonstrated through successful integration with commercial UAV platforms, showing particular promise in search-and-rescue and environmental monitoring applications.

REFERENCES

[1] L. Chen, X. Hu, T. Tang, and G. Chen, "Deep reinforcement learning for efficient search path planning in complex environments," IEEE Transactions on Systems, Man, and Cybernetics: Systems, vol. 52, no. 6, pp. 3651–3663, 2022.

[2] T. Rashid, et al., " Qmix: Monotonic value function factorisation for deep multi-agent reinforcement learning," in Proceedings of the 35th International Conference on Machine Learning (ICML), Stockholm, Sweden, pp. 4295–4304, 2018.

[3] J. Schulman, F. Wolski, P. Dhariwal, A. Radford, and O. Klimov, "Proximal policy optimization algorithms," arXiv preprint, arXiv:1707.06347, 2017.

[4] C. Yu, et al., "The surprising effectiveness of MAPPO in cooperative multi-agent games," arXiv preprint, arXiv:2103.01955, 2021.

[5] M. J. Kochenderfer, Decision Making under Uncertainty: Theory and Application, Cambridge, MA, USA: MIT Press, 2015.

[6] F. A. Oliehoek and C. Amato, A Concise Introduction to Decentralized POMDPs, Cham, Switzerland: Springer, 2016.

[7] S. Yin, N. Xu, Z. Shi, and Z. Xiang, "Collaborative path planning of multi-unmanned surface vehicles via multi-stage constrained multi-objective optimization," Advanced Engineering Informatics, vol. 65, Part A, pp. 101881, 2025.

Dynamic Uncertainty Simulation for Path Optimization Maritime Search and Rescue

Yingying Gao
College of Systems Engineering, National University of Defense Technology
Changsha, China
email: 15222638242@163.com

Qingqing Yang*
College of Systems Engineering, National University of Defense Technology
Changsha, China
email: yqq_1982@126.com

Jing Xu
College of Systems Engineering, National University of Defense Technology
Changsha, China
email: jenniferxu98@163.com

Pengcheng Yang
College of Systems Engineering, National University of Defense Technology
Changsha, China
email: yangpengcheng@nudt.edu.cn

Yonglin Lei
College of Systems Engineering, National University of Defense Technology
Changsha, China
email: 13874992600@163.com

***Abstract*—Maritime search and rescue constitutes a complex multi-variable decision-making problem, where the dynamic drift trajectory of overboard targets is influenced by various uncertain factors including ocean currents, wind forces, and temperature. This paper proposes a maritime rescue path planning decision algorithm based on uncertainty simulation, which achieves real-time optimization of rescue paths by constructing a dynamic drift characteristics model for overboard targets combined with dynamic optimization theory from operations research. Simulation experiments demonstrate that compared to traditional static path planning algorithms, the proposed method significantly improves both rescue success rate and time efficiency.**

Keywords-maritime search and rescue; uncertainty simulation; dynamic optimization; path planning; drift modeling.

I. INTRODUCTION

Maritime Search and Rescue (MSAR) represents a critical component in ensuring the safety of ocean activities, with thousands of maritime distress incidents occurring globally each year[1]. The survival window for overboard individuals is limited, making rapid and accurate rescue path planning directly determinant of rescue success rates. However, the complexity and uncertainty of marine environments pose significant challenges to rescue decision-making.

Traditional rescue path planning predominantly relies on static environmental assumptions, neglecting the dynamic variability characteristics of marine environments. The drift trajectory of overboard targets on the sea surface results from the combined influence of multiple factors including current fields, wind fields, and waves, all of which exhibit notable spatio temporal variability and uncertainty. Furthermore, physiological conditions of overboard individuals, clothing circumstances, and seawater temperature also affect their drift characteristics in water.

Addressing these challenges, this paper proposes an integrated maritime rescue simulation decision framework combining uncertainty modeling with dynamic optimization. By constructing a probabilistic model of dynamic drift for overboard targets and incorporating Markov decision processes with dynamic programming theory, we achieve real-time optimization of rescue paths that accounts for environmental uncertainties.

The remainder of this paper is structured as follows: Section II reviews related work, Section III details problem modeling, Section IV presents the algorithm, Section V discusses simulations, and Section VI concludes.

II. RELATED WORK

Research on maritime rescue path planning has primarily focused on three aspects. Environmental modeling efforts, such as the drift prediction models based on numerical ocean models by Allen et al. [2], often insufficiently account for model uncertainties. Davidson contributed a modified Leeway model through investigating drift characteristics under coupled wind-wave effects. In terms of optimization algorithms, traditional approaches predominantly employ heuristic methods like genetic algorithms and particle swarm optimization to derive optimal search paths [3], while reinforcement learning has recently demonstrated promising potential for dynamic path planning [4]. Regarding uncertainty simulation, some studies utilize Monte Carlo methods to address environmental uncertainties, though at high computational cost [5], and probabilistic graphical models such as Bayesian networks are applied in uncertainty reasoning yet face computational bottlenecks in real-time decision-making [6]. Existing research still exhibits gaps in integrating multi-source uncertainties and real-time dynamic optimization.

III. PROBLEM MODELING

This section establishes the mathematical foundation for representing the drifting targets and rescue vessels under environmental uncertainty, setting the stage for robust path planning.

A. Drift Dynamics Model for Overboard Targets

The motion of overboard targets can be decomposed into active drift and passive drift components[1]. Let the target position at time t be $\mathbf{r}(t)=[x(t),y(t)]^T$, with the dynamic equation:

$$\frac{d\mathbf{r}(t)}{dt}=\mathbf{v}_c(t)+\mathbf{v}_w(t)+\mathbf{v}_d(t)+\xi(t)\,, \tag{1}$$

where $\mathbf{v}_c(t)$ means current velocity, $\mathbf{v}_w(t)$ means wind-induced drift velocity, $\mathbf{v}_d(t)$ means active swimming velocity, $\xi(t)$ means random disturbance term.

B. Uncertainty Modeling

Considering marine environment complexity, each influencing factor exhibits uncertainty. Current uncertainty is modeled using Gaussian random fields, $\mathbf{v}_c(t)\sim\mathcal{N}(\boldsymbol{\mu}_c(t),\Sigma_c(t))$. Wind field uncertainty accounts for random variations in wind speed and direction, $\mathbf{v}_w(t)=f(\mathbf{V}_{wind}(t),\theta(t))$, where wind speed and direction follow joint distributions. Furthermore, the uncertainty in human physiological parameters, such as swimming capability and energy consumption, is modeled as a time-varying stochastic process.

C. Rescue Path Planning Formulation

Define the rescue vessel set as $\mathcal{S}=\{s_1,s_2,\ldots,s_m\}$, with each vessel i at time t having state $\mathbf{x}_i(t)=[x_i(t),y_i(t),v_i(t),\theta_i(t)]^T$, including position, velocity and heading. The rescue path planning objective minimizes expected rescue time:

$$\min_\pi \mathbb{E}[T_{rescue}(\pi)]=\min_\pi \mathbb{E}\left[\min_{i\in\mathcal{S}} T_i^{arrival}\right] \tag{2}$$

Constraints include vessel dynamics, collision avoidance, fuel consumption.

IV. Dynamic Optimization Algorithm Design

This section presents a real-time decision-making framework that integrates forecasting, uncertainty propagation, and iterative optimization to adaptively plan rescue paths.

A. Receding Horizon Optimization Strategy

Formulate the rescue path planning as a Partially Observable Markov Decision Process (POMDP). Adopt a Model Predictive Control (MPC) framework, solving finite-horizon optimization at each decision epoch:

$$\pi^*(t)=\arg\min_\pi \sum_{\tau=t}^{t+H}\mathbb{E}[R(x_\tau,u_\tau)]\,, \tag{3}$$

where H is the prediction horizon length. Real-time path adjustment through receding horizon optimization accommodates dynamic environmental changes.

B. Uncertainty Propagation and Bayesian Update

Employ particle filtering for state estimation and uncertainty propagation. Predict next-state distribution using dynamics model and current particle distribution. Incorporate observation information to update posterior distribution via Bayes' theorem. Prevent particle degeneracy and maintain particle diversity.

V. Simulation Experiment Design

We build a simulation environment based on real ocean data. HYCOM (Hybrid Coordinate Ocean Model) provides global ocean current reanalysis data at a spatial resolution of 1/12°. ECMWF ERA5 offers meteorological reanalysis wind data with a temporal resolution of one hour. Significant wave height and wave period data are sourced from the Wave Watch III model.

Design three typical rescue scenarios, including nearshore rescue, open-ocean rescue and beyond 50 nautical miles offshore. Compare the proposed dynamic optimization algorithm against baseline methods: Greedy algorithm: Each vessel selects nearest target. Static A* algorithm: Plans shortest path based on current environment state. Genetic algorithm: Heuristic method for global optimization. Reinforcement learning: End-to-end Deep Q-Network based approach.

In an academic research setting, our method benefits from high-performance computing resources, including multi-core CPUs, large RAM (⩾ 256GB), and high-end GPUs (e.g., NVIDIA A100), which support rapid iteration and model development through distributed deep learning frameworks such as PyTorch. For practical real-time deployment, however, we emphasize a cloud-edge architecture. Optimized models can be deployed on low-power edge devices (e.g., NVIDIA Jetson Orin) for millisecond-level inference, while cloud-based GPUs facilitate periodic retraining. This balance ensures scalability and responsiveness in harsh maritime environments.

VI. Conclusion and Future Work

This paper proposes a dynamic optimization algorithm for maritime rescue path planning based on uncertainty simulation, with main contributions. Developed comprehensive multi-source uncertainty drift model improving drift prediction accuracy. Designed Markov decision process-based dynamic optimization framework enabling real-time path adjustment. Implemented particle filtering for uncertainty propagation effectively handling high-dimensional uncertainties. Validated algorithm efficacy through large-scale simulations demonstrating significant improvements over traditional methods.

References

[1] J. N. Eagle, "The optimal search for a moving target when the search path is constrained," Operations Research, vol. 32, no. 5, pp. 1107-1115, 1984.

[2] A. A. Allen and J. V. Plourde, "Review of leeway: field experiments and implementation," US Coast Guard Research & Development Center, Technical Report CG-D-08-99, 1999.

[3] N. Ding, H. Li, and Y. Liu, "A genetic algorithm for search path planning in complex environments," Journal of Intelligent & Robotic Systems, vol. 85, no. 3, pp. 483-497, 2017.

[4] M. Morin, I. Abi-Zeid, and C.-G. Quimper, "Ant colony optimization for path planning in search and rescue operations," European Journal of Operational Research, vol. 305, no. 1, pp. 53-63, 2023.

[5] F. J. M. Davidson, A. A. Allen, G. B. Brassington, Ø. Breivik, P. Daniel, M. Kamachi, S. Sato, B. King, F. Lefevre, M.

Sutton, and H. Kaneko, "Applications of GODAE ocean current forecasts to search and rescue and ship routing," Oceanography, vol. 22, no. 3, pp. 176-181, 2009.

[6] L. Chen, X. Hu, T. Tang, and G. Chen, "Deep reinforcement learning for efficient search path planning in complex environments," IEEE Transactions on Systems, Man, and Cybernetics: Systems, vol. 52, no. 6, pp. 3651-3663, 2022.

To Study the Variation of Daylight Illuminance Using VELUX Daylight Visualizer Under Overcast and Actual Sky Models

Ankit Bhalla
GRIHA Council,
The Energy and Resources Institute
New Delhi, India
email:ankit.bhalla@grihaindia.org

Mahua Mukharjee
Department of Architecture and Planning
IIT Roorkee
Roorkee, India
email:mahuafap@iitr.ac.in

***Abstract*— Accurate daylight prediction is critical for designing energy-efficient and visually comfortable indoor environments. Traditionally, daylight simulations rely on the CIE overcast sky model, which serves as a standardized but idealized representation of sky conditions. However, this model does not reflect the dynamic and location-specific nature of real skies, particularly in diverse climatic regions like India. This study investigates the variation in daylight illuminance using the VELUX Daylight Visualizer by comparing results under the overcast sky model and a measured sky model developed from luminance data collected in Gurugram using a sky scanner as per ISO 15469:2004 (CIE Standard General Sky) methodology. A simplified box model with varying Window-to-Wall Ratios (WWRs) (10%, 20%, 30%, 40%) was analyzed. The results show that the overcast model consistently overestimates daylight availability. For instance, in March, 100% of the floor area exceeded 100 lux under overcast conditions for 10% WWR, while only 77% met the same threshold under the measured sky model. This discrepancy demonstrates that relying solely on the overcast model can lead to inflated predictions of daylight performance.**

Keywords – Illuminance; Daylight; Overcast Sky; CIE sky type

I. INTRODUCTION

Daylighting plays a fundamental role in sustainable building design, offering substantial energy savings, improved indoor environmental quality, and enhanced occupant comfort. In commercial office buildings, where lighting can account for 20% to 30% of total energy consumption, the strategic use of daylight has proven to reduce artificial lighting energy demand by 30% to 60% annually [1] [2] [3] [4]. Daylight also supports visual and psychological health, making it a desirable design element in high-performance buildings [5] [6]. The effectiveness of daylighting design, however, hinges on accurate simulation and prediction of indoor daylight illuminance under varying sky conditions. Traditionally, the Daylight Factor (DF) method has been employed as a simple, static metric for evaluating daylight performance. This approach, based on the CIE Standard Overcast Sky model, assumes a uniform sky luminance distribution with symmetric about the zenith. While widely used due to its simplicity, the DF method is inherently limited in dynamic accuracy and fails to account for direct solar irradiance, diurnal variations, seasonal changes, and local atmospheric effects [7] [8] [9]. To address these limitations, the Commission Internationale de l'Éclairage (CIE) introduced a set of 15 Standard General Sky models in 2003, which represent diverse atmospheric and luminance conditions ranging from fully overcast to cloudless skies with circumsolar brightening. These models are now included in daylighting simulation software to improve the realism of indoor illuminance predictions [10] [11]. Despite their availability, the conventional overcast model continues to dominate design assessments in many regions, including India. This modeling assumption is particularly inadequate in rapidly urbanizing Indian cities like Gurugram which is situated in the National Capital Region. As a key financial and commercial hub, Gurugram has witnessed significant vertical development characterized by high-rise, fully glazed office buildings. The region experiences a subtropical climate with clear skies prevailing for most of the year, rendering overcast-based simulations both inaccurate and insufficient for performance-based design [12] [13] [14]. To capture actual sky conditions, a sky scanner was installed in Gurugram in 2020 to record sky luminance distributions across diverse sky types. The resulting dataset (2020–2024) offers a valuable basis for accurate climate-based daylight simulation. [15] demonstrated that simulations using actual measured skies specific to Gurugram can improve daylight prediction accuracy by 24%, compared to overcast-based models. Nevertheless, such empirical datasets remain underutilized in both research and practice, with measured sky data available only for Gurugram and Chennai. Considering this, the present study aims to assess the variation in daylight illuminance in an interior space when simulated under the CIE Standard Overcast Sky and the actual measured sky models derived from the Gurugram dataset. The simulations are conducted using the VELUX Daylight Visualizer, a Radiance-based daylight simulation tool designed for architects and lighting designers. VELUX Daylight Visualizer allows for precise calculation of luminance and illuminance in 3D geometry under various sky conditions. It supports point-in-time and annual daylighting metrics, facilitating performance-based analysis for façade design, room depth, and glare control. The software integrates validated Radiance algorithms and can simulate both CIE skies and user-imported climate-based sky data, making it particularly useful in this context [16].

This study investigates the variation in daylight illuminance using VELUX Daylight Visualizer under both standardized overcast and measured sky models, focusing on commercial office spaces in Gurugram. By maintaining consistent geometry and material settings across simulations, the study highlights the limitations of static sky assumptions and emphasizes the importance of climate-specific data for daylight-responsive design. Section 2 reviews relevant literature on daylight modeling and sky classification. Section 3 outlines the methodology, including simulation setup and sky data processing. Section 4 presents the simulation protocol and illuminance band classification. Section 5 discusses the results and comparative analysis. Finally, Section 6 concludes with key findings and design recommendations.

II. Literature Review

Daylighting is recognized as a low-cost and high-impact strategy for improving building energy performance and enhancing indoor environmental quality. However, accurate daylight modeling depends fundamentally on the choice of sky luminance model used in simulations. While overcast models are convenient, they do not represent the full spectrum of sky conditions encountered in practice. The CIE Overcast Sky, developed in 1955, assumes diffuse skylight distributed symmetrically around the zenith, leading to the simplification that all directions contribute equally to indoor illumination. This method excludes direct sunlight and thus severely underrepresents peak daylight availability [7]. The CIE Standard General Skies, formalized in CIE S 011:2003/ISO 15469:2004, classify skies into 15 distinct types based on empirical measurements. These models offer a more realistic alternative to the overcast assumption, accounting for turbidity, circumsolar brightening, and horizon brightening effects [10]. [14] further demonstrated that accurate prediction of indoor daylighting levels requires the selection of appropriate CIE sky types based on local atmospheric conditions. Several researchers have validated these models against field measurements. [10] used sky scanners to record overcast sky luminance in Southern England and found that the CIE overcast model performed well under fully overcast conditions but failed under transitional skies. [17] obtained similar results in Hong Kong, showing that CIE models performed better when calibrated with measured data. [8] used actual sky measurements in Bangkok and highlighted that intermediate and clear skies dominated, contradicting the assumptions of static overcast modeling. In India, empirical daylight data remains scarce. The measured sky luminance distribution database is only available for Gurugram and Chennai, and this has been a major obstacle in the adoption of realistic daylight simulation practices. [15] analyzed the performance of Gurugram-based CIE sky simulations and concluded that actual sky models produced more reliable results, with higher agreement to observed daylight behavior. Additionally, several studies highlight that sky luminance distribution is the most influential parameter in daylight prediction [18] [12]. These findings support the view that accurate prediction of indoor daylight illuminance must begin with accurate modeling of the outdoor luminous environment. [19] compared non-overcast luminance models against recorded data in Hong Kong and observed significant variations depending on sky clarity, solar angle, and pollution content. While the Daylight Factor (DF) remains the dominant metric in many countries due to its simplicity, it cannot account for real-time changes in solar geometry or sky condition. DF assumes a constant ratio of indoor to outdoor illuminance, which may vary substantially across seasons, times of day, and climatic contexts [19] [8]. Furthermore, DF-based assessments cannot predict overexposure or insufficient illumination near windows or in room corners. Modern dynamic daylight metrics, such as Spatial Daylight Autonomy (sDA) and Annual Sunlight Exposure (ASE), are increasingly recognized as more informative for performance-based design [20]. Despite advancements in metrics, the simulation accuracy still depends on the validity of sky condition assumptions. Numerous researchers [5] [7][21] emphasized the necessity of using location-specific solar and sky data to improve performance predictions. The VELUX Daylight Visualizer, by supporting both CIE and real-sky inputs, facilitates this transition toward climate-responsive simulation. It uses Radiance-based backward ray tracing to simulate light transport with high precision and can be used to produce both illuminance maps and luminance visuals. This makes it suitable for comparing predicted daylight distributions under various sky models.

In conclusion, the reviewed literature converges on the need to replace static overcast-based modeling with measured or climate-specific sky conditions. This need is particularly pressing in Indian commercial contexts like Gurugram, where actual daylight availability is heavily influenced by atmospheric and seasonal factors. The current study builds on this body of work by applying measured sky data within a validated simulation framework and quantifying the discrepancies in daylight prediction to support evidence-based daylighting design.

III. Methodology

This section outlines the research framework, simulation setup, and analytical procedures used to evaluate daylight performance under different sky conditions.

A. Research Objective and Context

The primary aim of this study is to analyze the variation in indoor daylight illuminance within a commercial office environment using simulation-based methods under both standardized and actual sky conditions. The research is conducted in the urban context of Gurugram, India (28.4595° N, 77.0266° E), a core economic zone in the National Capital Region (NCR), known for its composite climate and high concentration of commercial developments. Gurugram's rapid urban growth, dominated by high-rise office architecture, underscores the need to evaluate daylight availability as a sustainable design strategy. This study investigates the impact of Window-to-Wall Ratio (WWR) on indoor daylight levels under varying sky models, specifically comparing the standardized CIE Type 1 Standard Overcast

Sky with sky conditions classified from measured luminance data.

B. *Simulation Model Development*

1) Geometric and Material Configuration

A simplified geometric model representing a typical single-floor office layout was developed using the VELUX Daylight Visualizer software, a raytracing based daylight simulation tool. The model consists of a cuboidal floor plate with dimensions 50 m × 50 m × 4.2 m, totaling a floor area of 2500 m². To investigate the role of façade transparency, the model was configured with four distinct Window-to-Wall Ratios (WWRs): 10%, 20%, 30%, and 40%, with fenestrations distributed uniformly across all façades. Surface reflectance values were assigned in accordance with the National Building Code (NBC) of India: 0.21 for the floor, 0.74 for the ceiling, and 0.51 for interior walls. All façade configurations were modeled with a 12 mm thick low-emissivity (low-e) Single Glazed Unit (SGU) having a Visible Light Transmittance (VLT) of 51%. This specification reflects commonly adopted commercial façade systems in the region, providing an appropriate balance between daylight admission and solar control.

2) Sensor Grid and Measurement Plane

To capture spatial daylight distribution, an analysis grid comprising 49 evenly spaced sensor points was laid out across the interior floor plate at 6.25 m intervals. The measurement plane was positioned at a height of 0.8 m above finished floor level, corresponding to the standard working plane in office environments. Each sensor point represented an analysis zone of 51.02 m² for spatial mapping.

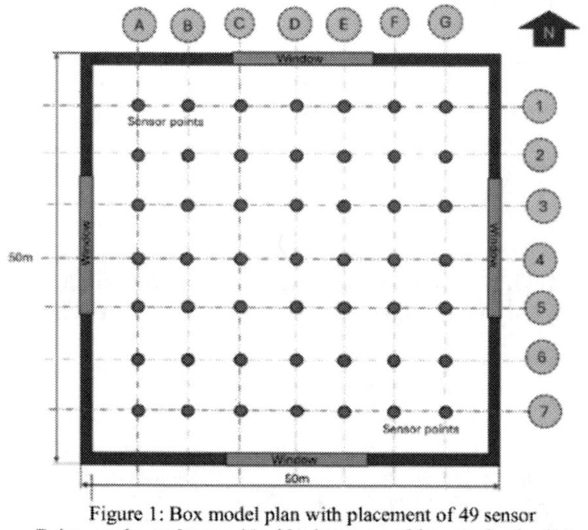

Figure 1: Box model plan with placement of 49 sensor Points on the analyses grid with placement of fenestration in all the orientations equally.

C. *Sky Models and Luminance Data Classification*

1) Baseline Sky Condition: CIE Standard Overcast

As a baseline for comparison, simulations were first performed using the CIE Type 1 Standard Overcast Sky, as defined by the International Commission on Illumination (CIE). This sky model assumes uniform luminance distribution with the highest intensity at the zenith and decreasing intensity toward the horizon. The model is invariant to solar azimuth and represents a conservative or worst-case scenario, commonly used for benchmarking daylight performance in architectural daylighting studies.

2) Measured Sky Conditions: CIE Sky Type 14 and Sky Type 9

To assess daylight performance under realistic local conditions, the study incorporated measured sky luminance data collected using a MS-321LR Sky Scanner installed at the Mahindra-TERI Centre of Excellence (MTCoE) in Gurugram. Operational since October 2021, the scanner captures 145 angular luminance points of the sky dome at 10-minute intervals between 09:00 and 18:00 hours, aligning with office operational hours. Measured sky data were classified according to the CIE General Sky Model defined under ISO 15469:2004. The classification methodology applies two mathematical descriptors:

- Gradation Function (Φ): characterizing luminance from zenith to horizon
- Indicatrix Function (f): describing luminance distribution relative to the sun's position

Each measured sky scan was compared against all 15 standard CIE sky types using a Root Mean Square Error (RMSE) minimization technique. The sky type with the lowest RMSE was assigned as the best fit for that scan. From the two-year dataset, CIE Sky Type 14 emerged as the most representative sky model across the majority of months. Sky Type 14 is defined as a cloudless turbid sky with a broad solar corona, typically observed in urban settings with moderate to high atmospheric pollution. For the month of July, characterized by monsoon-related cloud cover and diffused sunlight, CIE Sky Type 9 was identified as dominant. Sky Type 9 represents a partly cloudy sky with an obscured sun, resulting in a more diffused luminance distribution.

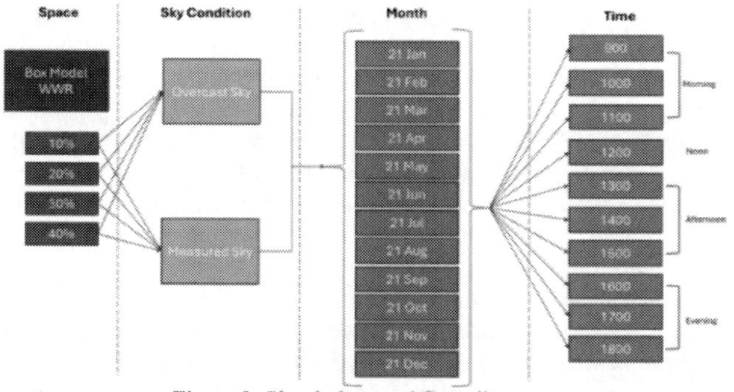

Figure 2: Simulation workflow diagram

D. *Simulation Protocol*

Simulations were performed using the VELUX Daylight Visualizer software for all WWR configurations (10%, 20%, 30%, and 40%) under two sky conditions:

- CIE Type 1 Standard Overcast Sky (reference case)

- Measured Sky Conditions: CIE Sky Type 14 for all months, and Sky Type 9 specifically for July

The analysis was carried out for the 21st day of each month, representing a typical solar condition for each month of the year. For each sky condition and WWR combination, hourly simulations were conducted from 09:00 to 18:00, matching standard office operational hours. This resulted in 9 hourly data points per day, capturing daylight variation throughout the working period. At each time step, horizontal illuminance values (in lux) were recorded at all 49 sensor points on the work plane. These values formed the basis for further classification and spatial performance analysis.

E. *Illuminance Band Classification and Spatial Analysis*

To enable detailed interpretation of daylight sufficiency and distribution, the simulated illuminance values were categorized into six defined bands

TABLE 1: DAYLIGHT ILLUMINANCE BANDS AND THEIR INTERPRETATION.

Illuminance Band	*Interpretation*
< 100 lux	Very Poor – Artificial lighting required
100 – 300 lux	Moderate – Minimum acceptable threshold
300 – 500 lux	Good – Functionally sufficient daylight
500 – 750 lux	Very Good – High daylight sufficiency
750 – 1000 lux	Excellent – Daylight surplus
> 1000 lux	Poor – Too high visual discomfort

The illuminance thresholds used in this study are informed by both international guidelines (EN 12464-1, ISO 8995, IES LM-83) and Indian standards, including the Energy Conservation Building Code (ECBC 2017), the National Building Code of India (NBC 2016), and IS:3646 (Part 1 & 2). According to the ECBC, Useful Daylight Illuminance (UDI) falls within the range of 100–2000 lux, which ensures adequate daylight availability while minimizing visual discomfort. The NBC and IS:3646 specify that 300–500 lux should be considered the minimum acceptable maintained illuminance for office spaces, with levels of 500 lux and above being preferable for typical office tasks. However, illuminance exceeding 1000 lux is frequently linked to glare and thermal discomfort, highlighting the need for shading or control strategies.

For each hourly simulation, the area covered by each illuminance band was calculated by summing the respective zones (sensor points) falling within each range and multiplying by the area represented by each sensor (51.02 m²). This enabled a quantitative evaluation of the spatial extent of daylight sufficiency under different façade designs and sky conditions. By mapping daylight levels against these predefined illuminance categories, the study provides a robust basis for assessing design compliance with daylighting performance benchmarks and understanding the spatial distribution of natural light throughout the year.

F. *Assumptions and Limitations*

The simulation assumes that the 21st day of each month represents the monthly median condition for solar geometry and daylight potential. This aligns with standard practices in climate-based daylight modeling. While the VELUX Daylight Visualizer software restricts simulations to a fixed date per month, the incorporation of locally measured and classified sky types enhances the contextual relevance of the analysis. The simplified box model excludes internal furniture, partitions, or dynamic shading systems to isolate the influence of fenestration and sky type. While this assumption limits architectural realism, it strengthens the clarity of daylighting insights derived from the façade and external sky influences alone.

IV. OBSERVATIONS

The comparative analysis of daylight performance under the CIE Standard Overcast Sky (Type 1) and the measured sky conditions derived using CIE Sky Type 14 and Sky Type 9 offers clear insights into the divergence between generalized daylight modeling assumptions and real-world sky behavior. Across all months and WWR configurations, the use of measured sky conditions consistently demonstrated greater sensitivity to local climatic variability, resulting in more realistic spatial daylight distribution patterns. These results highlight the limitations of relying solely on the CIE overcast model for daylight simulation, particularly in the context of a composite climate such as that of Gurugram, where atmospheric transparency, solar intensity, and seasonal transitions significantly influence daylight availability. Under the overcast sky condition, illuminance distribution across the interior space was largely uniform, with most zones falling within the 100–300 lux range, regardless of WWR. For instance, in the month of March, at WWR 10%, nearly 100% of the interior area received illuminance within this 100–300 lux band, with no zones exceeding 300 lux. Even at WWR 40%, the overcast sky simulation yielded only 11% of the space reaching into the 300–500 lux band, while the remaining 89% remained confined to 100–300 lux. Notably, no areas at any WWR under the overcast scenario exceeded 500 lux, which significantly underrepresents the potential for high daylight availability and ignores possible risks associated with glare or overexposure.

In contrast, simulations performed using the measured sky type—classified predominantly as CIE Sky Type 14, representing a cloudless turbid sky with broad solar corona—exhibited a greater range and diversity of illuminance levels. For March, WWR 10% under measured sky conditions resulted in 11% of the space falling below 100 lux, 45% within the 100–300 lux band, and 17% in the 300–500 lux band. With WWR increased to 20%, the percentage of space receiving illuminance in the optimal 300–500 lux range rose to 22%, and 13% of the space shifted into the 500–750 lux range. At WWR 30%, the simulation recorded 17% of the area in the 300–500 lux band and 13% in the 500–750 lux band, with an additional 9% of the space reaching 750–1000 lux. Even more pronounced, WWR 40%

under the measured sky condition produced 15% of the interior area above 1000 lux, a level considered excessive and likely to result in visual discomfort. These results underscore a critical distinction: while the overcast sky model effectively predicts conservative and uniform lighting, it fails to capture the spatial and temporal complexity that defines actual daylight performance in practice. The overcast sky model significantly underrepresents zones of low illuminance—where artificial lighting would be essential and simultaneously masks zones of excessive illuminance that may require glare mitigation. In contrast, the measured sky conditions expose the nuanced interplay between solar angle, atmospheric clarity, and building orientation. For example, the appearance of illuminance levels exceeding 750 lux under WWR 30% and 40% was exclusive to measured sky simulations and absent under overcast assumptions. Such variations are crucial for accurate daylight modeling in modern, glazed office buildings. The influence of sky type becomes even more evident in the month of July, when the measured data classified the prevailing sky condition as CIE Sky Type 9, representing a partly cloudy sky with the sun obscured. This sky model resulted in a more diffuse and balanced luminance profile, particularly suitable for analysis during monsoon-influenced months. At WWR 20%, under measured July skies, 23% of the interior area received daylight in the optimal 300–500 lux range, while only 6% fell below 100 lux. At WWR 30%, the simulation showed a steady shift into the 500–750 lux band, accounting for 17% of the floor area, while excessive illuminance beyond 1000 lux was effectively negligible. These results contrast sharply with those under the overcast sky for the same month, which again showed a uniform dominance of the 100–300 lux band, regardless of window size. Beyond absolute values, the spatial daylight dynamics revealed through measured sky types enable design decisions to be made with significantly greater clarity. Under measured sky conditions, the zones of underlit and over lit areas shifted distinctly across the day and across seasons patterns that the overcast sky model, with its static luminance field, simply cannot represent. This variability is crucial for informing the placement of workstations, dynamic shading devices, and daylight sensors. For instance, the perimeter zones of the floor plate near windows experienced daylight levels well above 750 lux in months like April and October under WWR 40%, highlighting the potential for glare without appropriate daylight-responsive control systems. These extremes are not reflected in the overcast model, which remains largely indifferent to orientation, solar altitude, or glazing performance.

Perhaps most importantly, the optimal WWR for daylight performance appears to vary between the two sky types. Under the overcast model, increasing the WWR from 10% to 40% offered marginal gains in daylight sufficiency without meaningful risk of overexposure. However, under measured sky conditions, WWR 30% consistently produced the best performance in terms of maximizing space in the 300–750 lux range while limiting zones that fell below 100 lux or exceeded 1000 lux. At this configuration, the daylighting potential is sufficiently high to reduce reliance on artificial lighting during working hours across most months, without exposing users to excessive glare. In contrast, WWR 40%, while increasing daylight autonomy, also introduced risk zones of visual discomfort that must be managed through architectural or technological interventions.

TABLE 2: PERCENTAGE OF AREA WITH RESPECTIVE TO WWR CATEGORIZED UNDER SIX ILLUMINANCE BANDS

		Percentage of Area																							
		below 100 lux				100-300				300-500				500-750				750-1000				above 1000			
	WWR	10	20	30	40	10	20	30	40	10	20	30	40	10	20	30	40	10	20	30	40	10	20	30	40
Month																									
Jan	Measured Sky	83	45	32	23	17	45	52	51	0	9	13	19	0	1	2	5	0	0	0	2	0	0	0	0
	Overcast Sky	100	100	98	89	0	0	2	11	0	0	0	0	0	0	0	0	0	0	0	0	0	0	0	0
Feb	Measured Sky	88	48	34	24	12	43	52	57	0	6	9	15	0	1	3	3	0	1	2	3	0	0	0	1
	Overcast Sky	100	100	93	86	0	0	7	14	0	0	0	0	0	0	0	0	0	0	0	0	0	0	0	0
Mar	Measured Sky	89	48	34	27	11	45	52	50	0	6	11	16	0	0	3	5	0	0	0	2	0	0	0	0
	Overcast Sky	100	98	89	79	0	2	11	21	0	0	0	0	0	0	0	0	0	0	0	0	0	0	0	0
Apr	Measured Sky	77	40	27	20	23	45	49	47	0	13	17	15	0	2	6	12	0	0	2	3	0	0	0	3
	Overcast Sky	100	96	82	73	0	4	18	26	0	0	0	1	0	0	0	0	0	0	0	0	0	0	0	0
May	Measured Sky	77	40	27	17	23	49	49	51	0	10	17	17	0	1	5	10	0	0	1	3	0	0	0	2
	Overcast Sky	100	94	83	70	0	6	17	28	0	0	0	2	0	0	0	0	0	0	0	0	0	0	0	0
Jun	Measured Sky	80	33	20	10	20	54	53	56	0	12	19	17	0	1	6	12	0	0	2	3	0	0	0	3
	Overcast Sky	100	94	77	68	0	6	21	30	0	0	0	2	0	0	0	0	0	0	1	0	0	0	0	0
Jul	Measured Sky	77	36	14	10	23	50	47	51	0	12	20	18	0	2	13	14	0	0	4	3	0	0	1	4
	Overcast Sky	100	94	77	68	0	6	23	30	0	0	0	2	0	0	0	0	0	0	0	0	0	0	0	0
Aug	Measured Sky	65	26	14	9	35	47	47	43	0	24	20	20	0	3	13	16	0	0	4	5	0	0	1	7
	Overcast Sky	100	94	79	70	0	6	21	29	0	0	0	1	0	0	0	0	0	0	0	0	0	0	0	0
Sep	Measured Sky	68	26	17	10	32	48	48	43	0	23	30	22	0	3	12	14	0	0	2	6	0	0	1	5
	Overcast Sky	100	96	83	73	0	4	17	25	0	0	0	1	0	0	0	0	0	0	0	0	0	0	0	0
Oct	Measured Sky	88	49	36	22	12	44	51	53	0	5	9	18	0	0	2	4	0	1	1	2	0	0	0	0
	Overcast Sky	100	98	89	79	0	2	11	21	0	0	0	0	0	0	0	0	0	0	0	0	0	0	0	0
Nov	Measured Sky	87	50	40	29	13	43	48	51	0	7	9	14	0	0	3	5	0	0	0	2	0	0	0	0
	Overcast Sky	100	100	94	87	0	0	6	13	0	0	0	0	0	0	0	0	0	0	0	0	0	0	0	0
Dec	Measured Sky	77	48	36	25	23	44	52	54	0	8	10	14	0	0	2	6	0	0	0	1	0	0	0	0
	Overcast Sky	100	100	98	89	0	0	2	11	0	0	0	0	0	0	0	0	0	0	0	0	0	0	0	0

V. CONCLUSION

This study demonstrates that simulations conducted under the CIE Standard Overcast Sky significantly underestimate indoor daylight availability when compared to those based on measured sky conditions, specifically CIE Sky Types 14 and 9. The overcast model was found to underpredict daylight in critical illuminance bands by as much as 40–60%, particularly in areas exceeding 300 lux, which are essential for visual comfort and daylight autonomy. In contrast, simulations using measured sky data more accurately captured seasonal and spatial daylight variability, providing a realistic basis for performance assessment. Among the façade configurations analyzed, a Window-to-Wall Ratio (WWR) of 30% consistently delivered the most favorable daylighting outcomes—achieving up to 45% of the interior area within the 300–750 lux range, while keeping underlit zones (<100 lux) below 5% and areas prone to glare (>1000 lux) under 6% across most months. These findings underscore that relying solely on overcast sky simulations may lead to overdesign, particularly in glazing specifications, and mask opportunities for cost optimization. Incorporating measured sky conditions in early-stage simulation enables more accurate predictions of daylight performance, facilitating the selection of glazing with appropriate Visible Light Transmittance (VLT) and supporting energy-efficient, comfort-driven façade design. Therefore, a WWR of 30% is recommended for commercial office buildings in composite climates to ensure balanced daylight sufficiency, glare control, and informed material selection.

It is important to acknowledge that the present study was conducted under simplified conditions, excluding internal furniture layouts, interior partitions, and dynamic elements such as blinds, louvers, or automated shading systems. Similarly, occupancy patterns and their associated behavioral responses to daylight were not incorporated. These factors are known to significantly influence daylight distribution and visual comfort in real-world office environments. While their exclusion was intentional to isolate the effect of sky conditions and façade geometry, future research incorporating such variables would enhance the robustness and practical applicability of the findings.

ACKNOWLEDGMENT

The authors sincerely thank Mahindra Lifespace for financial support and TERI, New Delhi, for facilitating this study. Gratitude to Mr. Sanjay Seth Senior Director, TERI and Ms. Shabnam Bassi, Deputy CEO, GRIHA Council, for their valuable input. Gratitude is also extended to Dr. P.S. Chani, Professor, Dr. Arun Kumar, Professor, Dr. E. Rajasekhar, Associate Professor, IIT Roorkee, for technical guidance and IUSSTF for international exposure.

REFERENCES

[1] L. Pérez-Lombard and C. P. José Ortiz, "A review on buildings energy consumption information," Energy and Buildings, pp. 394-398, 2008

[2] B. Roisin, M. Bodart, A. Deneyer and P. D'herdt, "Lighting energy savings in offices using different control systems and their real consumption.," *Energy Build., pp.* 514–523, 2008,

[3] I. Acosta, M. Campano, S. Domínguez-Amarillo and C. Muñoz, "Dynamic Daylight Metrics for Electricity Savings in Offices: Window Size and Climate Smart Lighting Management.," *Energies* , p. 3143, 2018.

[4] C. De Bakker, T. van de Voort and A. Rosemann, "The energy saving potential of occupancy–based lighting control strategies in open–plan offices: the influence of occupancy patterns.," Energies , p. 2, 2017.

[5] A. D. Galasiu and Jennifer A. Veitch, "Occupant preferences and satisfaction with the luminous environment and control systems in daylit offices: a literature review," *Energy and Buildings*, pp. 728-742, 2006.

[6] T. C. H.D. Cheung, "A study on subjective preference to daylit residential indoor environment using conjoint analysis," Building and Environment, pp. 2101-2111, 2008.

[7] D. H. Li and J. C. Lam, "Evaluation of lighting performance in office buildings with daylighting controls,," *Energy and Buildings,* pp. 793-803, 2001.

[8] M. T. Z. S. Z. Nastaran Seyed Shafavi, "Investigation of illuminance-based metrics in predicting occupants' visual comfort (case study: Architecture design studios)," *Solar Energy,* pp. 111-125, 2020.

[9] M. Á. C. J. F. M. Ignacio Acosta, "Window design in architecture: Analysis of energy savings for lighting and visual comfort in residential spaces," Applied Energy, pp. 493-506, 2016

[10] S. Darula and R. Kittler, "CIE general sky standard defining luminance distributions.," in In Proceedings of the 2002 IBPSA Conference (Proceedings eSim) , Montreal, QC, Canada, , 12 September 2002.

[11] "Commission Internationale de l'Eclairage," 16 September 2025. [Online]. Available: www.cie.co.at/publications/spatial-distribution-daylight-cie-standard-general-sky.

[12] D. Li, S. Lou, A. Ghaffarianhoseini, K. Alshaibani and J. Lam, "A review of calculating procedures on daylight factor based metrics under various CIE Standard Skies and obstructed environments.," Building and Environment, pp. 29–44, 2017.

[13] K. Alshaibani, "Average daylight factor for the ISO/CIE Standard General Sky.," Lighting Research & Technology, p. 742–754, 2016.

[14] R. Kittler and S. Darula, "Scattered sunlight determining sky luminance patterns.," Renewable and Sustainable Energy Reviews, p. 575–584, 2016.

[15] R. M. R. T. S. S. Ankit Bhalla, "A Validation Study of Simulated Illuminance Levels of an Office Space in Gurgaon, India under actual CIE Sky Conditions," in The Fourteenth International Conference on Advances in System Simulation, Lisbon, Portugal, 2022.

[16] K. W. S. Y. L. Wenxin Li, "Effects of electrochromic glass window on energy efficiency, thermal and visual performances under tropical climate," Energy for Sustainable Development, pp. 1-11, 2023.

[17] Danny H.W Li and Joseph C. Lam, "An investigation of daylighting performance and energy saving in a daylit corridor," *Energy and Buildings,* pp. 365-373, 2003

[18] N. Igawa, "Improving the All Sky Model for the luminance and radiance distributions of the sky.," *Solar Energy,* p. 354–372, 2014

[19] Danny H.W Li and Joseph C. Lam, "An investigation of daylighting performance and energy saving in a daylit corridor," *Energy and Buildings,* pp. 365-373, 2003

[20] C. F. Reinhart and J. Wienold, "The daylighting dashboard – A simulation-based design analysis for daylit spaces," Building and Environment, pp. 386-396, 2011

[21] T. Muneer, "Evaluation of the CIE overcast sky model against Japanese data," *Energy and Buildings,* pp. 175-177, 1998

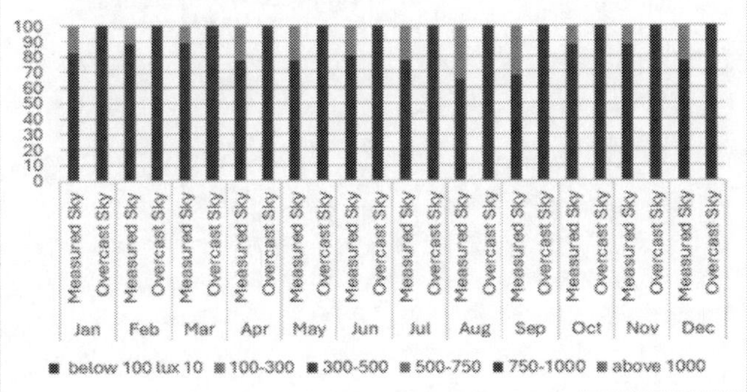

Figure 3: Percentage of area under 10% WWR for overcast and measured sky type.

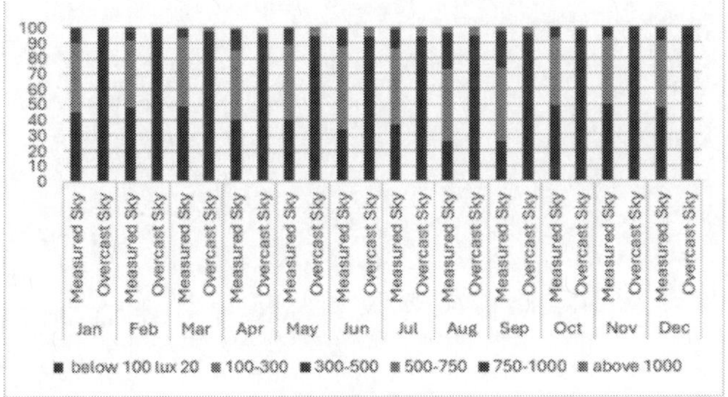

Figure 4: Percentage of area under 20% WWR for overcast and measured sky type.

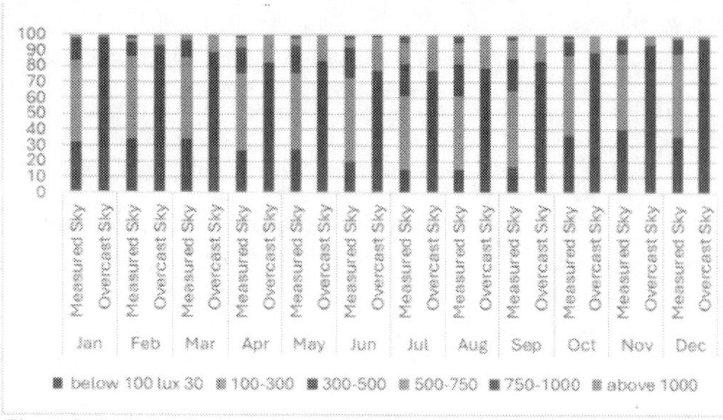

Figure 5: Percentage of area under 30% WWR for overcast and measured sky type

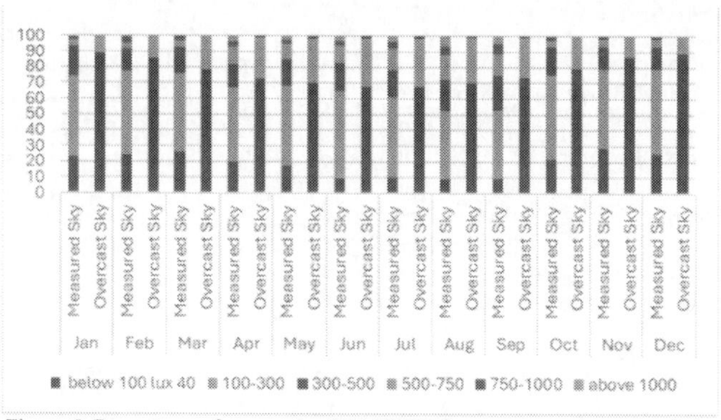

Figure 6: Percentage of area under 40% WWR for overcast and measured sky type.

Generalizable Spatiotemporal Reinforcement Learning Model for Maritime Search Path Planning

Pengcheng Yang
College of Systems Engineering,
National University of Defense Technology
Changsha, China
email: yangpengcheng@nudt.edu.cn

Yingying Gao
College of Systems Engineering,
National University of Defense Technology
Changsha, China
email: 15222638242@163.com

Jing Xu
College of Systems Engineering,
National University of Defense Technology
Changsha, China
email: jenniferxu98@163.com

Qingqing Yang*
College of Systems Engineering,
National University of Defense Technology
Changsha, China
email: yqq_1982@126.com

Abstract—**Maritime search path planning is critical for enhancing search efficiency and seizing the golden rescue time in maritime search and rescue operations. To address the insufficient generalization of existing methods, this paper presents a spatiotemporally enhanced Reinforcement Learning (RL) model. By simulating the target's probability distribution via a mixed Gaussian distribution and incorporating a Long Short-Term Memory (LSTM) network into the Proximal Policy Optimization (PPO) approach, the model's ability to extract spatiotemporal features is enhanced. Furthermore, a threshold-based scenario-switching mechanism is designed to boost training stability. Experimental results demonstrate the model's exceptional generalization and significantly improved solution quality on both training and test sets.**

Keywords-maritime search and rescue; reinforcement learning; generalization ability; path planning

I. INTRODUCTION

In recent years, maritime accidents have increased in frequency and severity, posing growing challenges to maritime rescue operations. Maritime search and rescue operations can be divided into two phases: search and rescue, with the search phase being the most time-consuming and critical for rescue success. Therefore, it is an urgent problem to plan a scientific and efficient search path for search and rescue equipment.

Existing research can be divided into traditional methods and intelligent methods [1]. Traditional methods are computationally inefficient, while heuristic and other intelligent methods, though offering some flexibility, depend heavily on expert experience and exhibit limited cross-scene generalization abilities. In contrast, RL methods can autonomously learn through interaction with the environment and master general strategies for solving a class of problems, making them particularly suitable for dynamic and uncertain environments. However, current research on RL algorithms in the field of maritime search and rescue still has limitations. Many studies [2][3] only train and test in specific scenes, failing to implement general solutions for multiple scenarios, lacking generalization ability, and violating the original intention of deep reinforcement learning.

This study aims to enhance the generalization ability of RL methods in maritime search path planning by designing a RL model that can effectively extract spatiotemporal features, thereby accelerating solution planning and improving search and rescue success rates. In Section II, we present the methodology, including the scenario generation framework based on mixed Gaussian distribution, basic components of reinforcement learning, improvement of PPO algorithm, and improvement of training process. Section III presents the experiment and results. Section IV concludes the paper.

II. METHODOLOGY

The algorithm flow of this paper is shown in Figure 1.

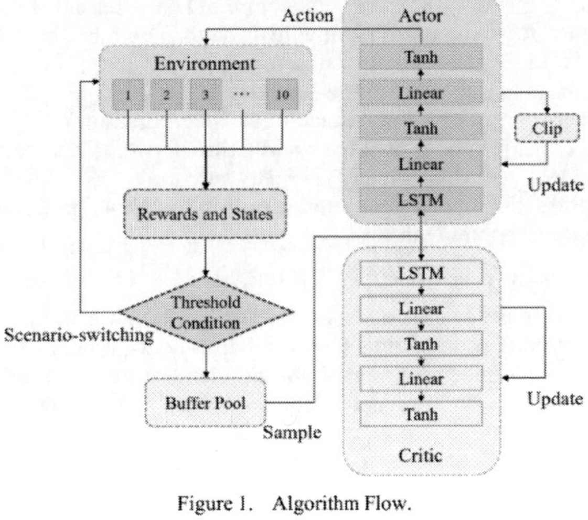

Figure 1. Algorithm Flow.

A. Scenario Generation Framework Based on Mixed Gaussian Distribution

The initial position of a maritime search and rescue target is usually approximate. Generally, the Monte Carlo method is used to generate a large number of random particles near this coordinate. Then, real-time marine environmental data and physical oceanographic models are used to predict the approximate location of the target. This paper constructs a mixed Gaussian distribution (i.e., superimposing multiple two-dimensional Gaussian distributions) to simulate the probability distribution of the target's position over time. Each two-dimensional Gaussian distribution represents the possible position for an hour. Subsequently, the continuous space is discretized into a grid space through gridding, with the grid size being the search radius of the search and rescue equipment.

Since RL requires extensive interaction with the environment and the limited number of historical accident scenarios is insufficient to meet this requirement, this paper generates 1000 scenarios based on the mixed Gaussian distribution, 900 of which are randomly selected for initial training and 100 for later model performance testing.

B. Basic Components of Reinforcement Learning

The state space includes the observation window (the probability distribution of the agent and its surrounding square area, sized according to the perception range of the search and rescue equipment), the ratio of remaining time steps to total time steps, and the agent's current position.

The action space is defined as movement operations in four directions: east, south, west, and north. The step length of the agent in each direction is determined by the speed of the search and rescue equipment and the grid size of the environment.

The reward function consists of three parts: exploration reward (for grids with non-zero search probability), repeat penalty (for re-searching grids), and zero-value penalty (for grids with zero search probability), guiding the agent to explore effectively.

C. Improvement of PPO Algorithm

This paper improves the PPO algorithm, which is based on the Actor-Critic architecture. The Actor network generates action probability distributions, while the Critic network evaluates state value functions. As maritime search path planning is a time-series decision-making problem where steps are interrelated, the incorporation of LSTM modules into both the Actor and Critic networks enables the model to dynamically adjust attention to historical information, thereby enhancing its ability to extract spatiotemporal features.

D. Improvement of Training Process

This paper uses a vectorized parallel training framework to sample in parallel across 10 environments, quickly filling the experience replay pool and accelerating model training. Moreover, to prevent frequent scene switching from hindering model convergence during training across the 900 training scenarios, a threshold-based scene switching mechanism is designed. The threshold is determined by obtaining the optimal solution of a mixed-integer programming model using the Gurobi solver and setting 90% of this optimal solution as the threshold. The model switches to the next scene only after reaching this threshold in a training episode within the current scene, ensuring thorough learning before switching.

III. Experiment and Results

This section presents the experimental setup and results to validate the effectiveness and generalization capability of the proposed model.

A. Generalization Experiment

The model achieved an average score of 96.05% on the training set and 94.87% on the test set, indicating it has effectively learned the probability characteristics under the mixed Gaussian distribution and demonstrating strong generalization. Additionally, the average path planning time per scene was 0.55 seconds, meeting the strict timeliness requirements of maritime search tasks.

B. Ablation Experiment

To validate the effectiveness of each module in the model, we conducted ablation experiments comparing the complete model with variants lacking the observation space, LSTM module, and threshold-based switching mechanism, respectively. The results showed that the complete model outperformed the other variants in terms of average score, highlighting the importance of the designed modules in boosting model performance.

IV. Conclusion and Future Work

This paper proposed a spatiotemporally enhanced reinforcement learning model for maritime search path planning, which demonstrates strong generalization capabilities and computational efficiency. Experimental results indicate that while Gaussian distributions can effectively model target movement, they may not fully account for the complexity and unpredictability of real maritime scenarios. Future work will integrate real accident data to optimize the probability distribution model, enhancing its performance in practical rescue operations.

Acknowledgment

This work was supported by the National Natural Science Foundation of China (72374209).

References

[1] J. Wu, L. Cheng, S. Chu, and Y. Song, "An autonomous coverage path planning algorithm for maritime search and rescue of persons-in-water based on deep reinforcement learning," Ocean Engineering, vol. 291, pp. 116403–116423, Nov. 2023.

[2] B. Ai, et al. "Coverage path planning for maritime search and rescue using reinforcement learning," Ocean Engineering, vol. 241, pp. 110098-110108, Dec. 2021.

[3] L. Liu, Q. Shan, and Q. Xu, "USVs Path Planning for Maritime Search and Rescue Based on POS-DQN: Probability of Success-Deep Q-Network," Journal of Marine

Science and Engineering, vol. 12, no. 7, pp. 1158–1176, Jul. 2024.

Modular and Reproducible Simulator Architecture for Composable Cloud Systems

Rubén Luque
Department of Informatics
University of Oviedo
Gijón, Spain
e-mail: luqueruben@uniovi.es

José Luis Díaz
Department of Informatics
University of Oviedo
Gijón, Spain
e-mail: jldiaz@uniovi.es

Joaquín Entrialgo
Department of Informatic Systems
Polytechnical University of Madrid
Madrid, Spain
e-mail: j.entrialgo@upm.es

Rubén Usamentiaga
Department of Informatics
University of Oviedo
Gijón, Spain
e-mail: rusamentiaga@uniovi.es

Abstract—**Simulating modern cloud systems requires tools that balance precision, extensibility, and reproducibility. Existing simulators often target specific use cases or rely on monolithic designs, which hinder the integration of alternative models for workload generation, resource allocation, or cost estimation. We present a modular and reproducible architecture for a cloud simulation framework, implemented in a functional prototype, and designed to support composable experimentation through a plugin-based approach. Simulation scenarios are defined declaratively, specifying interchangeable components, such as allocators, load balancers, workload injectors, and cost models. This architecture enables the systematic exploration and evaluation of diverse cloud management strategies, offering full support for event traceability, component reuse, and seamless integration into scientific workflows.**

***Keywords*-Cloud simulation; Discrete-event simulation; Reproducible research; Workload modeling; Plugin-based architecture.**

I. Introduction

Cloud computing has become the dominant paradigm for deploying scalable and elastic services. However, the growing heterogeneity of modern infrastructures, including container orchestration platforms, serverless computing, and hybrid cloud-edge deployments, introduces new challenges for modeling and evaluating such systems in a systematic and repeatable manner. In this context, discrete-event simulation remains a fundamental tool for studying resource allocation policies, autoscaling strategies, load balancing mechanisms, and cost evaluation models.

This paper introduces a declarative, plugin-oriented architecture for cloud simulation and evaluates it using `Nuberu`, an internal prototype that embodies the proposed design.

The main contributions of this paper are:

- The design of a modular and reproducible simulation architecture based on dynamic plugin discovery and decoupled component integration.
- An extensible plugin system that supports declarative simulation configuration through YAML (Yet Another Markup Language) files and static interface validation through Python `Protocols`.
- A practical validation scenario that demonstrates the framework's support for traceability, component reuse, and reproducibility, and showcases its applicability across diverse runtime configurations.

The remainder of this paper is organized as follows: Section II reviews related simulation frameworks; Section III presents the simulator architecture; Section IV details the plugin system and extensibility model; Section V provides a simple yet comprehensive use case to validate the architectural design; and Section VI concludes the paper, summarizing key findings and outlining directions for future work.

II. Related Work

Simulation has long been a fundamental tool for evaluating cloud infrastructures, as real-world experimentation is often prohibitively expensive, time-consuming, and difficult to reproduce. Numerous simulation frameworks have been developed to support the study of cloud systems, each focusing on specific aspects, such as resource provisioning, scheduling policies, or cost modeling.

CloudSim [1] is one of the most established simulators, providing a general-purpose Java framework for modeling datacenters, Virtual Machines (VMs), and application workloads. Despite its configurability, CloudSim lacks a plugin architecture, is tightly coupled to Java workflows, and requires code modification to explore alternative policies, which limits its adaptability and reproducibility.

SimGrid [2] is another mature toolkit for modeling large-scale distributed systems, supporting diverse paradigms, such as High Performance Computing (HPC) and Grid computing. While it enables precise modeling of network and computing resources and has been widely adopted in the systems research community, its focus is broader than cloud infrastructures, and its extensibility relies on low-level Application Programming Interfaces (APIs) rather than composable modules.

Beyond these foundational tools, several recent surveys [3]–[7] systematically review cloud simulation frameworks, identifying common limitations and areas for future research. Mansouri et al. [3] evaluated 33 simulators and concluded that no single tool covers all required dimensions, calling for improvements in Mobile Cloud Computing (MCC) [3][8], federated environments [9], and emerging paradigms, such as edge, fog, and Internet Of Things (IoT) [10][11]. Other studies [4][5] stress the lack of integrated support for security, dynamic behavior, or complex task prioritization, and emphasize the need for reproducibility, flexibility, and modularity in future frameworks.

More recently, several simulators written in Python have gained attention for their accessibility and extensibility. *Yet Another Fog Simulator (YAFS)* [10] simulates microservice deployments over user-defined network topologies, using the SimPy engine, and supports modular control over service placement and routing policies. Although it exhibits high flexibility for customizing placement, routing, and scheduling strategies, allowing dynamic scenario definition via class extension and functions integration, it lacks an explicit plugin system for external and decoupled integration of new core components. As a result, adding new functionality in YAFS often requires more intrusive modifications to the core codebase. *Cloudy* [12], by contrast, introduces a hybrid discrete-time and event-driven simulator with native Graphics Processing Unit (GPU) support and integration plans for optimization and machine learning (ML) libraries. However, its extensibility depends on manual template duplication, and it lacks a unified declarative configuration system. Finally, *ECLYPSE* [13], a preprint that has not undergone peer review, focuses on simulating composable cloud architectures with an emphasis on reproducibility. Its extensibility is achieved through a highly modular architecture that leverages object-oriented design principles, such as inheritance, and Python's dynamic capabilities, such as decorators, rather than relying on an explicit, separate plugin ecosystem.

These Python-based initiatives highlight the community's growing interest in modern, flexible, and scriptable simulation platforms. However, to the best of our knowledge, none of them adopts a modular, plugin-based architecture as the one we propose for simulating cloud environments. This makes our approach a novel contribution to the field.

Table I summarizes and contrasts key features of representative simulators in the domain, highlighting their support for modularity, configuration mechanisms, extensibility, and reproducibility, along with their limitations and typical application areas. As shown, none of the existing solutions fully meets all desired characteristics, especially in terms of reproducibility and plugin support.

TABLE I. SIMULATORS COMPARISON

Simulator	Modularity	Declarative Config	Plugin Support	Reproducibility	Limitations	Use Cases
CloudSim	○	○	○	◐	(a)	VM scheduling, provisioning
SimGrid	◐	◐	◐	◐	(b)	HPC, distributed simulation
YAFS	◐	◐	○	●	(c)	Fog, IoT strategy evaluation
Cloudy	◐	○	○	◐	(d)	Cloud + ML, GPU workloads
ECLYPSE	●	○	◐	●	(e)	Edge-cloud prototyping
Nuberu (proto)	●	●	●	●	(f)	Reproducible workflows

Legend of symbols:
● Fully supported
◐ Partially supported
○ Not supported

Limitation notes:
(a) Rigid architecture, low modularity.
(b) Low extensibility, low-level abstractions.
(c) No plugin interface, core modification required.
(d) No declarative config, manual extension required.
(e) Tightly coupled modules, no plugin API.
(f) See Section VI.

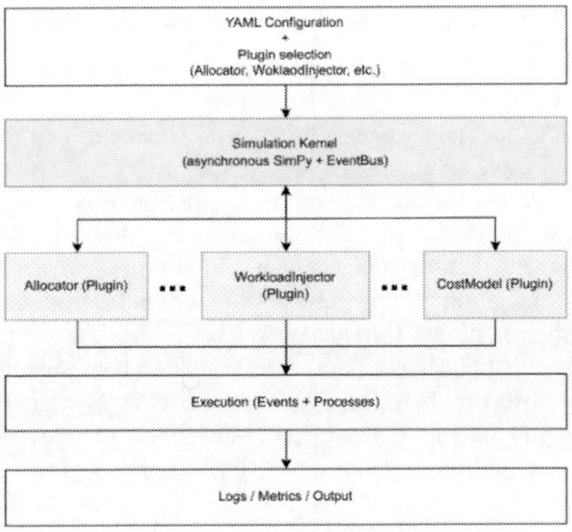

Figure 1. Conceptual high-level architecture

III. SYSTEM ARCHITECTURE

The proposed architecture targets cloud simulation and centers on a discrete-event simulation engine, a global event bus, and a set of pluggable components. This design minimizes coupling between simulation logic and system policies, allowing researchers to prototype, compare, and reproduce complex deployment strategies with minimal implementation effort.

Figure 1 shows a conceptual view of the architecture, structured in layers of abstraction. The uppermost layer corresponds to the declarative experiment definition, where the simulation scenario and plugin selection are specified. The simulation kernel is responsible for orchestrating component instantiation and execution using asynchronous event-driven logic. Plugins encapsulate functional policies and interact only through the EventBus. The bottom layer collects structured outputs, thereby enabling traceability and reproducible analysis.

A. Core Simulation Engine

The simulation kernel follows a discrete-event model similar to `SimPy` library [14], but adopts Python's native `async/await` syntax instead of generator-based event handling. This design choice significantly improves the readability and maintainability of complex simulation flows, particularly those that involve multiple concurrent components, such as virtual machines, containers, and request dispatchers.

B. Component Model and Plugin Architecture

This architecture distinguishes between two user roles: developers, who create alternative implementations of pluggable components by writing plugins that conform to predefined interfaces, and analysts, who design simulation scenarios by selecting among available plugins without modifying the core system. In practice, a single user may assume both roles, developing custom components and designing simulation scenarios.

The simulation framework distinguishes between core components, which define the structure and control flow of the system, and pluggable components, which encapsulate specific, customizable behaviors. Core components include the discrete-event simulation engine, the communication primitives (e.g., event bus and channels) and essential modules, such as the workload injector, allocator, and infrastructure manager. These components are not pluggable themselves, but delegate critical functionality—such as workload characteristics, allocation strategy, or cost modeling—to user-defined plugins.

The mechanisms for dynamic discovery, registration, and static validation of these plugins are detailed in Section IV.

C. Event Bus and Inter-component Communication

Components communicate through a central event bus, implemented as a publish/subscribe mechanism over asynchronous message queues. Each event is categorized by a predefined topic (e.g., `VM_STARTED`, `REQUEST_COMPLETED`) and includes metadata, such as simulation time, origin, and payload. This decoupled communication model ensures that components remain independent and composable, facilitating experimentation and instrumentation without introducing tight coupling or global state dependencies.

The event bus is not limited to simulation components: additional observers (e.g., loggers, metric collectors, or debugging tools) can be implemented and subscribed to relevant event topics at runtime without modifying existing logic.

D. Simulation Configuration

The simulation runtime is configured declaratively via a YAML specifying parameters such as the simulation duration, the names of the plugins to be loaded for each functional component, and the input data, such as workloads, infrastructure specifications, performance data or allocation strategies. It can also define external data sources, such as workload traces in custom formats, to be parsed and injected at runtime by compatible plugins. This enables integration with external tools, such as cost optimizers, whose solutions can be imported through the appropriate plugin.

The architecture follows a *microkernel-inspired* design, in which the simulation engine acts as a lightweight orchestrator. Pluggable components are dynamically instantiated, operate in isolated asynchronous processes, and communicate exclusively through event-based interactions. This design allows for flexible composability and simplifies the development and integration of experiment-specific logic without entangling it with the simulation kernel.

IV. Plugin System and Extensibility

A. Plugin Discovery and Registration

The architecture uses the `pluggy` library [15] to support dynamic plugin discovery using Python's `entry_points` mechanism. Each plugin is an installable python package which registers itself in the `pyproject.toml` file under a specific namespace (e.g., `application_model.llm`, `cost_model.default`), which enables the simulation framework to identify the type and logical name of each component. Once installed in the Python environment, plugins are automatically discovered at runtime without requiring any additional code modification.

Multiple plugins of the same type can be installed and selected declaratively through the YAML configuration file.

If a plugin declared in the YAML configuration cannot be found or does not conform to the expected interface, the simulation engine is designed to abort execution and issue a descriptive error. This validation occurs at startup time, before any event execution, ensuring that core simulation behavior remains consistent and reproducible, even when user-defined extensions are used in the configuration. Non-essential third-party plugins, such as auxiliary observers or loggers, may fail gracefully with a warning, allowing the simulation to proceed when their absence does not compromise correctness.

B. Interface Contracts via Protocols

Each pluggable component in the architecture adheres to two complementary interface mechanisms. First, a *hook specification* (`hookspec`) is defined using `pluggy`, which declares the methods that a plugin must implement to be properly registered and invoked at runtime. Second a Python `Protocol` interface is used for each plugin type, enabling static type checking and improved developer experience. These protocols specify the required methods (e.g., `get_workloads()`, `apply_allocation()`, `compute_cost()`) and allow for static verification using tools, such as `mypy`.

This dual-layer interface ensures runtime compatibility via `pluggy`, while also providing static guarantees, editor support, and better documentation through `Protocol`. Together, these mechanisms improve reliability, reduce integration errors, and facilitate the rapid development of new components.

V. Experimental Validation: Comparing Optimized Allocations with Simulated Behavior

To demonstrate how the proposed architecture supports rigorous, scenario-driven evaluation, we present a case study executed with *Nuberu*, a prototype that instantiates our design. The goal is to show how the framework can expose hidden assumptions in external decision-making tools, such as mathematical optimizers, and thus guide their refinement.

Optimizers based on mathematical models, such as linear programming, often rely on idealized assumptions about workload, resource performance, and system behavior. This section investigates to what extent such optimized allocations remain effective when deployed in a more realistic simulated

TABLE II. PERFORMANCE IN REQUEST PER SECOND (RPS) OF EACH CONTAINER CLASS ON EVERY VM INSTANCE CLASS

C. Class / VM I. Class	cc0app0	cc0app1	cc1app0	cc1app1	cc2app0	cc2app1
c5.2xlarge	2.10	0.46	4.30	0.96	6.35	1.63
c5.large	2.10	0.46	4.30	0.96	6.35	1.63
c5.xlarge	2.10	0.46	4.30	0.96	6.35	1.63
c6i.2xlarge	2.29	0.50	4.71	1.02	6.82	1.76
c6i.large	2.29	0.50	4.71	1.02	6.82	1.76
c6i.xlarge	2.29	0.50	4.71	1.02	6.82	1.76

environment. By simulating the deployment plan produced by the optimizer under multiple runtime conditions, we aim to identify discrepancies, stress points, and potential modeling oversights. This not only validates the practical viability of the computed solution but also highlights the role of simulation as a complementary tool for refining optimization strategies.

A. Description of the scenario to simulate

The scenario to be simulated is the output of an optimizer, *Conlloovia* [16], that solves a linear programming problem to allocate container replicas on VMs to minimize cost while ensuring the throughput of each application reaches or exceeds its 95th percentile over the forecast load trace. Inputs include:

- VM instance classes (including cost, cores and memory),
- container classes (defining CPU/memory requirements),
- and throughput performance matrices for each container class/VM instance class pair (see Table II).

As an example, we analyze a one-hour segment from one of the scenarios presented in Section 5.4 of [16]. It involves two deployed applications, app0 and app1, each with a one-hour request trace that exhibits different dynamics: app0 maintains a stable average load of 39 rps with a 95th-percentile (p95) of 44 rps, whereas app1 shows a variable load whose average rate changes over time, with a p95 of 117 rps (see Figure 2). The optimizer's solution deploys 38 VMs across three instance types and 126 container replicas from three classes (one for app0 and two for app1), as depicted in Figure 3.

Using a custom plugin, the simulator can read this allocation directly from the files generated by *Conlloovia* and use it to: bootstrap the VMs, start the containers, inject traffic (using a user selected mode), and route requests through a configurable load balancer. Each container simulates service time based on the performance data, and metrics are collected throughout.

B. Experimental design

To assess the flexibility and analytical power of the simulator, we simulate the same scenario under 16 configurations combining four binary dimensions

1) **Load injection (Load)**: either from the original trace (replaying realistic variability) or as a synthetic Poisson process which ensures the same p95 throughput value used by the optimizer.

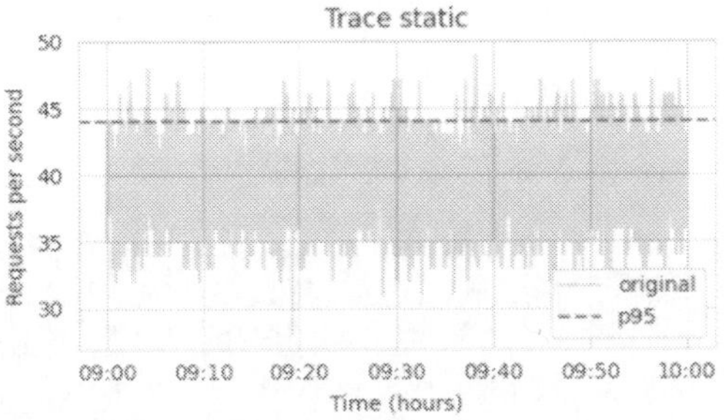

(a) Workload for app0

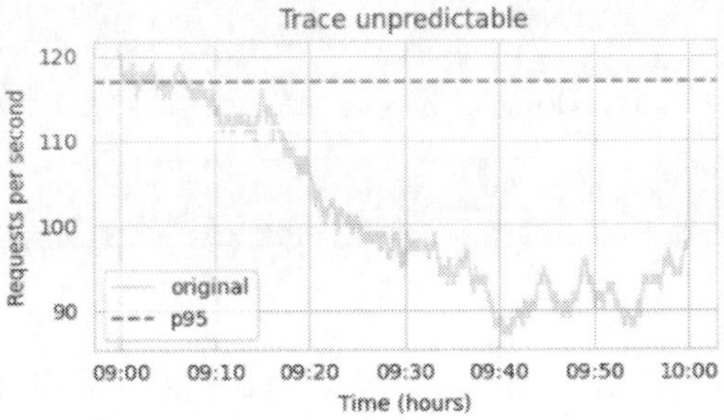

(b) Workload for app1

Figure 2. Plot of the workloads for each application

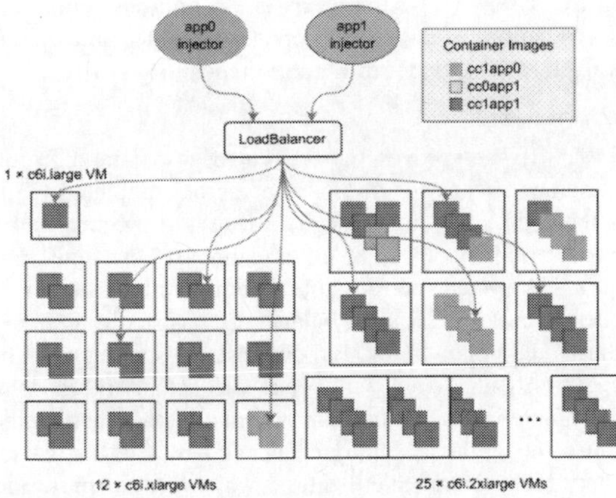

Figure 3. Scenario to simulate

2) **Load Balancing (LB)**: either a simple Round-Robin (RR) or a Smooth Weighted Round-Robin (SWRR), as the one used in nginx [17], which takes into account the performance differences between containers to assign appropriate weights.
3) **Queuing model (Q)**: either none (requests are dropped if busy) or bounded queues of size 1000 per container.
4) **Termination policy (Term)**: either 'hard' (containers are terminated immediately) or 'drain' (containers are kept alive to complete queued requests).

TABLE III. SUMMARY OF KEY METRICS (SUCCESS RATE AND TOTAL COST) FOR THE 16 SIMULATION SCENARIOS.

Q	Term	LB	Load	app0	app1	cost
0	drain	RR	poisson	82.6%	95.0%	$10.66
			trace	100.0%	98.5%	$10.63
		SWRR	poisson	82.6%	94.8%	$10.66
			trace	100.0%	94.4%	$10.63
	hard	RR	poisson	82.6%	94.9%	$10.62
			trace	100.0%	98.5%	$10.62
		SWRR	poisson	82.6%	94.8%	$10.62
			trace	100.0%	94.3%	$10.62
1000	drain	RR	poisson	100.0%	99.8%	$16.56
			trace	100.0%	99.8%	$16.53
		SWRR	poisson	100.0%	100.0%	$10.66
			trace	100.0%	100.0%	$10.63
	hard	RR	poisson	100.0%	99.2%	$10.62
			trace	100.0%	99.2%	$10.62
		SWRR	poisson	100.0%	100.0%	$10.62
			trace	100.0%	100.0%	$10.62

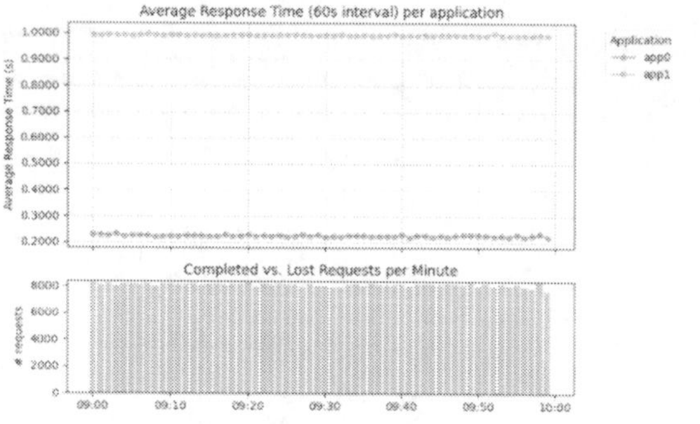

(a) Synthetic workload with Poisson arrivals

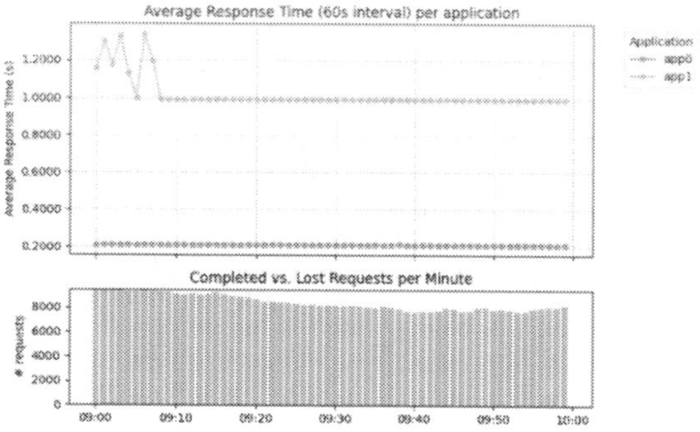

(b) Trace based workload

Figure 4. Response time and number of requests completed for the scenarios with SWRR balancing, large queues and 'hard' termination (last two rows of Table III)

This design allows us to evaluate how an optimized deployment responds under diverse execution settings and policies.

Each of the 16 simulations is defined through a YAML file that declares the scenario parameters, input data sources (e.g., system specification and optimal allocation), and the plugin components responsible for parsing external formats, such as Conlloovia. All experiment definitions, input traces and simulation results used to create the tables and figures in this paper are available in a public repository [18].

C. Discussion

Table III summarizes two key metrics obtained from the 16 simulated scenarios: the percentage of completed requests and the total simulated cost. The results provide a compact overview of how different combinations of runtime parameters affect system performance. Configurations that include queueing, and SWRR load balancing consistently deliver the highest completion rates. By contrast, in scenarios with no queues, only the ones which use the actual traces achieve high completion rates. Poisson arrivals degrade performance, because the optimal solution generated by Conlloovia relies on very high container utilization, which in turn presupposes perfectly synchronized request arrivals.

Queues absorb demand spikes and improve request completion, though at the cost of higher response times. The drain policy avoids loss of in-flight or queued requests but prolongs VM usage and increases cost.

Interestingly, the simulated costs match exactly the optimizer's predictions in all scenarios using hard termination, since containers are shut down precisely as scheduled. However, in scenarios with drain termination, VMs remain active longer to complete pending requests, resulting in slightly higher costs. The RR scheduler results in the highest cost because it ignores container performance, leading to long queues of pending requests in the slower containers. These take longer to drain at the end of the simulation, thereby increasing the cost. SWRR balancing proves superior in these scenarios by distributing the load more proportionally across containers with heterogeneous performance, resulting in shorter queues.

Figure 4 shows the evolution of average response times and request completion rates for the SWRR load balancer under a 'hard' termination policy. Subfigure 4a corresponds to a synthetic workload generated as a Poisson arrival process with $\lambda = 34.563$ rps for app0 and $\lambda = 100.718$ rps for app1, ensuring a p95 of 44 rps and 117 rps, respectively, matching the throughput guaranteed by Conlloovia's solution. Subfigure 4b uses a trace-based workload from [16], where the number of requests per second varies over time and is read from Comma Separated Values (CSV) files. In this case, the request rate can be at times above the p95 throughput expected by the solver. This is most noticeable for *app1*, which experiences pressure during the initial minutes, resulting in increased response times. In contrast, *app0* remains stable throughout, even during short periods when its demand exceeds the p95 threshold.

Together, these results confirm the value of simulation not just for performance validation but as a diagnostic tool to uncover modeling assumptions that may not hold under realistic or adverse conditions.

VI. Conclusion and Future Work

This paper has introduced a modular, extensible architecture for cloud simulation frameworks that is explicitly designed to support reproducible and composable experimentation. Based on decoupled components, dynamic plugin discovery, and declarative configuration, the design enables researchers to prototype and compare alternative models for workload generation, resource allocation, and cost evaluation without modifying the simulation core.

By capturing the experimental setup in version-controlled configuration files and generating structured simulation traces, the proposed architecture aligns with the FAIR principles, Findable, Accessible, Interoperable, and Reusable [19]. This foundation enables both local reproducibility and broader community validation of alternative orchestration strategies.

The framework is under active development, with future releases providing curated plugins and scenarios. This work serves as a foundation for reproducible and extensible cloud simulation. Although the current prototype does not yet simulate network communication, I/O operations, or energy consumption, and no validation against real cloud deployments has been performed, it can already handle hundreds of VMs and thousands of requests with acceptable overhead. A complete evaluation of scalability and runtime efficiency is planned as part of future work. Upcoming extensions will enable more complex simulation scenarios. Firstly, we plan to incorporate models for network and I/O operations to support richer and more realistic simulations. Secondly, we will expand the plugin ecosystem with curated modules for common use cases, including auto-scalers, Large Language Model (LLM) serving patterns, spot-instance strategies, and multi-tenant execution. Finally, we will validate the architecture through large-scale comparative studies and evaluate its suitability for hybrid cloud-edge deployments.

ACKNOWLEDGMENT

This research was funded by the project PID2021-124383OB-I00 of the Spanish National Plan for Research, Development and Innovation from the Spanish Ministerio de Ciencia e Innovación.

References

[1] R. N. Calheiros, R. Ranjan, A. Beloglazov, C. A. F. D. Rose, and R. Buyya, "Cloudsim: A toolkit for modeling and simulation of cloud computing environments and evaluation of resource provisioning algorithms," *Software: Practice and Experience*, vol. 41, pp. 23–50, 2011. DOI: https://doi.org/10.1002/spe.995.

[2] H. Casanova, A. Legrand, and M. Quinson, "SimGrid: A generic framework for large-scale distributed experiments," *Tenth International Conference on Computer Modeling and Simulation (uksim 2008)*, pp. 126–131, 2008. DOI: 10.1109/UKSIM.2008.28.

[3] N. Mansouri, R. Ghafari, and B. M. H. Zade, "Cloud Computing simulators: A comprehensive review," *Simulation Modelling Practice and Theory*, vol. 104, p. 102 144, Nov. 2020, ISSN: 1569-190X. DOI: 10.1016/j.simpat.2020.102144.

[4] I. Bambrik, "A survey on Cloud Computing simulation and modeling," *SN Computer Science*, vol. 1, no. 5, p. 249, Aug. 2020, ISSN: 2661-8907. DOI: 10.1007/s42979-020-00273-1.

[5] S. Lata and D. Singh, "Cloud simulation tools: A survey," *AIP Conference Proceedings*, vol. 2555, no. 1, p. 030 003, Oct. 2022, ISSN: 0094-243X. DOI: 10.1063/5.0109181.

[6] F. Fakhfakh, H. H. Kacem, and A. H. Kacem, "Simulation tools for cloud computing: A survey and comparative study," *2017 IEEE/ACIS 16th International Conference on Computer and Information Science (ICIS)*, pp. 221–226, 2017. DOI: https://doi.org/10.1109/ICIS.2017.7959997.

[7] S. V. Margariti, V. V. Dimakopoulos, and G. Tsoumanis, "Modeling and simulation tools for fog computing - a comprehensive survey from a cost perspective," *Future Internet*, vol. 12, p. 89, 2020. DOI: https://doi.org/10.3390/fi12050089.

[8] M. Shiraz, A. Gani, R. H. Khokhar, and E. Ahmed, "An extendable simulation framework for modeling application processing potentials of smart mobile devices for mobile cloud computing," in *2012 10th International Conference on Frontiers of Information Technology*, Dec. 2012, pp. 331–336. DOI: 10.1109/FIT.2012.66.

[9] A. Núñez *et al.*, "iCanCloud: A flexible and scalable cloud infrastructure simulator," *Journal of Grid Computing*, vol. 10, no. 1, pp. 185–209, Mar. 2012, ISSN: 1572-9184. DOI: 10.1007/s10723-012-9208-5.

[10] I. Lera, C. Guerrero, and C. Juiz, "YAFS: A simulator for IoT scenarios in fog computing," *IEEE Access*, vol. 7, pp. 91 745–91 758, 2019. DOI: https://doi.org/10.1109/ACCESS.2019.2927895.

[11] X. Zeng *et al.*, "IOTSim: A simulator for analysing IoT applications," *Journal of Systems Architecture*, Design Automation for Embedded Ubiquitous Computing Systems, vol. 72, pp. 93–107, Jan. 2017, ISSN: 1383-7621. DOI: 10.1016/j.sysarc.2016.06.008.

[12] A. Siavashi and M. Momtazpour, "Cloudy: A Pythonic cloud simulator," *2024 32nd International Conference on Electrical Engineering (ICEE)*, pp. 1–5, 2024. DOI: https://doi.org/10.1109/ICEE63041.2024.10667881.

[13] J. Massa *et al.*, "ECLYPSE: A Python framework for simulation and emulation of the cloud-edge continuum," *ArXiv*, vol. abs/2501.17126, pp. 1–16, 2025. DOI: https://doi.org/10.48550/arXiv.2501.17126.

[14] SimPy Development Team, "Simpy: Discrete event simulation for python," Version 4.1.2, 2025, Available from: https://simpy.readthedocs.io/ [retrieved: July, 2025].

[15] pytest-dev, "Pluggy: A minimalist production ready plugin system," Version 1.5.0, 2025, Available from: https://pluggy.readthedocs.io/ [retrieved: July, 2025].

[16] J. Entrialgo, M. García, J. García, J. M. López, and J. L. Díaz, "Joint autoscaling of containers and virtual machines for cost optimization in container clusters," *Journal of Grid Computing*, vol. 22, pp. 1–24, 2024. DOI: https://doi.org/10.1007/s10723-023-09732-4.

[17] M. Dounin, "Upstream: Smooth weighted round-robin balancing," Commit, nginx source tree, May 2012, Available from: https://github.com/phusion/nginx/commit/27e94984486058d73157038f7950a0a36ecc6e35 [retrieved: July, 2025].

[18] R. Luque, J. L. Díaz, J. Entrialgo, and R. Usamentiaga, "Nuberu simulation results – experiments repository," 2025, Available from: https://github.com/asi-uniovi/nuberu-experiments-results [retrieved: July, 2025].

[19] M. D. Wilkinson *et al.*, "The FAIR guiding principles for scientific data management and stewardship," *Scientific Data*, vol. 3, p. 160 018, 2016. DOI: 10.1038/sdata.2016.18.

Spatially Partitioned Robust Optimization for Energy-Efficient Underwater Wireless Sensor Networks under Simulation-Informed Network Conditions

Ozhan Eren and Aysegul Altin-Kayhan
Department of Industrial Engineering
TOBB University of Economics and Technology
Ankara, Turkiye
e-mail: {ozhaneren | aaltin}@etu.edu.tr

***Abstract*—Underwater Wireless Sensor Networks (UWSNs) have attracted considerable attention for decades, owing to their broad spectrum of application areas. Despite technological advances, designing energy-efficient underwater communication architectures remains a key challenge due to the harsh and dynamic environment. Among the various factors influencing the performance of UWSNs, data traffic load emerges as a critical component, particularly in relation to the operational lifetime. Additionally, with their increasing deployment, Autonomous Underwater Vehicles (AUVs) are integrated into UWSNs in various roles. However, their presence introduces new challenges that require the design of robust sensor network configurations capable of effectively detecting and interacting with AUVs. This paper addresses a novel simulation-driven and uncertainty-aware design scheme for energy-efficient UWSNs. Building on prior studies of data traffic uncertainty in wireless sensor networks and AUV mobility, this paper employs a simulation environment that captures the integrated interactions among mobile targets, sensor nodes, and seabed topography to evaluate the proposed network model. Furthermore, recognizing that the unrestricted mobility of navigating vehicles can cause variations in data generation rates across the network, we apply balanced 3D K-means partitioning to structure the network for uncertainty modeling. The proposed robust optimization framework is evaluated against a deterministic baseline under varying traffic conditions induced by vehicle movement. To capture uncertainty at multiple scales, we incorporate parameters representing sensor-specific deviations and regional conservativeness, enabling examination of their impact on solution stability. Results indicate that the robust framework consistently outperforms the deterministic approach across varying levels of traffic deviation under the applied spatial partitioning scheme.**

Keywords-Simulation; spatial partitioning; underwater wireless sensor networks; traffic uncertainty; robust optimization.

I. Introduction

Underwater Wireless Sensor Networks (UWSNs) have become essential for diverse underwater applications, including environmental monitoring, offshore exploration, scientific investigation, and marine operations involving submarine detection, AUV-assisted monitoring, and maritime observation for situational awareness [1]–[4]. Comprising spatially distributed acoustic sensor nodes, UWSNs are designed to observe and transmit underwater phenomena to a base station, often through multi-hop communication schemes. Due to the inherent challenges in accessing and replacing deployed sensor nodes, energy efficiency is a critical design consideration.

Recent advancements in underwater acoustic communication and the integration of heterogeneous underwater platforms have significantly expanded the capabilities of UWSNs. Nevertheless, these networks still face persistent operational challenges, especially in dynamic and mission-oriented environments. The need to detect and track mobile entities such as submarines and AUVs creates sensing demands that vary spatially and temporally. As these entities move through the monitored area, nearby nodes experience fluctuating sensing activity, resulting in uneven data generation and shifting traffic patterns. Such imbalances result in localized energy depletion, reduced network availability, and premature degradation of system performance [5]. Therefore, understanding how target mobility affects sensing dynamics and communication load is crucial for developing resilient UWSNs.

Our primary goal is to design an event-driven UWSN capable of monitoring a designated underwater area through a robust optimization approach. For a comprehensive literature review on the topic, the interested reader is referred to [6], where a preliminary formulation was introduced to address uncertainty using a global robustness framework. Building upon this foundation, the current study extends the analysis by incorporating spatial heterogeneity through a region-based modeling strategy. To better capture spatial variability in uncertainties, we partition the 3D underwater network into sub-regions, allowing region-wise deviations for detailed analysis of localized uncertainties. Several spatial partitioning methods, such as grid-based schemes, clustering algorithms, and Voronoi tessellations, have been explored in underwater studies [7]–[9]. In this study, we adopt a balanced 3D K-means clustering approach to achieve spatial division that reflects the structure and operational characteristics of underwater environments. This method provides a practical and effective means to form spatially compact and evenly sized regions, facilitating the application of localized deviation scenarios and enabling clearer analysis of their region-specific impacts on network behavior [10].

More specifically, we address the problem of minimizing the maximum initial battery allocation to sensors while ensuring sustained network operation over a specified time period. The robust design framework determines energy allocations that remain feasible across all admissible data rate variations, guided by a reference lifetime defined during the configuration phase. In contrast, the nominal design which does not consider uncertainty may lead to premature network failure under slight deviations from expected sensing rates. Subsequent evaluation shows that the robust design consistently achieves network lifetimes at or near the reference lifetime, demonstrating improved resilience and reliability compared to the nominal approach.

Finally, we present detailed analyses illustrating the performance of both robust and deterministic designs during the implementation phase, based on comprehensive tests conducted across a wide range of scenarios.

The major contributions of this study are as follows:

- We utilize a comprehensive simulation framework that integrates underwater vehicle movements, sensor deployment, and detailed seabed topography derived from real-world bathymetric data. This allows realistic estimation of sensing rates as they vary with sensor locations and target trajectories, forming a critical input for our robust model.
- We introduce a novel robust optimization framework for UWSNs featuring balanced 3D K-means spatial partitioning. This approach captures localized uncertainty and traffic load variations more precisely, enhancing the network's resilience and performance.
- We present comprehensive test results on the performances of the nominal design made without considering the uncertainty in the configuration phase and the robust design under a polyhedral uncertainty definition in different sensing rate scenarios when they are put into practice. The test results indicate that minor variations in sensing rates substantially impair the performance of the deterministic design, whereas the robust design consistently preserves the expected performance and extends operational longevity relative to the deterministic approach.

The remainder of this paper is organized as follows. Section II presents the main components of our optimization framework. We begin by introducing an optimization model for the deterministic design of underwater networks in Section II-A, followed by the robust counterpart formulation that enables analysis under uncertainty in Section II-B. Section II-C then describes the simulation environment used to derive sensor data generation rates. Computational results and performance analysis are provided in Section III, organized around the configuration and implementation phases. Finally, Section IV concludes the study with a summary and directions for future research.

II. Problem Definition

A. The Network Model

In this section, we will first present the classical mathematical model for the problem of efficient energy allocation to sensors. Next, we will block out how we integrate the uncertainty in detection rates into the model within the framework of robust optimization. In all models, we assume that the sensors and sink possess all the necessary capacity to process the data that they are supposed to transmit and receive, respectively. As indicated in [11] and [12], we consider only transmitting and receiving energy consumption, which are dominant with respect to other forms of consumptions like sensing and processing. The channel characteristics are considered ideal and the number of retransmissions due to failures is negligible [13]. We present the notation used in the paper in Table I.

Given the data sensing rates of the sensors, the following mathematical model ($E_{\max}^{\det}$) aims to determine the initial energy allocations for the sensors, which ensures the energy-efficient operation of the network over default network lifetime T:

TABLE I. Sets, parameters, and decision variables.

Sets	
N	Set of sensor nodes
N_G	Set of all nodes in the network, i.e., $N \cup \{BS\}$, where BS denotes the base station
$\mathscr{R}$	Set of sensor subsets (regions), i.e., $\mathscr{R} = \{R_1, R_2, \ldots\}$ with $R_j \subseteq N$
R_j	A subset of sensors forming region R_j, i.e., $R_j \in \mathscr{R}$
$\mathscr{J}$	Index set of regions, i.e., $\mathscr{J} = \{1, 2, \ldots, \lvert\mathscr{R}\rvert\}$
$\mathscr{S}$	Set of sensing rate vectors within feasible intervals satisfying regional sum constraints
A	Set of directed one-hop connections: $A = \{(i,j) : i \in N, j \in N_G \setminus \{i\}, d_{ij} \leq R\}$
G	Directed graph representing the network, i.e., $G = (N_G, A)$
$\mathscr{U}$	Uncertainty set of feasible sensing rate vectors
Parameters	
d_{ij}	Euclidean distance between $i \in N$ and $j \in N_G$
T	Default network lifetime in configuration
R	Transmission range for sensors (m)
e_{ij}^{TX}	Energy cost of transmission from $i \in N$ to $j \in N_G$ per bit (mJ/bit)
e_{ji}^{RX}	Energy cost of reception by $i \in N$ from $j \in N$ per bit (mJ/bit)
s_k	Sensing rate of sensor $k \in N$ (bit/s)
s_{nom}^k	Nominal sensing rate of sensor $k \in N$ (bit/s)
s_{dev}^k	Sensing rate deviation of sensor $k \in N$ (bit/s)
α	Regional uncertainty budget
β_{kj}	Binary parameter indicating whether sensor k belongs to region R_j, where $j \in \mathscr{J}$
Variables	
f_{ij}^k	Proportion of s_k sensed by $k \in N$ transmitted on $(i,j) \in A$
e_i	Initial energy to be allocated to $i \in N$ (mJ)
$e_{\max}^{rob}$	Maximum energy assigned to a sensor in N under the robust model (mJ)
$e_{\max}^{det}$	Maximum energy assigned to a sensor in N under the deterministic model (mJ)
μ_{ik}, λ_{ik}	Deviation duals
θ_{ji}	Regional budget dual variable

$$min \quad e_{\max}^{\det} \tag{1}$$

$s.t.$

$$\sum_{(i,j)\in A} f_{ij}^k - \sum_{(j,i)\in A} f_{ji}^k = \begin{cases} 1 & \text{if } i = k \\ -1 & \text{if } i = BS \\ 0 & \text{otherwise} \end{cases}$$

$$\forall i \in N_G,\ k \in N \tag{2}$$

$$\sum_{k\in N}\left[\sum_{(i,j)\in A} Te_{ij}^{TX} f_{ij}^k s_k + \sum_{(j,i)\in A} Te_{ji}^{RX} f_{ji}^k s_k\right]$$

$$\leq e_i \qquad \forall i \in N \tag{3}$$

$$e_{\max}^{\det} \geq e_i \qquad \forall i \in N \tag{4}$$

$$f_{ij}^k \geq 0 \qquad \forall (i,j) \in A,\ k \in N \tag{5}$$

$$e_i \geq 0 \qquad \forall i \in N \tag{6}$$

B. The Network Model for Polyhedral Sensing Rates

The polyhedral uncertainty model is widely adopted in robust optimization due to its favorable balance between computational efficiency and strong worst-case protection. It enables reformulation into linear programs, preserving the complexity of deterministic models and allowing scalable solutions using standard optimization techniques. Compared to ellipsoidal sets [14], which require second-order or semi-definite programming, the polyhedral approach offers greater tractability [15].

Unlike probabilistic methods that rely on distributional assumptions and often lead to nonconvex or chance-constrained formulations, the polyhedral model guarantees feasibility without stochastic knowledge [16]. It also flexibly captures parameter dependencies, supporting diverse use cases.

To apply localized uncertainty, sensor nodes were partitioned into spatially compact, equally sized groups using the balanced K-Means method, which has demonstrated effectiveness across various domains [17][18]. This structure facilitates region-specific deviation modeling in underwater network design by minimizing intra-cluster distances while maintaining uniform group sizes.

The balanced K-Means algorithm divides the sensor set N into k clusters of equal size n_i, minimizing intra-cluster variance. At each iteration t, cluster centroids are updated as $C_i(t+1) = \frac{1}{n_i}\sum_{j\in C_i(t)} x_j$. Sensors are then reassigned via a weighted bipartite matching process that minimizes the total squared distance to centroids, subject to $|C_i| = n_i$. This is achieved using a virtual slot index $a \in [1, n]$ with edge weights defined as $W(a,i) = \text{dist}(x_i, C_{(a \bmod k)+1})^2$ for all $i \in [1, n]$ [10].

Unlike standard K-Means, the equal-size constraint introduces global dependencies, requiring iterative reassignments to balance cluster sizes and minimize variance. This ensures a fair and symmetric robustness formulation by avoiding region-specific scaling and simplifying constraints [10][19].

Under this formulation, deviations are restricted to one region at a time. To prevent over-conservatism from overly broad uncertainty sets, we adopt a region-based version of the Γ-uncertainty model [15], enabling tractable and focused robustness without excessive conservatism.

We define the polyhedron of feasible sensing rates as the set of all s_k satisfying $s_k^{\text{nom}} \le s_k \le s_k^{\text{nom}} + s_k^{\text{dev}}$ for each sensor $k \in N$, and for all regions $R_j \in \mathscr{R}$, the sum of sensing rates within R_j satisfies $\sum_{k\in R_j} s_k \le (1+\alpha)\sum_{k\in R_j} s_k^{\text{nom}}$. More explicitly, $\mathscr{U} = \{s_k \in \mathscr{S} : s_k^{\text{nom}} \le s_k \le s_k^{\text{nom}} + s_k^{\text{dev}}\ \forall k \in N;\ \sum_{k\in R_j} s_k \le (1+\alpha)\sum_{k\in R_j} s_k^{\text{nom}}\ \forall R_j \in \mathscr{R}\}$. This formulation allows for individual deviations while controlling aggregate sensing rates regionally, balancing robustness with practical conservatism.

The worst-case realization of the left-hand side in the energy constraint leads to the robust counterpart constraint $\max_{s\in\mathscr{U}} \sum_{k\in N} s_k \cdot a_{ik} \le e_i$, where $\mathscr{U}$ is the uncertainty set defined by the intervals and regional budget constraints, and a_{ik} denotes the energy consumption at node i associated with the sensing activity of node k, represented in the original constraint as $\sum_{(i,j)\in A} Te_{ij}^{\text{TX}} f_{ij}^k + \sum_{(j,i)\in A} Te_{ji}^{\text{RX}} f_{ji}^k$. We now dualize the inner maximization problem. The primal form of this inner maximization is:

$$\max_{s_k} \quad \sum_{k\in N} s_k \cdot a_{ik} \tag{7}$$

$s.t.$

$$s_k^{\text{nom}} \le s_k \qquad \forall k \in N \tag{8}$$

$$s_k \le s_k^{\text{nom}} + s_k^{\text{dev}} \qquad \forall k \in N \tag{9}$$

$$\sum_{k\in N} \beta_{kj} s_k \le (1+\alpha)\sum_{k\in N} \beta_{kj} s_k^{\text{nom}} \qquad \forall j \in \mathscr{J} \tag{10}$$

$$\beta_{kj} \in \{0,1\} \qquad \forall k \in N,\ \forall j \in \mathscr{J} \tag{11}$$

Introducing dual variables $\mu_{ik} \ge 0$ for the upper bounds, $\lambda_{ik} \ge 0$ for the lower bounds, and $\theta_{ji} \ge 0$ for the regional constraints, the dual of this linear maximization becomes:

$$\min_{\mu,\lambda,\theta} \quad \sum_{k\in N} \mu_{ik}(s_k^{\text{nom}} + s_k^{\text{dev}}) - \sum_{k\in N} \lambda_{ik} s_k^{\text{nom}} + (1+\alpha)\sum_{j\in\mathscr{J}} \theta_{ji} \sum_{k\in N} \beta_{kj} s_k^{\text{nom}} \tag{12}$$

$s.t.$

$$\mu_{ik} - \lambda_{ik} + \sum_{j\in\mathscr{J}} \theta_{ji}\beta_{kj} \ge a_{ik} \quad \forall k \in N \tag{13}$$

$$\mu_{ik}, \lambda_{ik} \ge 0 \qquad \forall i \in N, k \in N \tag{14}$$

$$\theta_{ji} \ge 0 \qquad \forall j \in \mathscr{J}, i \in N \tag{15}$$

Consequently, replacing the original constraint with its dual leads to the robust energy constraint. The resulting compact LP model, which represents the robust counterpart of $E_{\max}^{\text{det}}$, is denoted by $E_{\max}^{\text{rob}}$:

$$min \quad e_{\max}^{\text{rob}} \tag{16}$$

$s.t.$

$$\sum_{k\in N}\Big[\mu_{ik}(s_k^{\text{nom}} + s_k^{\text{dev}}) - \lambda_{ik} s_k^{\text{nom}} + \sum_{j\in\mathscr{J}} \theta_{ji}(1+\alpha)\beta_{kj} s_k^{\text{nom}}\Big] \le e_i \qquad \forall i \in N \tag{17}$$

$$e_{\max}^{\text{rob}} \ge e_i \qquad \forall i \in N \tag{18}$$

$$(2), (5), (6), (13) - (15).$$

C. Simulation Model

The simulation framework developed for underwater sensor networks encompasses several critical stages to capture the complex interactions between sensors, underwater vehicles, and the seafloor environment. These stages ensure realistic modeling of detection processes and yield the data generation rate as a key uncertainty parameter to support the accuracy of robust network model.

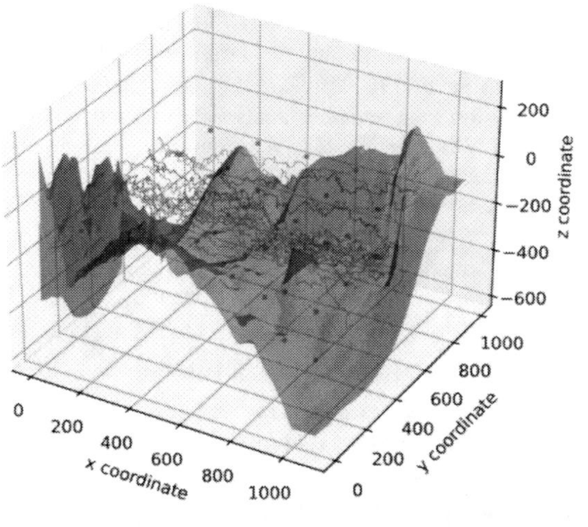

Figure 1. Trajectories of AUVs in 3D underwater environment

The process begins with generating detailed bathymetric maps to accurately characterize the underwater terrain. Underwater vehicles are initialized at random locations, and their trajectories are simulated based on predefined mobility rules formulated to emulate smooth underwater motion. A network of 40 sensors is deployed in a grid-like fashion with terrain-aware feasibility checks and appropriate detection radii to ensure sufficient coverage [20]. Each sensor is assumed to possess both an absolute detection area, which is designed to be tangential to those of neighboring nodes, and a surrounding probabilistic zone where the likelihood of detection decays with distance due to signal attenuation. This dual-layer sensing model captures detection uncertainty beyond the immediate sensing range, resulting in a more precise representation of sensing behavior.

Sensor detection durations are evaluated over discrete time intervals, integrating continuous environmental monitoring with event-driven sensing triggered by the transitions of underwater vehicles. In each run, a total of 100 underwater vehicles follow their trajectories, during which sensors remain actively engaged in monitoring and record the cumulative durations of the detection process. These values are normalized by the total simulation time to compute individual data generation rates. To account for environmental variability, the process is independently repeated 30 times using different random seeds, and the consistency observed across these repetitions confirms the reliability of the estimated sensing rates used in the optimization model. The modular simulation framework, implemented in Python and conceptually detailed in [6], supports flexible modeling of sensor coverage, AUV mobility, and energy-aware operations, thereby providing a reliable foundation for both current analyses and potential extensions involving more detailed energy models. The energy model adopted in this study is based on the 10-level discrete power scheme described in [21], in which each level defines a communication range along with the corresponding energy cost per bit for both transmission and reception, thereby capturing distance-dependent energy consumption. Figure 1 presents an overview of the simulation environment along with the intruder trajectories.

III. Computational Results

In this section, we present the results of numerical experiments conducted in two main phases. First, we examine the impact of incorporating uncertainty into energy allocation decisions during the configuration phase. Second, we compare the performance of robust and deterministic network designs in terms of operational lifetime once deployed. These analyses aim to evaluate the network's capability to maintain performance when exposed to potential uncertainties after configuration.

In the deterministic model, all parameters are assumed to be known with complete accuracy. In contrast, the robust model takes into account possible deviations in the data generation rate, which is based on event-driven measurements observed throughout the simulation. The maximum battery allocations for both the deterministic and robust models are obtained by solving their respective linear programming formulations, denoted as $E^{\text{det}}_{\text{max}}$ and $E^{\text{rob}}_{\text{max}}$, respectively. The goal in both cases is to minimize the highest amount of energy allocated to any single sensor. As expected, the robust model does not yield a better objective value than the deterministic one, since it is designed to handle more demanding and uncertain conditions. Then, we evaluate the practical performance of both configurations by comparing their optimal results across various cases to assess trade-offs and identify the most effective design strategy.

We performed all computations on a 2.50 GHz machine with 16 GB. The optimization problems were solved by IBM ILOG CPLEX Optimization Studio Version: 20.1.0 under a runtime limit of 720 seconds.

A. Configuration Phase: Maximum Energy Allocation

The aim of this section is to analyze how variations in data generation rates, characterized by different uncertainty sets, affect the maximum battery allocation values (E^{max}) as determined by both the deterministic model ($E^{\text{max}}_{\text{det}}$) and the robust model ($E^{\text{max}}_{rob}$) during the configuration phase. In both models, the default network lifetime is fixed at 100 seconds.

To assess the sensitivity of the robust framework in comparison to the deterministic one, we vary the regional uncertainty budget $\alpha \in \{0.01, 0.05, 0.10, 0.20\}$ within a selected region. Additionally, sensors are allowed to deviate individually by up to three standard deviations (σ) to reflect node-specific uncertainty bounds. For each (α, σ) combination, a robust provisioning is generated to enable lifetime analysis in Section III-B.

These uncertainty parameters determine the level of conservatism in the robust design: larger values lead to broader uncertainty sets, thereby requiring more energy provisioning to guard against adverse scenarios. Although the robust model yields more conservative objective values during the configuration phase, it consistently ensures reliable performance in implementation. In contrast, the deterministic design shows greater performance degradation even under minor deviations.

At this stage, considering the standard deviation bands σ_i (for $i = 1, 2, 3$) with $\sigma_1 < \sigma_2 < \sigma_3$, it is observed that the maximum battery capacity increases against higher σ_j, while all other parameters remain constant. A similar trend is evident across the localized conservativeness levels α_i, though the growth follows a sublinear pattern in percentage terms. This suggests that higher regional conservativeness entails relatively modest additional battery provisioning during the configuration phase, while still ensuring robustness. Although variations in α contribute to the observed gains, the deviation level σ emerges as the primary factor driving regional disparities, as illustrated in Figure 2.

In this context, for the least conservative scenario ($\alpha = 0.05$, σ_1), the average increase in maximum battery allocation under the robust configuration relative to the deterministic baseline is 2.97%. Under the most conservative setting ($\alpha = 0.20$, σ_3), this increase reaches 9.85%.

Region-wise analysis further reveals that sub-region R_1 consistently requires the highest battery allocation, whereas R_3 necessitates the lowest, across all σ levels. This pattern is likely related to the higher sensitivity of critical constraints in R_1 to input deviations. In particular, several nodes in R_1 appear to operate near their feasibility limits. In such cases, even small perturbations can activate binding constraints with high dual values, amplifying their influence on battery provisioning and, in turn, the objective function.

B. Implementation Phase: Network lifetime

This section analyzes the performance of networks designed with both models, as described in Section

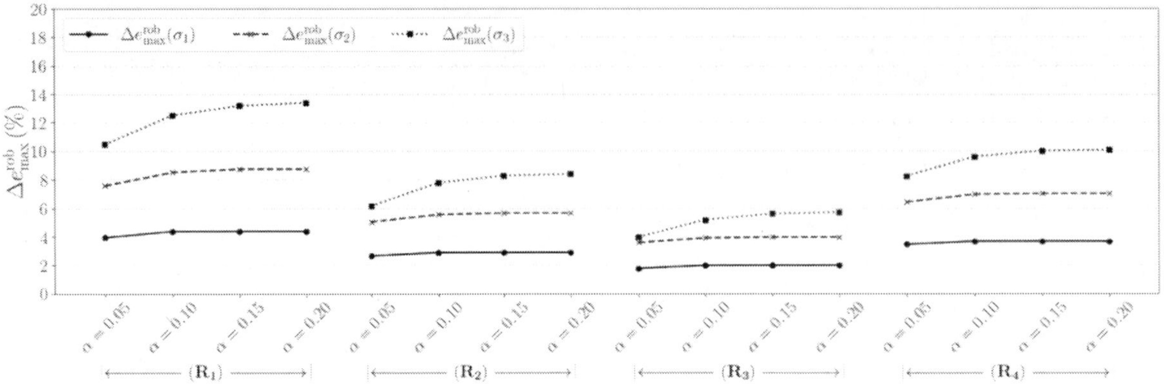

Figure 2. Percentage change of optimal battery capacity across different α and σ values in each sub-region R_j.

III-A, under predetermined parameter combinations. Consequently, given the battery capacities of the sensors and the data transmission paths, the functional duration of each design will be calculated under different data sensing rates and compared with the reference lifetime value T, specified during the design phase. Based on the uncertainty set encompassing the applicable sensing rate vectors for the given network configuration, and for specified values of σ, we generate the set $s' = \{s'_k : k \in N\}$ by selecting sensors whose sensing rates are allowed to deviate from their nominal values and reach the corresponding upper bounds within the predefined sub-regions.

Then, we solve formulations (19) and (21) to determine the lifetime of the deterministic and robust designs in each case, respectively. Herein $f^k_{ij,\text{det}}$ and $f^k_{ij,\text{rob}}$ denote the transmission paths, while e^i_{det} and e^i_{rob} represent the battery capacities obtained by solving E^{det}_{max} and E^{rob}_{max}. Hence, we solve LP models since the only unknowns are T_{det} and T_{rob}.

$$\max\ T_{\text{det}} \tag{19}$$

s.t.

$$\sum_{k\in N}\left[\sum_{(i,j)\in A} T_{\text{det}} e^{TX}_{ij} f^k_{ij,\text{det}} s'_k + \sum_{(j,i)\in A} T_{\text{det}} e^{RX}_{ji} f^k_{ij,\text{det}} s'_k\right] \le e^i_{\text{det}} \qquad \forall i \in N \tag{20}$$

and

$$\max\ T_{\text{rob}} \tag{21}$$

s.t.

$$\sum_{k\in N}\left[\sum_{(i,j)\in A} T_{\text{rob}} e^{TX}_{ij} f^k_{ij,\text{rob}} s'_k + \sum_{(j,i)\in A} T_{\text{rob}} e^{RX}_{ji} f^k_{ij,\text{rob}} s'_k\right] \le e^i_{\text{rob}} \qquad \forall i \in N \tag{22}$$

The sensor network is partitioned into four disjoint regions $R_j \subseteq N$ (for $j = 1,2,3,4$), satisfying $\bigcup_{j=1}^{4} R_j = N$ and $|R_j| = 10$ for each j. Deviation bands are applied precisely to the sensors within each active R_j, consistent with the robust configuration. The network lifetime achieved under the robust configuration closely approaches or slightly underperforms the reference lifetime value of 100 seconds across all cases, as observed in Figure 3.

Under nominal conditions, where no deviations occur, higher values of α in the robust configuration extend network lifetimes by provisioning additional capacity. When deviations arise, as illustrated in Figure 3, increased α enhances the model's ability to maintain feasible operation durations and mitigate premature battery depletion. This adaptive behavior is achieved by conservatively allocating battery capacity, selectively restricting the total magnitude of deviations within regions characterized by spatially correlated risks.

Building on this, the analysis based on parameters α and σ highlights the critical importance of incorporating sensing rate variability through robust optimization to enhance network availability and reliability under high uncertainty. For instance, in the baseline scenario with ($\alpha = 0.05$, σ_1), the deterministic configuration exhibits network lifetimes approximately 9.44%, 11.15%, 11.94%, and 11.97% shorter across regions R_1 to R_4, respectively, compared to the robust model. As uncertainty intensifies, reflected by larger α and σ values, these differences increase substantially, reaching reductions of 14.72%, 17.93%, 15.30%, and 21.75% in the most extreme cases. From the α perspective, the robust design closely approaches the reference lifetime under low σ conditions. However, as σ increases, the model requires more conservative allocations to accommodate higher uncertainty, making it more difficult to achieve the reference lifetime. This reflects the inherent trade-off between robustness and performance in the presence of increased variability. Ultimately, region-wise analysis indicates that lifetime variability increases across each region as the levels of α or σ increase.

Together, these findings confirm that the robust design effectively sustains network lifetime close to the reference target despite any considered level of uncertainty, balancing conservatism with operational efficiency.

IV. Conclusion and Future Work

This paper proposes a robust optimization framework for the design of an UWSN focused on target detection, ensuring energy efficiency and network reliability under uncertainty. Utilizing a simulation-based robust optimization framework with real-world bathymetric data, we

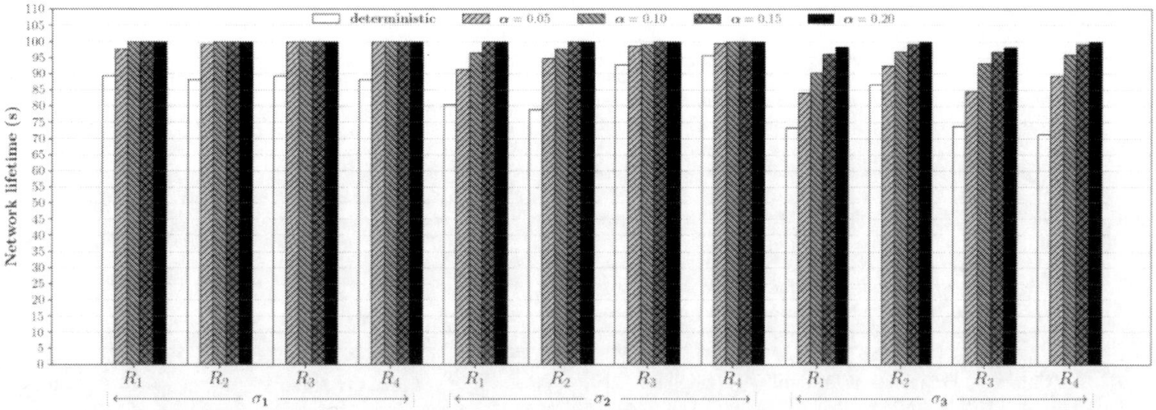

Figure 3. Comparison of deterministic and robust lifetime performance for a 40-sensor network across varying parameters

address uncertainties in sensing rates stemming from both regional and individual sensor deviations, and evaluate their impact on overall network performance. To enhance this framework, we integrate a region-based deviation model that provides a more comprehensive assessment of spatial vulnerabilities across the network.

This study develops an uncertainty set grounded in system-specific data obtained through simulation, leveraging a polyhedral formulation that improves the scalability of the proposed method and enhances its suitability for practical applications.

Results from comprehensive tests indicate that even minimal variations in sensing rates can severely compromise deterministic designs, causing early network failures. In contrast, the robust design consistently delivers sustained long-term performance, substantially exceeding the reliability of deterministic methods, even in the presence of varying regional and localized spatial instabilities.

Following the worst-case scenario implementations that are localized within one of the designated regions, future work may explore more comprehensive deviation models to address increasingly complex and unstructured conditions across networks with varying numbers of sensors. These include sensors deviating outside the active region, mixed-region cases, and over-budget scenarios exceeding the predefined uncertainty limits. Additionally, alternative deployment and partitioning strategies can be employed to evaluate their impact on robustness and enable comparative analyses.

REFERENCES

[1] I. Akyildiz, D. Pompili, and T. Melodia, "Underwater acoustic sensor networks: Research challenges," *Ad Hoc Networks*, vol. 3, no. 3, pp. 257–279, May 2005.

[2] A. F. Harris and M. Zorzi, "Modeling the underwater acoustic channel in ns2," in *Proceedings of the 2nd International Conference on Performance Evaluation Methodologies and Tools*, ser. ValueTools '07, Nantes, France: ICST (Institute for Computer Sciences, Social-Informatics and Telecommunications Engineering), 2007, pp. 1–8.

[3] I. Vasilescu, K. Kotay, D. Rus, M. Dunbabin, and P. Corke, "Data collection, storage, and retrieval with an underwater sensor network," *SenSys 2005 - Proceedings of the 3rd International Conference on Embedded Networked Sensor Systems*, pp. 154–165, Nov. 2005.

[4] E. Felemban, F. Shaikh, U. Qureshi, A. Sheikh, and S. Qaisar, "Underwater sensor network applications: A comprehensive survey," *International Journal of Distributed Sensor Networks*, vol. 2015, pp. 1–14, Nov. 2015.

[5] F. D'Andreagiovanni and A. Nardin, "Towards the fast and robust optimal design of wireless body area networks," *Applied Soft Computing*, vol. 37, pp. 971–982, Apr. 2015.

[6] O. Eren and A. Altin-Kayhan, "A simulation-informed robust optimization framework for the design of energy efficient underwater sensor networks," *Ad Hoc Networks*, vol. 178, p. 103 933, 2025..

[7] K. Kumar Gola, N. Chaurasia, B. Gupta, and D. Singh Niranjan, "Sea lion optimization algorithm based node deployment strategy in underwater acoustic sensor network," *International Journal of Communication Systems*, vol. 34, no. 5, e4723, 2021.

[8] K. Sunil Kumar, D. Singh, and V. Anand, "Strategic node deployment scheme for maximizing coverage area and network lifetime in uasns using voronoi-fuzzy c-means and salp swarm optimization," *IEEE Sensors Journal*, vol. 24, no. 10, pp. 16 926–16 934, 2024.

[9] L. Santoro, D. Brunelli, and D. Fontanelli, "Unveiling the undersea: A collaborative approach to monitoring underwater objects," in *2024 IEEE International Workshop on Metrology for Industry 4.0 IoT (MetroInd4.0 IoT)*, 2024, pp. 76–81.

[10] M. I. Malinen and P. Fränti, "Balanced k-means for clustering," in *Structural, Syntactic, and Statistical Pattern Recognition*, Berlin, Heidelberg: Springer Berlin Heidelberg, Aug. 2014, pp. 32–41.

[11] F. D'Andreagiovanni and A. Nardin, "Towards the fast and robust optimal design of wireless body area networks," *Applied Soft Computing*, vol. 37, pp. 971–982, 2015.

[12] B. Braem *et al.*, "The need for cooperation and relaying in short-range high path loss sensor networks," in *2007 International Conference on Sensor Technologies and Applications (SENSORCOMM 2007)*, 2007, pp. 566–571.

[13] M. R. Bharamagoudra and S. S. Manvi, "Deployment scheme for enhancing coverage and connectivity in underwater acoustic sensor networks," *Wireless Personal Communications*, vol. 89, pp. 1265–1293, 2016.

[14] A. Ben-Tal and A. Nemirovski, "Robust solutions of uncertain linear programs," *Operations Research Letters*, vol. 25, no. 1, pp. 1–13, 1999.

[15] D. Bertsimas and M. Sim, "The price of robustness," *Operations Research*, vol. 52, no. 1, pp. 35–53, 2004.

[16] M. Raayatpanah, T. Weise, J. Wu, M. Tan, and P. Pardalos, "Robust optimization for minimizing energy consumption of multicast transmissions in coded wireless packet networks under distance uncertainty," *Journal of*

Combinatorial Optimization, vol. 46, no. 4, pp. 815–838, Aug. 2023.

[17] Y. Zhang, H. Sun, and J. Yu, "Clustered routing protocol based on improved k-means algorithm for underwater wireless sensor networks," in *2015 IEEE International Conference on Cyber Technology in Automation, Control, and Intelligent Systems (CYBER)*, 2015, pp. 1304–1309.

[18] D. Arthur and P. Date, "Balanced k-means clustering on an adiabatic quantum computer," *Quantum Information Processing*, vol. 20, no. 9, p. 294, 2021.

[19] R. de Maeyer, S. Sieranoja, and P. Fränti, "Balanced k-means revisited," *Applied Computing and Intelligence*, vol. 3, no. 2, pp. 145–179, 2023.

[20] A. Aljughaiman, "Grid deployment scheme for enhancing network performance in underwater acoustic sensor networks," *IEEE Access*, vol. 11, pp. 112 973–112 987, 2023.

[21] M. Cobanlar, H. Yildiz, V. Akram, O. Dagdeviren, and B. Tavli, "On the trade-off between network lifetime and k-connectivity based reliability in uwsns," *IEEE Internet of Things Journal*, pp. 24 444–24 452, Jul. 2022.

Traditional Statistics and Machine Learning in Social Network Analysis: A Comparative Reanalysis of Social Network Data on Energy Transition Decisions

Mart Verhoog
Marketing and Communication Department
IU International University of Applied Sciences
Cologne, Germany
e-mail: mart.verhoog@iu.org

Abstract - **The goal of this idea contribution is to provide a systematic head-to-head comparison of regression-based inference and Machine Learning (ML) prediction in applied Social Network Analysis (SNA) for energy transition research, addressing a gap that has not yet been explored. The problem is relevant because methodological choices affect how actor influence and decision-making are interpreted in networked household energy-efficient refurbishments. While regression models offer explanatory clarity, ML models often deliver higher predictive accuracy; yet their joint evaluation in this domain remains missing. This study proposes a structured pipeline combining regression baselines with ML models, such as Random Forests, Support Vector Machines (SVMs), and Gradient Boosting. Model performance will be evaluated using R^2 and the Receiver Operating Characteristic – Area Under the Curve (ROC-AUC), while interpretability will be assessed through SHapley Additive exPlanations (SHAP) values. The expected outcome is a sharper understanding of trade-offs and complementarities between inference and prediction in energy transition networks, informing methodological integration in computational social science.**

Keywords - Social Network Analysis; Machine Learning; Traditional Statistics; Comparative Methods; Interpretability and Prediction

I. INTRODUCTION

Statistical reasoning has long underpinned empirical social science. Yet today, the term "artificial intelligence" is often used loosely, conflating traditional methods with data-driven techniques simply because they run in complex software environments. This paper critically engages with that trend by comparing traditional statistics and ML approaches within a shared empirical context - Social Network Analysis (SNA) of decision-making in energy-efficient home refurbishments.

While statistical modeling prioritizes explanatory clarity and hypothesis testing, ML focuses on pattern detection and predictive power. Recent studies (e.g., Hossain [1], Sakib et al. [2]) have shown how ML methods like LASSO, Random Forests, and SVMs improve predictive accuracy, especially in complex or high-dimensional settings. However, to our knowledge, no prior work has conducted a head-to-head comparison of regression-based inference and ML-based prediction in applied SNA of energy transition networks. This study seeks to fill that gap by re-analyzing a large, previously published dataset using both methodological paradigms.

The remainder of this idea contribution first introduces the methodological paradigms (Section II), then outlines the dataset and empirical frame (Section III), presents the research question (Section III), and concludes with expected contributions and next steps (Section IV).

II. TRADITIONAL STATISTICS AND MACHINE LEARNING: DEFINITIONS AND TENSIONS

A. *Traditional Statistical Inference*

Methods like linear and logistic regression rely on assumptions, such as linearity, homoscedasticity, and independence. These methods enable interpretability and quantification of uncertainty—key strengths in hypothesis-driven research.

B. *Machine Learning and Predictive Modeling*

ML models like Random Forests and SVMs are assumption-light and often outperform traditional models in predictive contexts. Though often less interpretable, new tools (e.g., SHAP values) are improving transparency.

C. *Convergence and Complementarity*

Techniques like regularized regression (LASSO, Ridge) and decision trees bridge the gap between interpretability and flexibility. These "hybrid" models illustrate growing convergence.

D. *Prior Comparative Research*

Studies in psychology, epidemiology, and sociology (e.g., Jang & Lee [3]; Di Franco & Santurro [4]) show ML often provides superior predictive power while traditional models offer theoretical alignment. Comparable SNA studies remain scarce - underscoring this study's relevance.

III. SOCIAL NETWORK ANALYSIS: THE EMPIRICAL FRAME

A. *Dataset and Context*

The analysis draws on a dataset from Verhoog (2017) covering approximately 700 cases of household decisions regarding energy-efficient refurbishment. The data capture not only household characteristics but also the role of professional stakeholders, such as building merchants, engineers, energy consultants, and financial institutions. Alongside these actor variables, the dataset includes the technical and efficiency status quo of the dwelling and the homeowners' attitudes toward refurbishment.

For instance, a household's decision to invest in energy-efficient refurbishment may depend not only on the building's technical condition and the homeowner's attitudes, but also on the involvement of professionals—whether consultants, engineers, merchants, or financial institutions—within the decision network. This combination of contextual, attitudinal, and network-related information provides a suitable empirical frame for comparing traditional statistical inference and Machine Learning (ML) prediction in applied Social Network Analysis (SNA)

B. *Feature Engineering*

Multiple SNA metrics (degree, betweenness, closeness centrality; network size; density; interaction intensity) will serve as predictors. These are complemented by contextual variables and preprocessed via normalization and encoding for compatibility with both methods.

C. *Modeling Approach*

The original analysis employed regression and factor methods. The reanalysis will apply ML models, such as Random Forests, Support Vector Machines (SVMs), and Gradient Boosting, with optional extensions to Neural Networks. The comparative pipeline will include preprocessing of SNA metrics (normalization and encoding), model training with cross-validation, hyperparameter tuning via grid search, and evaluation on a hold-out test set. Model performance will be evaluated using R^2 and the Receiver Operating Characteristic – Area Under the Curve (ROC-AUC), while interpretability will be assessed through SHapley Additive exPlanations (SHAP) values. Results from these ML models will be benchmarked directly against baseline regression models to enable a head-to-head comparison of inference and prediction.

D. *Research Question*

This study asks to what extent can Machine Learning uncover structural patterns in energy transition networks that traditional statistics may overlook, and under what conditions do their results converge or diverge?

This overarching question is addressed through three dimensions:

1. Network conditions – when do ML models achieve higher predictive accuracy than regression models?
2. Feature relevance – which network features emerge as most influential in ML compared to regression?
3. Interpretability – can tools, such as SHAP reconcile predictive accuracy with explanatory clarity in applied SNA for energy transition research?

IV. Expected Contribution and Next Steps

This idea contribution aligns with SIMUL 2025 themes by providing one of the first head-to-head comparisons of regression-based inference and ML-based prediction in applied SNA for energy transition research. In line with the research question, the study will clarify (i) under which network conditions ML offers superior predictive accuracy, (ii) how feature importance differs between ML and regression, and (iii) whether interpretability tools can bridge predictive and explanatory approaches. While the analysis centers on one empirical dataset, the approach is adaptable to other energy transition networks, which may enhance its broader relevance. These insights will highlight methodological synergies and trade-offs, advocating a hybrid perspective that combines theory-driven and data-driven approaches in studying decision-making in energy transition networks.

Immediate next steps are the preparation of the dataset and the construction of the modeling pipeline (Python: scikit-learn, NetworkX, SHAP). This will involve feature engineering of network metrics, cross-validation and hyperparameter tuning for multiple ML models, and systematic benchmarking against regression baselines to generate comparative performance and interpretability results. The findings will inform a full paper for the computational social science and organizational modeling community.

References

[1] A. Hossain, "Utilizing machine learning and causal graph approaches to address confounding factors in health science research: a scoping review", *F1000Research*, vol. 14, art. no. 129, 2025, doi: 10.12688/f1000research.159632.1.

[2] S. Sakib et al., "Comparative analysis of machine learning algorithms used for translating aptamer-antigen binding kinetic profiles to diagnostic decisions", *ACS Sensors*, vol. 10, no. 2, pp. 907–920, Feb. 2025, doi: 10.1021/acssensors.4c02682.

[3] D. Jang and B. Lee, "When machine learning meets social science: A comparative study of ordinary least square, stochastic gradient descent, and support vector regression for exploring the determinants of behavioral intentions to tuberculosis screening", *Asian Communication Research*, vol. 19, no. 3, pp. 101–118, Dec. 2022, doi: 10.20879/acr.2022.19.3.101.

[4] A. Di Franco and M. Santurro, "From big data to machinel learning: an empirical application to the sociology of health", *Athens Journal of Social Sciences*, vol. 10, no. 1, pp. 33–50, 2023.

[5] M. Verhoog, *Controlling Actors and Decisions in Construction Networks*, Springer Gabler, Wiesbaden, 2017.

A Framework for Demonstrating and Mitigating CAN Injection Attacks in Vector CANoe: a Case Study Using ABS

Uma Kulkarni
Institute for Secure Cyber-Physical Systems
Hamburg University of Technology
Hamburg, Germany
email: uma.kulkarni@tuhh.de

Sibylle Fröschle
Institute for Secure Cyber-Physical Systems
Hamburg University of Technology
Hamburg, Germany
email: sibylle.froeschle@tuhh.de

***Abstract*—Modern vehicles rely heavily on the Controller Area Network (CAN) for communication between electronic control units, yet CAN lacks inherent security features like authentication, making it susceptible to attacks, such as message injection. In this paper, we develop a means of simulating and visualizing the effect of an attack on the communication traffic and the actual system and the effect of a countermeasure. Our tool is based on Vector CANoe simulation and demonstrates a CAN message injection attack and a simple rule-based Intrusion Detection System (IDS). The setup includes a custom Graphical User Interface (GUI) for interactive demonstration. This framework serves as an educational tool and a foundation for future research into more advanced attack and defense scenarios. This work takes a step towards developing simulation platforms or frameworks for security of in-vehicle networks that are flexible and based on industry suitable toolchains.**

Keywords - Controller Area Network (CAN); In-vehicle Network Security; Simulation; Demonstration for Education

I. Introduction and Background

Vehicles today are increasingly dependent on in-vehicle communication networks such as the Controller Area Network (CAN) bus to support functionalities ranging from basic engine control to advanced driver assistance systems. While the CAN protocol was originally designed for reliability and efficiency, it lacks built-in security features such as authentication, encryption and message integrity [1]. This makes it vulnerable to a range of cyber-attacks including spoofing, injection, and Denial-of-Service (DoS) [2][3][4]. The growing concern over automotive cybersecurity has prompted researchers and engineers to explore both, attack vectors and countermeasures.

However, there remains a gap between experimentally established attacks and targeted security concepts and being able to demonstrate and explore them in flexible and configurable environments such as those used by the automotive industry in their development processes. Vector CANoe provides a powerful platform to model, simulate and analyse automotive networks, making it well-suited for such exploratory work [5].

This paper presents a simulation-based demonstration using CANoe that showcases a common CAN bus attack and the impact of an Intrusion Detection System (IDS) designed to mitigate it. The setup simulates normal traffic on the CAN network, introduces a malicious node injecting abnormal messages, and then analyzes the detection capability of a rule-based IDS. The objective is to provide a practical framework for visualizing both vulnerabilities and potential defense mechanisms within the CANoe environment. This demonstration can be useful in teaching as well as serve as a starting point to build complex real-time simulation framework for other attack and countermeasure demonstrations.

The rest of the paper is structured as follows: Section II explains the methodology, Section III describes the demonstration itself followed by conclusion and future work in Section IV.

II. Methodology

This section outlines the experimental setup created in Vector CANoe to simulate a CAN bus environment, demonstrate the attack and the IDS. The demo contains the baseline network configuration, attack implementation, IDS integration and the Graphical User Interface (GUI).

(1) Configuration: The simulation is built on the sample

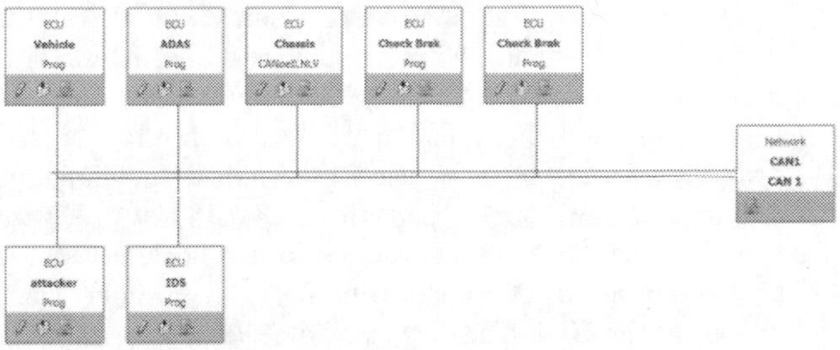

Fig. 1. Simulation set-up showing the CAN network.

configuration *ABS Brake Control* provided with the CANoe installation. The simulation, as seen in Figure 1, mainly consists of an embedded Simulink model for the *Chassis* block that simulates the application of brakes by providing the brake moment depending on two signals, status of ABS and brake activation. Other physical properties, such as mass of the vehicle are input as parameters to the model. The two *Check Brak* nodes are used for testing the Antilock Brake System (ABS) performance. The environment consists of two vehicles: the vehicle under consideration and a trailing vehicle. We added two Communication Access Programming Language (CAPL) programs *Vehicle* and *ADAS* that perform the functions such as setting the car in cruise control, calculating the distance between the vehicle under consideration and the trailing vehicle among other things.

(2) Attack Simulation: We use the attacker model from [3]. The attack is simulated with the addition of a node called *attacker* which represents a compromised gateway. The behaviour is simulated in CAPL. The attacker can now inject malicious messages on the CAN with the aim to bring down the *Vehicle speed* suddenly causing an accident on the highway. When the attack is active, if the *Vehicle speed* is high (in this case more than `130 kmph`), *Brake Input* messages are injected at intervals of `50ms` for `3s`.

(3) IDS Simulation: We have implemented a simple rule-based IDS here. This is realised as an additional CAPL node. It utilises the periodic property of the *Brake Input* message. Since the time interval between two consecutive legitimate *Brake Input* messages is known, any message occurring on the bus between this is flagged.

(4) GUI: We developed the GUI to facilitate the demonstration.

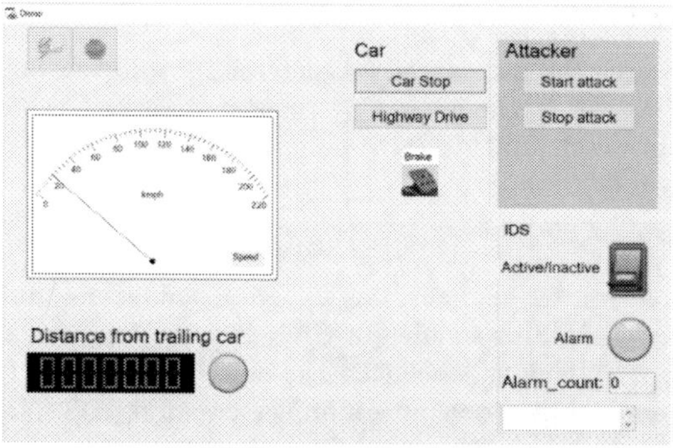

Fig. 2. GUI developed to facilitate the demonstration.

Here, the dial shows the current speed of the vehicle in `kmph`. The *Highway Drive* button provides a quick way to accelerate the vehicle to constant high speed and set the vehicle in cruise control like motion. The *Car Stop* button provides a quick way to decelerate the vehicle until it reaches a speed of `0`, i.e. it stops. The *Brake* button is used to simulate standard brake pedal action. The *Attacker* part of the GUI shown in Figure 2 provides the means to start the attack during the demonstration. The activation and deactivation of IDS can be done via the *IDS* part of the GUI. The distance from the trailing car is also displayed in `m` with an indicator LED showing if the distance is safe (green), is in warning limits (yellow) or dangerous (red).

III. Demonstration and Results

The steps of the demonstration flow are as follows: Without IDS: (1) Start the config from the GUI. (2) Press *Highway Drive* and wait till cruise control. (3) Press *Start attack*. (4) Observe - The warning LED goes from green to yellow to red and the cars in animation collide. See Figure 3. CAN message injection can be seen in the trace and graphics window in Display Desktop as shown in Figure 4(a), where the attack was started at around 53s after simulation start. With IDS: (1) Stop and Start config from the GUI. (2) Press *IDS* - see that IDS indicator is ON. (3) Press *Highway Drive* and wait till cruise control. (4) Press *Start attack*. (5) Observe - As

(a) Safe distance. (b) After attack.

Fig. 3. Demonstration results - cars animation

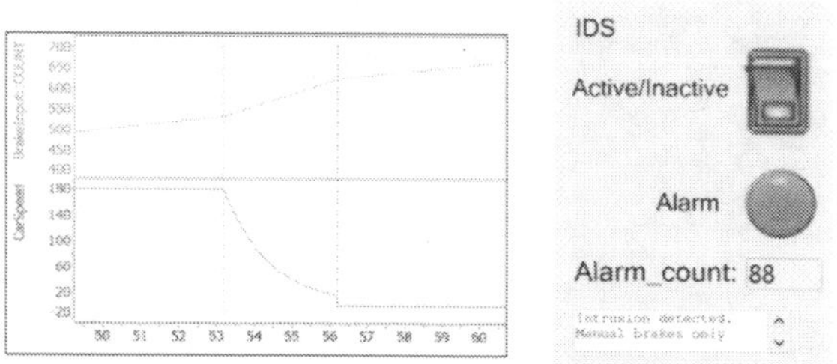

(a) Graph shows increased Brake input messages between 53s and 56s and corresponding decrease in vehicle speed when IDS is inactive.

(b) IDS section of GUI when IDS is active and attack is attempted.

Fig. 4. Demonstration results

shown in Figure 4(b), *Alarm* LED indicates that intrusion is detected. Warning text is displayed for the driver. Alarm count maintains history as long as Config is running (analogous to car ECUs being reflashed and reset). Cars in animation do not collide. From this point on, there is no effect of Start attack. Brake by wire is deactivated as a preventive measure but manual brake application is possible with the pedal and can be observed as a short dip in speed and also small dip in distance from trailing car. The cars continue to drive safely.

IV. Conclusion and Future Work

We have presented in this paper a CANoe-based simulation framework demonstrating a CAN bus injection attack and a rule-based IDS designed to mitigate it. This demonstration provides an effective means to visualise the said attack and countermeasure and observe the effects. Future work can be pursued in two directions. One is to add other attacks such as those exploiting fault-confinement to the demonstration and other security concepts. Second is to extend the demonstration to include real-time simulations with Hardware-in-the-loop (HIL) for more accurate analysis of attacks and IDS implementations.

References

[1] *CAN Specification, Robert Bosch GmbH, Postfach*, vol. 50, p. 15, 1991.

[2] K. Koscher, A. Czeskis, F. Roesner, S. Patel, T. Kohno, S. Checkoway, D. McCoy, B. Kantor, D. Anderson, H. Shacham *et al.*, "Experimental security analysis of a modern automobile," in *2010 IEEE symposium on security and privacy*. IEEE, 2010, pp. 447–462.

[3] S. Fröschle and A. Stühring, "Analyzing the capabilities of the CAN attacker," in *Computer Security–ESORICS 2017: 22nd European Symposium on Research in Computer Security, Oslo, Norway, September 11-15, 2017, Proceedings, Part I 22*. Springer, 2017, pp. 464–482.

[4] Z. Tang, K. Serag, S. Zonouz, Z. B. Celik, D. Xu, and R. Beyah, "Eracan: Defending against an emerging can threat model," in *Proceedings of the 2024 on ACM SIGSAC Conference on Computer and Communications Security*, 2024, pp. 1894–1908.

[5] J. Hayward, A. Tomlinson, and J. Bryans, "Adding cyberattacks to an industry-leading can simulator," in *2019 IEEE 19th International Conference on Software Quality, Reliability and Security Companion (QRS-C)*. IEEE, 2019, pp. 9–16.